'With technologies like AI now driving hotel performance and guest experiences, *Tech-Enabled Hospitality* is a must-read for non-tech professionals in the hospitality industry wanting to understand today's changes.'
Floor Bleeker, hotel tech expert

'If profit, guest experience and long-term relevance matter to you, this is your next read. Every page feels like you're sat in on a master-class. No filler, just stuff you can use.'
Mark Simpson, Founder, Boostly

'Reading this felt like clearing the cache of my brain after hearing one too many sales pitches from ChatGPT wrappers posing as innovative startups. It's sharp, focused and, most importantly, actually useful. This one will very likely age well.'
Simone Puorto, Head of Emerging Trends and Strategic Innovation, Hospitality Net

'A smart, timely guide for anyone serious about the future of travel and accommodation. Gillingham distils complexity into insight, offering both clarity and vision at a moment of accelerating change.'
David Peller, former Global Managing Director, Amazon Web Services Travel and Hospitality

'A timely and insightful book that captures how technology is reshaping both short-term rentals and hotels. Drawing on expert perspectives from across the industry, it offers practical guidance and fresh thinking for the future of hospitality. A must-read for anyone serious about staying ahead in this space.'
James Varley, Founder and CEO, Host Planet

'A watershed work by one of the most respected voices in travel tech. The book offers the most comprehensive research and insights our industry has seen to date. It is essential reading for anyone seeking to understand the current landscape of travel technology – the challenges we face, the opportunities ahead and, most importantly, the solutions that will shape the future. A must-read for forward-thinking professionals in hospitality and travel.'
Terry Whyte, The Vacation Rental Software Guy

'A landmark text and required reading for anyone building or backing hospitality tech. A thorough, strategic and expertly written deep dive into the sector's key dynamics.'
Richard Vaughton, Founding Partner, Yes Consulting and The Avio Goup

'The bridge our industry needs right now – a must-read for any hospitality professional navigating the digital shift. It shows how to adopt tech without losing the human touch. A practical guide to making smarter tech investments, rooted in the real world of hotel operations and guest experience – my kind of read!'
Danica Smith, Founder and CEO, MorningStar GX, and GAIN Adviser

Tech-Enabled Hospitality

*Strategies to elevate guest experience
and operational efficiency*

Jessica Gillingham

KoganPage

First published in Great Britain and the United States in 2025 by Kogan Page Limited

Kogan Page
Kogan Page Ltd, 2nd Floor, 45 Gee Street, London EC1V 3RS, United Kingdom
Kogan Page Inc, 8 W 38th Street, Suite 902, New York, NY 10018, USA
www.koganpage.com

EU Representative (GPSR)
Authorised Rep Compliance Ltd, Ground Floor, 71 Baggot Street Lower, Dublin D02 P593, Ireland
www.arccompliance.com

Kogan Page books are printed on paper from sustainable forests.

ISBNs

Hardback   978 1 3986 2034 6
Paperback   978 1 3986 2028 5
Ebook   978 1 3986 2035 3

British Library Cataloguing-in-Publication Data

A CIP record for this book is available from the British Library.

Library of Congress Control Number

2025021173

Typeset by Integra Software Services, Pondicherry
Printed and bound by CPI Group (UK) Ltd, Croydon CR0 4YY

CONTENTS

ACKNOWLEDGEMENTS

This book could not have been written without the time, insight and stories of the operators and tech leaders who each allowed me to interview them and draw on their expertise. I'm forever grateful to Alessandra Leoni, Andrew Evers, Andrew McGregor, Antoine Serrurier, Antonia Bernhardt, Begum Agca Okutgen, Dale Smith, David Kelso, David Peller, Floor Bleeker, Frans Garoarsson, Graham Donoghue, Hans Meyer, Hjörtur Valgeirsson, James Cornwell, James Lemon, Jason Fudin, Jean-Paul Godfroy, Jeremy Slater, Jessica Matthias, Kent Hatcher, Klaus Kohlmayr, Leah Rankin, Markus Mueller, Nils Mattisson, Nolan Mondrow, Oliver Stern, Rachel Fearon, Richard Vaughton, Roman Pedan, Ryan Killeen, Saber Kordestanchi, Shahar Goldboim, Spencer Hanlon, Steve Collins, Steve Davis, Terry Whyte, Thibault Masson, Uli Pillau, Willem Rabsztyn and Wouter Geerts. Thank you.

Thank you to my husband Steven for keeping the home fires burning while I was distracted writing this book and to Hugo and Margot for just being who they are.

Thank you to the incredible Abode Worldwide team for keeping the 'office' fires burning while I have been busy with the book and inspiring me to always go deeper into the world of hospitality technology each and every day.

Thank you to Jeylan Ramis for your support through the process. Susan Furber and Kogan Page for trusting me to write this book, and for putting faith in a first-time book author to get this done.

My biggest thanks go to Matthew Parsons, who has gone above and beyond to help me write this book. From shaping the interviews to spotting insights and themes that I missed. From editing to encouragement and moral support. Your support has been invaluable over the months of being in the making. Thank you!

Introduction

Someone recently said to me that hotels are in the business of selling *sleep*. And that sleep quality depends more on the guest and their sensibilities than on the hotel and what it offers. There is truth in this. However, this view negates the rest of what a hotel offers: the concept of *hospitality*, which, in simple terms, is the welcoming of guests and the provision of a home away from home for those guests.

Today, the global lodging industry is at a crossroads when it comes to providing hospitality. The *delivery* of hospitality is changing and technology is at the forefront of that change. In response to shifting consumer preferences, rising operational costs, increased competition and talent retention struggles, technology now sits at the heart of hospitality.

A new movement, *'tech-enabled'* hospitality, has arrived. Hospitality delivery has been made better, more efficient and, in some cases, more personalized *because of technology*.

Tech is changing hospitality on two core fronts. First, hotel and short-term rental (STR) managers now have the tools available to streamline, automate and improve operations: the nuts-and-bolts side of hospitality. Second, guests are looking to experience new levels of connection, communication and marketing while engaging with properties – before, during and after their stays. Lodging has been one of the last frontiers to adopt digitization, lagging behind what most consumers experience in their daily lives – but it is now beginning to catch up.

As Wouter Geerts, Director of Research and Intelligence at Mews, said to me, 'Hoteliers need to look at technology not as an inhibitor in their operations but as an enabler.'

He continues: 'You need to invest in technology. What a guest sees in their daily lives when they go to the supermarket or when they go on their phones and connect to apps that give them a very personalized experience, they will expect the same in a hotel.'

In some cases, technology enhances and supports personal interaction in hospitality, and in other cases, it is being deployed to remove the human element altogether and provide a fully automated, 'staffless' experience for guests.

Floor Bleeker, hotel technology expert and former group CTO for Accor, told me, 'There is a certain view that technology should not replace humans or human interactions but enhance them. I believe it can and will be much more disruptive than that.'

The purpose of this book is not to make a judgement about whether tech should or shouldn't remove the human element of hospitality – my purpose has been to provide different examples of how tech is achieving, and will continue to achieve, either – or *both*. It is up to the hospitality provider to decide which model best fits its guest profile and operational model.

The changing nature of hospitality and how it is elevated through technology fascinates me, and exploring this cultural shift is what has spurred me to write this book.

And make no mistake, at this point in time, culture and mindsets are intrinsically linked to innovation. Artificial intelligence (AI) is now 'cool', Beyond's co-founder David Kelso told me. Generative AI – or more precisely ChatGPT – has brought it back into the spotlight.

Hoteliers also need to appreciate how different generations of guests and workers view technology and be empathetic when integrating new systems and ways of working into their business. As Ulrich Pillau, co-founder and CEO of Apaleo, highlights, 'It's not only about putting new technology into place. It's also about changing your mindset on how you run your business.'

In the process of researching this book, I've spoken with a diverse group of professionals, including founders, CTOs, hotel operators, STR managers and seasoned tech experts to illustrate the changing nature of today's hospitality. You'll hear voices from Canada, the United States, the United Kingdom, Dubai, Iceland, France, Finland, Australia, Belgium, Austria, Sweden, Switzerland and Singapore.

I have used examples of hotels and STR operations throughout the book and spoken with technology leaders across both categories. There are two reasons for this: over recent years, there has been an explosion of STR properties available for guests to book. Second, the distinction between hotels and STR accommodation is becoming less apparent to consumers. With online travel agencies now offering both STRs and traditional hotels side by side, guests can compare the merits of both lodging types before booking. We are seeing a growing number of hotels offering rentals as part of their portfolios, and non-traditional hospitality providers, such as multifamily providers, now doing short stays.

In the last few years, we have witnessed an explosion of new tools and platforms entering the hospitality space. Each new software category or advanced tool aims to solve an operations problem, or provide a better experience for guests. This book has been written to guide hospitality professionals navigating this new chapter. Its hope is to offer practical insights into how technology, leveraged well, can deliver, either as a replacement or as an enhancement, the human-centric service that hospitality has been built upon.

Through real-world examples, expert interviews, and deep dives into key technological areas such as Property and Revenue Management Systems, guest communications and AI, this book provides a comprehensive roadmap for hospitality owners, operators, mid- to senior-level professionals, and hospitality students wanting to understand the new technology landscape. Whether you are at the beginning of your tech adoption journey or looking to refine your existing tech stack, you will find strategies, tools and lessons that resonate with your challenges and aspirations and give a greater understanding of the movement towards 'tech-enabled' hospitality.

Hospitality technology has been changing fast. But the past few years have also taught us that predicting the future is a fool's game. We don't know how technology will change hospitality in the near future, let alone in the next five to ten years. But what we can do is look at how hospitality is changing *now* and what operators and tech leaders are doing *today* to make the most of a tech-enabled world.

I hope you find this book, with its practical examples and candid narratives with some of the brightest minds in hospitality today, informative, interesting, but, above all, transformative.

1

The new hospitality landscape

Buoyed by global growth and widespread technological adoption, the hospitality industry is at an exciting crossroads. As Klaus Kohlmayr, Chief Evangelist at IDeaS, observed during my interview with him, 'The long-term prospects of hospitality are very positive. With the growth of disposable income and the middle class over the next 15 years, the industry is set to grow by at least 3, 4 or 5 per cent every year.' This optimistic trajectory signals not only increased opportunities for hoteliers and short-term rental (STR) operators and investors but also a parallel expansion for the many technology providers striving to meet the growing demands of the sector.

Throughout this book, I explore the developing and changing nature of both hospitality and hospitality technology and what it means to be an operator or tech innovator today. My hope is that the book achieves this by capturing the stories and insights of more than 30 leaders across property management solutions, security, access, guest communications, marketing, payments, revenue management, sustainability and, of course, the operators themselves. Those brands on the front lines are navigating the constant balance between providing for guests and ensuring operational excellence that delivers margins.

No two hospitality businesses are alike, and their technology needs vary accordingly. A single hotel with a few rooms is relatively easy to manage without complicated tech. But for 10 properties, or more than a dozen homes if you are an STR operator, you are more likely to need software tools to gather and analyse data effectively and to implement processes and standards. With scale also come economies of scale. This plays out across all lodging types – whether that is traditional hotels, aparthotels, vacation rentals or even hostels.

'It is a fascinating time for hospitality. Everyone is incredibly bullish on the long term for the industry. People have an inherent need to travel. They want to explore the world. They continue to set aside chunks of their household incomes and their company budgets to do so. But it's also an industry that was probably relatively exposed during Covid and now is seeing potentially a second softening of demand.'

James Lemon, Global Industry Lead – Hospitality, Travel & Leisure, Stripe

Democratization of hospitality technology

One of the most promising and exciting trends in the industry is the democratization of technology. Cloud-based and Software as a Service (SaaS) models have opened up access to sophisticated tools, making it easier for operators of all sizes to integrate technology into their operations. Whether it's implementing a basic Property Management System (PMS) or leveraging advanced business intelligence platforms, the right technology enables businesses to thrive by improving decision making, optimizing operations and delivering better guest experiences.

The modular flexibility of SaaS solutions also means that operators can scale incrementally. A boutique hotel might start with an entry-level PMS and add advanced features – such as Revenue Management Systems (RMSs), housekeeping apps or guest communication platforms – as it expands. This scalability ensures that technology investments remain cost-effective and aligned with operational needs, no matter the size and growth stage of the business.

As Leah Rankin, Chief Product Officer for SiteMinder, notes, innovations like AI and revenue management tools are no longer exclusive to large chains. Even independent operators can now access solutions that optimize pricing, enhance guest personalization and streamline operations. This levelling of the playing field empowers small and medium-sized enterprises (SMEs) to compete with established brands, promoting innovation across the sector. This change is good for operators, teams and – of course – guests.

The rise of no-code and low-code platforms has further accelerated this trend. These platforms enable operators without technical expertise to customize and deploy digital solutions quickly, empowering small businesses to address specific challenges efficiently. By lowering barriers to adoption, these tools encourage widespread use of technology and democratize innovation. Even though, as we all know, hospitality is a hard business to do well, tech eases some of the pressures for the operators.

TECH LEADER INSIGHT

Why the barriers to innovation are coming down – Klaus Kohlmayr, Chief Evangelist, IDeaS

Hospitality companies that fail to innovate on a technological level are at risk of losing customers – and that risk is accentuated as digitization increasingly spreads faster and faster into our everyday lives.

The truth of the matter, according to Klaus Kohlmayr, is that the hotel industry is a follower rather than a leader when it comes to technology adoption, although there are signs that this could soon change.

Kohlmayr, who has been charting the hospitality landscape for more than two decades and is currently the Chief Evangelist and Development Officer at revenue management software specialist IDeaS, thinks two factors are stifling technology innovation: fragmentation and prioritization.

'There is fragmentation between managers, asset managers, brand owners and real estate owners, because priorities are not always aligned on where money should be invested,' he says. 'And spending prioritization means having to choose between: am I going to buy new hotels, build new hotels, renovate my existing portfolio, or am I going to invest in technology?'

The risk of failing to innovate is that hotels will fail to meet customer expectations.

'If I'm used to interacting with my airline, taxi or retail company in a certain way, and that is not possible with the [hotel] brand of my choice, then I'm going to vote with my feet and go somewhere else,' he adds.

Admittedly, hospitality brands are at varying stages in offering a seamless digital journey, but Kohlmayr argues that within the broader travel landscape, airlines are further ahead. In other sectors, banks have also done 'a pretty good job of moving the customer journey and customer interaction to fully digitized and digital methods'.

Playing catch-up

While Kohlmayr's day job may see him focus on pricing, he has a strategic background and holds a Bachelor of Science in Hotel Management. He also studied business at Henley Management College; real estate investment and asset management at Cornell University's School of Hotel Administration; and finance and strategy at Singapore Management University.

From this vantage point, he appears to be optimistic about the future, thanks to the recent transition of software to the cloud. This has meant that software has become more readily available, cheaper to implement and, most importantly, is giving more hotel brands opportunities to innovate.

'About 20 years ago, a typical hotel-based system would probably have been six figures, and would not have been a Software as a Service (SaaS) solution,' he says. 'The migration to SaaS lowers the total cost of ownership, is easier to install and easier to budget for, which obviously led to a wider adoption of technology across the industry. We're now seeing, finally, a shift to the cloud in general in the hotel industry, which will further accelerate the adoption of advanced next-generation systems going forward.'

He also notes that the larger hotel groups are investing billions of dollars into upgrading their tech stacks, particularly around Customer Relationship Management (CRM) systems.

'We're just starting to see that translating into a better customer experience. But it's not yet adopted throughout the entire technology, the entire industry,' he adds.

Merchandising future

The end game is for a hotel to digitize a customer's journey, translating that into a more personalized offering, leading to more chances to sell things that the guests want.

'On the commercial side, it's going to be transformative,' Kohlmayr says. 'As more companies adopt a digital-first mindset, that allows them to create a more personalized experience with better merchandising capabilities, which then increases revenue and profitability. There's a lot that can be done through technology to make the operation side more efficient and increase margins.'

As for revenue management, Kohlmayr plays down the AI hype.

'AI has been used by revenue management companies, like IDeaS, forever,' he says. 'We've had AI as part of our solution from day one. Already with *2001: A Space Odyssey*, the movie from Stanley Kubrick, people talked about talking to a computer and talking to AI. So it's not new.'

He argues that revenue management companies have been using AI for at least the past 35 years, but what is 'new' is how professionals are currently engaging, interacting and communicating with the technology through voice or generative-type interfaces.

'Where that's going to come to the forefront is obviously how you're interacting with technology and how you're getting to answers quicker,' he says. 'Today, a revenue manager has to go through tables and charts and graphs. Tomorrow they'll be able to ask the system, why is my forecast XYZ, or can you change my pricing from A to B? Or can you adjust this or that?'

Another innovation includes the ongoing progress in RMSs to price function, space and group requests and manage other spaces within a hotel rather than rooms alone.

And that all comes full circle to personalization, providing hotels with the opportunity to sell anything they want, whether space, feature or add-on – placing it right in front of the customer.

The growing affordability of modern solutions and rising customer expectations may prove an inflection point that positions the hospitality sector as a leader in technological innovation, as opposed to a follower.

A changing guest demographic

As we think about the future of hospitality and lodging, we recognize that in order to stay ahead, hospitality operators must plan for the generational shift in their customer base. As Alessandra Leoni, Head of Commercial at Resident Hotels, noted in her interview with me, 'In 10 or 15 years, today's children will be tomorrow's guests, bringing new expectations and behaviours.' Anticipating these changes is essential for long-term success. Tomorrow's guests, born into a digital-first world, will demand seamless, technology-integrated experiences that blend personalization with efficiency.

This evolving demographic underlines the importance of understanding guest needs at a granular level. Businesses that fail to adapt risk losing relevance as they struggle to attract and retain new customers. Embracing innovation while preserving the essence of hospitality – a warm, human-centric experience – will be key.

Generational shifts also bring varied preferences for sustainability practices, technology use and guest/operator engagement. Hotels and STR operators must be agile enough to cater to new travellers who value eco-conscious choices, seamless mobile experiences and varied levels of desire or bandwidth for contact. Investing in data-driven insights can help operators stay ahead of these evolving preferences.

Beyond technology, these shifts also require rethinking operational strategies. Future travellers may prioritize health and wellness experiences, immersive cultural engagements and meaningful connections to the places they visit. Operators can meet these needs by integrating wellness services, curating local experiences and embedding sustainability into their business models.

It's also critical to prepare for the influence of digital-native Gen Z and Gen Alpha travellers, who bring a new level of expectation for transparency and personalized service. This includes integrating user-generated content, reviews and direct feedback into marketing and operational decisions. Engaging with these generations requires building authentic, socially responsible brands that align with their values and offer consistent, tailored service. It also requires technology that can curate, assimilate and disseminate information.

A second big trend that has impacted hospitality is the move towards a more flexible and remote workforce. People have always relocated for work or taken 'business trips', which has traditionally meant serviced apartments or hotels – but today's traveller might be a remote worker combining work and leisure, so is looking for a more 'home-like' experience over a corporate stay. Travellers are also looking to join communities and stay in short-term let co-living apartments that have built-in community experiences.

UNDERSTANDING THE KEY STAKEHOLDERS IN HOTELS

Franchise holder (franchisee): An independent business operating a hotel under a brand's name. Franchisees pay fees and adhere to brand standards while maintaining ownership or operational control, leveraging the reputation and resources of larger hospitality companies. Tech deployment decisions are likely to be made at a franchisee level.

Hotel brand (flag): A recognized name under which the hotel operates (e.g. Marriott, Hilton, IHG). Brands provide marketing, reservation systems and operational guidelines. Many brands do not own the hotels but operate under franchise agreements.

Hotel operator: Responsible for the day-to-day operations, including staffing, guest services and financial performance. Operators can be independent companies (third-party operators) or part of the brand. They ensure brand standards and manage the guest experience.

Hotel owner: The entity or individual who owns the physical hotel property. They may operate independently or lease their property to an operator or a brand. Owners focus on asset appreciation, real estate value and revenue generation from the property.

'After Covid, the behaviour of the guest changed. We saw a change where people valued more privacy, and in some cases privacy above service.'
Hjörtur Valgeirsson, Chief Operating Officer, Íslandshótel

The imperative of technology adoption

The hospitality industry has often been criticized for its slow techno-logical adoption. However, the tide is now turning, with concerns that technology might disrupt the guest experience and provide a 'lesser service' being largely overblown. Instead, technology has been used to amplify what hospitality does best: provide optionality, efficiency and personalization, providing experiences through service and product. 'The industry needs to grasp the value of hospitality tech and how it enhances both guest and staff experiences,' James Lemon, Global Industry Lead – Hospitality, Travel & Leisure for payment firm Stripe, notes. This perspective underscores the necessity of bridging the knowledge gap for operators to fully realize the potential of their technology investments.

Increased technology adoption addresses operational pain points. Tools like AI-powered chatbots, self-service kiosks and mobile check-ins enhance guest convenience while reducing pressure on staff. These innovations also provide data-driven insights for strategic decision making.

Moreover, technology adoption enables a seamless fusion of operational efficiency and guest satisfaction. A PMS integrated with AI can potentially analyse booking patterns to optimize room assignments, predict peak occupancy periods and allocate resources effectively.

For staff, technology reduces repetitive tasks, allowing them to focus on high-touch interactions with guests. Automated scheduling tools can optimize housekeeping schedules based on guest check-outs, while real-time notifications ensure maintenance teams address issues promptly.

At the strategic level, adopting cutting-edge technology such as dynamic pricing systems and demand forecasting tools can drive revenue growth. These systems utilize machine learning to analyse market trends, competitor pricing and historical data, enabling operators to adjust room rates in real time. This ensures pricing remains competitive while maximizing profitability.

Finally, technology adoption can support sustainability goals, which are increasingly vital to modern hospitality. Smart energy management systems, Internet of Things (IoT)-enabled devices and digital guest directories help reduce a property's environmental footprint. These innovations align with guests' growing preferences for eco-friendly practices and contribute to a positive brand image.

By integrating technology thoughtfully, operators can create an ecosystem where operational efficiency, guest satisfaction and sustainability coexist harmoniously. Ultimately this positions hospitality businesses to thrive in a competitive and ever-evolving market.

UNDERSTANDING THE KEY STAKEHOLDERS IN STRs

Hybrid and flexible stay operators: Brands that blend hospitality with residential living, offering tech-enabled stays with hotel-like amenities in multifamily residential spaces, often leasing entire buildings or floors for STR operations at scale.

Institutional and multifamily investors: Large investors and developers integrating STRs into multi-unit residential or hotel-style buildings, focusing on professionalizing STRs with dedicated technology stacks.

Property owner: The owner of the rental property, which can range from a single home to multi-unit apartments. Owners may manage the property themselves or hire an operator.

STR manager: The property manager manages the daily operations of rental properties, including pricing, guest communication, cleaning and maintenance. Operators can be individual hosts, local property managers or large-scale management companies.

'It's important that hotels get on the wagon of new technology. There are a lot of new platforms, a lot of startups, a lot of mature startups that are available nowadays that replace some of the manual admin work.'

Alessandra Leoni, Head of Commercial, Resident Hotels

Contrasts in technology adoption: hotels vs STRs

The STR sector and how it is managed, marketed and operated varies quite wildly from hotels. This is largely due to its fragmented nature, the sheer number of small operators serving the market and the nuances around managing disparate units. Unlike consolidated hotel chains, STR operators may lack the resources to invest in advanced systems, so what has developed in response to the needs of STR businesses has been a rise in the number of tech startups that solve operational challenges. Over the last eight to ten years, and really since Airbnb took off in 2013, more and more solutions established on more affordable unit price-based SaaS models have entered the market.

The tech-stack sophistication in the STR market is still behind hotels and relative market penetration of tech tools is still low. However, today, the STR sector is rethinking its models and growing far more sophisticated in its technology use and understanding. Metrics like revenue per available night (RevPAN) are gaining traction, aligning operational strategies with those of hotels. By adopting innovative approaches, STR operators can enhance their competitiveness and profitability, using technology to unlock new opportunities.

Another promising development in the STR space is the integration of hybrid models that combine short-term and long-term rentals. By leveraging dynamic software tools and adjusting to guest feedback, these operators can maximize revenue streams, diversify portfolios and mitigate risk while catering to diverse guest personas.

Hybrid models also facilitate better resource utilization. For example, properties can switch between short-term and long-term bookings depending on demand patterns, enabling them to fill gaps in occupancy and maximize income. This flexibility can be enhanced through integrated software that provides real-time insights into market trends and forecasts. We are now also seeing multifamily and other long-term rental products shift towards offering elements of flexible rentals, with short lets favoured across more than just lease-up periods to provide stronger yields for asset owners.

Furthermore, the adoption of smart technology has begun to reshape the STR experience. Automation of remote guest check-ins, digital concierges and real-time support through chatbots elevate the service standards of STR properties, narrowing the gap between them and traditional hotels.

Despite these advancements, challenges remain. STR operators often face difficulty in integrating disparate systems, leading to inefficiencies and potential missed opportunities. Addressing these gaps requires the development of more accessible and interoperable solutions tailored to the unique needs of STR businesses. Industry collaboration and partnerships with tech providers could accelerate this process.

UNDERSTANDING KEY HOTEL TYPES

Boutique hotels: Smaller, design-driven hotels offering unique, upscale experiences with a strong focus on individuality and personalized service.

Budget hotels: Affordable accommodation with basic amenities, focusing on cost-conscious travellers and short stays.

Business hotels: Located in city centres or business districts, catering to business travellers with services like meeting rooms, high-speed internet and business centres.

Chain hotels: These are part of larger hotel groups with standardized services, centralized operations and strong brand recognition (e.g. Marriott, Hyatt, Hilton).

Extended-stay hotels: These are designed for long-term stays and offer amenities like kitchenettes, laundry facilities and spacious living areas, appealing to business travellers and relocating families. They could also fit the STR category and are also called serviced apartments or aparthotels.

Independent hotels: Privately owned and operated without a brand affiliation, allowing for unique guest experiences and personalized service but requiring self-managed marketing and operations.

Luxury hotels: High-end properties offering premium amenities, exceptional service and exclusive experiences, often associated with well-known luxury brands.

Resort hotels: These are properties in vacation destinations that offer extensive recreational amenities such as pools, spas, golf courses and entertainment.

Select-service hotels: A hybrid between full-service and limited-service hotels, offering essential amenities like breakfast, fitness centres and meeting spaces, but without the extensive services of full-service properties, providing cost-effective yet comfortable accommodation.

REAL-WORLD EXAMPLE

How Zoku solves the hybrid hospitality conundrum

Zoku, named after the Japanese word for family, tribe or clan, is a European extended stay accommodation operator. Its signature 'Lofts' are micro-apartments featuring a raised bed area, fully equipped kitchen, work/dining table and a living area. The company also aims to create a vibrant community through shared rooftop social spaces, co-working areas and regular events. Its first property in Amsterdam opened in 2016, with other locations including Copenhagen, Vienna and Paris opening within the last few years.

Challenges and opportunities

Many hospitality brands have their eye on a particular demographic: the hybrid worker, whether that's a digital nomad, business traveller or even a local resident.

EY's 2024 Mobility Reimagined Survey reveals that employees and employers largely agree that remote and hybrid work will persist, long after the pandemic. The global number of digital nomads was estimated at 40 million in 2023, according to the WYSE Travel Confederation, and is expected to rise to 60 million by 2030.[1]

The hybrid worker has many appealing qualities. They tend to stay for longer and spend more during their stay at a property compared to a leisure guest who's there just to sightsee. This is particularly true if the employer is picking up the bill.

But a challenge for many accommodation operators focused on this segment is in figuring out how to provide the right mix of working environment, hotel-quality stay and community feel.

Zoku embarked on its mission to address the challenges faced by modern business travellers and remote workers a few years before the pandemic.

'These are people who need to live and work in a city from a few days to a few months, which means that the place they stay at actually needs to be suitable for both living and working,' notes Hans Meyer, Zoku co-founder and managing director. 'Hotels are traditionally fantastic places to sleep, have a quick bite to eat and that's about it. And that's when I realized there was a huge opportunity here.'

Zoku also offers co-working areas, which can be used daily or monthly. Between 80 and 90 per cent of its co-working members live locally in that same city and work from home about three days a week. 'And they can get lonely in those three days,' Meyer says. 'So, for one or two of those days each week, they join us to work from our rooftop at Zoku.'

When technology plays catch-up

The hospitality technology landscape is vast, and software developers tend to provide solutions for almost every scenario. When they don't, accommodation operators take a DIY approach, overlaying existing technology with their own workaround solutions.

But in some cases, it's a waiting game. This is currently the situation with Europe's Zoku. Although founded in 2016, there doesn't appear to be an all-in-one solution to satisfy its admittedly unique co-working-meets-hotel proposition from an operational perspective as well as revenue management.

It has left Hans Meyer frustrated.

Hotel technology is generally focused on selling rooms by the night, but Meyer says Zoku needs to create revenue per square metre on a 24/7 basis. 'Our model is not seven nights. Our model is 168 hours per week where we try to stack different business models on the same square metre. This is the model going forward; however, the technology is not there yet.'

Many travel technology companies are exploring this area, focusing on helping hotels maximize revenue from their spaces, not just beds. For now, Zoku works with a PMS and separate co-working software, but in the future wants to have it all housed within one system.

'Wouldn't it be great to have just one,' says Meyer. 'And that system provides a kind of a frictionless experience for the guests and at the same time saves a lot of time on the operational side, which gives our team the opportunity to really facilitate people in the best possible way.'

The solution

Zoku is focusing on enabling as many social interactions as possible with guests. The goal for its technology is to free up as much time as possible for staff to spend on mundane tasks so they can spend more time focused on residents.

Self-service check-in is available, for example, but Meyer sees a future where there's no check-in process at all, and believes guests will be able to just walk in and feel at home.

'When we first did our research for Zoku, we learned that 9 out of 10 people who go to a city where they don't speak the local language or know anyone start to feel disconnected within one week of being away. This is because they start to miss their friends and family, ultimately leading to feelings of loneliness,' he says.

As a result, Zoku's apartment hotels host regular events, such as live music nights, yoga sessions or motivational speakers. 'The community part is a very fundamental part of our concept,' Meyer adds. It also designs large social spaces for its hotels to facilitate these types of activities and help guests connect during their stay.

It also pays close attention to the design of its hotels.

The company designed a different room product, which it calls 'Lofts', and they play a key role. 'If you look at traditional hospitality, hotels are basically focusing on selling the rooms by the night. This means that, in 99.9 per cent of hotel rooms or studio apartments worldwide, the bed is always the most dominant piece of furniture,' Meyer says.

Therefore, the Zoku team designed the bed area so that, as well as being elevated, it can be screened off when needed. The kitchen table then becomes the focus of the room, which Meyer argues creates a more residential or workspace feeling.

While traditional serviced apartments or corporate housing provide adequate living spaces for longer-stay guests, Meyer says that few promote social interaction among the residents.

The result, according to Meyer, is that Zoku hotels can become 'a kind of social glue, bringing together both our residents and the local neighbourhood'.

For Meyer, the concept of space will only grow in importance in the future, and he tips that AI will rapidly shake up revenue management with more powerful forecasting and predictive analysis.

Integrating AI into guest communication will also help shorten the time it takes to answer guest customer queries across different systems down to minutes or even seconds. This would free up the staff to focus on more meaningful interactions rather than handling repetitive tasks that could be automated.

'That's the kind of efficiency and service I believe will define the future of hospitality,' Meyer concludes.

Conclusion

Zoku's niche proposition reminds hospitality professionals not to lose sight of the basics: namely, ensuring guests feel welcome throughout their stay, not just when they arrive. This is even more relevant for longer-stay guests.

Technology is already enhancing the experience, such as offering self-check-in, which allows team members to spend more time making guests feel at home instead of managing a repetitive process. But Zoku equally demonstrates that much more software development is needed to further improve the experience for the hybrid guest.

UNDERSTANDING STR BUSINESS MODELS

Co-hosting: A partnership where the property owner handles some tasks while a co-host (often another local host or small operator) manages day-to-day operations.

Franchise model: Similar to hotels, independent operators manage properties under a recognized STR brand, adhering to brand standards while leveraging marketing and operational support.

Full-service management: A professional management company oversees all marketing, guest relations and maintenance operations for a fee or commission.

Hybrid management: A flexible model where operators manage select services (such as pricing, booking and guest communication) while property owners retain control over specific elements like maintenance and on-the-ground guest services.

Lease arbitrage: Operators lease properties from owners and rent them as STRs, profiting from the difference between rental income and lease costs.

Owner-managed: Property owners handle all aspects of operations, including marketing, guest services, cleaning and maintenance.

New models for growth and flexibility

Emerging brands are redefining hospitality by capitalizing on flexible, tech-enabled business models. Companies like Europe's Bob W demonstrate how adaptive reuse of non-hotel buildings – such as converting office spaces into boutique accommodation – can drive growth without competing directly with established chains for prime real estate.[2] This agility allows new players to innovate rapidly, using technology to deliver unique guest experiences.

New models challenging the normal perceptions of hotels and what they offer are also developing. We are seeing more and more hotels looking to become something other than a place that just offers a nice welcome and a bed for the night. They are growing into mixed-use properties that may offer co-working facilities, like Ennismore's Working From_ brand. Originally inspired by the comfy sofas at The

Hoxton and the fact that they were attracting non-resident workers, Ennismore decided to lean in and launch the add-on co-working brand with the know-how of a hospitality brand to offer more to the market.

Other hotel brands are focused on being hubs for local communities. Hans Meyer of Zoku observes, 'If you look at hotel F&B [food and beverage], it's quite common that 90 per cent of the revenue is from hotel guests and 10 per cent is from outside guests. With us, it's 50/50.' This highlights how some operators are transforming hospitality spaces into multifunctional hubs that appeal to both travellers and locals, adding a new layer of flexibility and community engagement to their business models.

Flexibility in business models also extends to technology adoption. By prioritizing modular and interoperable systems, operators can adapt to changing market demands quickly. The ability to innovate and remain flexible is critical. Operators who embrace these new models and technologies will be well positioned to capture emerging opportunities and navigate the challenges of a dynamic market that is experiencing rapid change.

'What I love about this industry is that everyone's here because they want to deliver a great customer experience, which is for the guests. But we're also here to deliver that across the board for the hotel, the guest, as well as our partners, which ultimately brings that solution together.'

Leah Rankin, Chief Product Officer, SiteMinder

The role of loyalty in the digital age

Brand loyalty remains a cornerstone of hospitality, even as booking behaviours evolve. While customers may not exhibit loyalty to specific booking methods, they remain loyal to brands that deliver exceptional experiences. Hoteliers today are looking to cultivate direct relationships with guests so they can strengthen their brand loyalty. Personalized marketing, differentiation and service delivery are core ways that hotel and STR brands harness loyalty – or don't.

Modern loyalty programmes go beyond traditional points-based systems. Instead, they focus on creating emotional connections with guests. For instance, brands can implement tiered rewards systems that unlock exclusive benefits, such as access to premium rooms or personalized concierge services. Taking things a step forward, Ennismore has shown creative leadership by developing the 'Dis-loyalty' members app which advocates against tiers and points and gives every member access to discounts and value-adds. The goal is also to make members feel part of a wider 'club'.

The dominance of online travel agencies (OTAs) presents both opportunities and challenges for hotels and STR brands. While OTAs drive bookings, their monopolistic tendencies can create barriers for independent operators seeking to own the customer relationship. Encouraging direct bookings through enhanced digital experiences and loyalty programmes is key for reducing dependence on OTAs and supporting sustainable growth.

One significant challenge with OTAs is their reluctance to share guest data, limiting operators' ability to personalize experiences and build direct relationships. To counter this, many hoteliers are investing in direct booking strategies, leveraging tools like user-friendly websites, mobile apps and targeted marketing campaigns. These efforts aim to showcase the unique value of booking directly, such as exclusive perks, lower rates for members or more flexible cancellation policies.

Lastly, strengthening guest loyalty through exceptional service remains a powerful strategy for reducing OTA dependence. As Steve Davis, CEO of Operto, suggests, 'At the end of the day, operators are gunning for five-star reviews, repeat bookings and word-of-mouth recommendations.' By focusing on creating memorable experiences and cultivating direct relationships, hospitality operators can mitigate the challenges posed by OTA dominance and secure a sustainable future.

'As a technologist, it feels like we're on the cusp of a lot of big changes.'

Kent Hatcher, Director of Product, Mint House

KEY TAKEAWAYS

Democratization of hospitality technology: Cloud-based and SaaS models have opened doors for operators of all sizes to adopt advanced tools so that they can run better, more efficient businesses and meet guest expectations.

Barriers to innovation: Challenges such as fragmentation and misaligned priorities may slow technological adoption, but the shift to cloud-based solutions is helping the industry innovate more effectively.

Playing catch-up: The hospitality sector has lagged behind industries like airlines and banking in adopting digital transformation, but advances in customer journey digitization are narrowing this gap.

A changing guest demographic: Younger, digital-native travellers are demanding personalized, seamless and tech-integrated experiences, prompting operators to rethink their strategies.

New models for growth: In response to changing guest motivations and to capitalize on new opportunities, some operators are looking at different ways to utilize space, creating community hubs, co-working hubs, hybrid properties and more.

The imperative of technology adoption: Technology is not a luxury but a necessity, offering benefits like operational efficiency, enhanced guest satisfaction and alignment with sustainability goals.

Contrasts in adoption: Hotels and STRs face distinct technological challenges and opportunities, with the latter sector now adopting tools to enhance competitiveness and profitability.

Real-World Example – Zoku: This European brand is leading hybrid hospitality to create a new model for 'space' and the opportunity for blending work, living and community interaction.

Notes

1   WYSE Travel Confederation (2023) WYSE Travel Confederation: Growth and developments in the digital nomad market since Covid-19, WYSE News, 16 January, www.wysetc.org/2023/01/growth-and-developments-in-the-digital-nomad-market-since-covid-19/ (archived at https://perma.cc/H4TU-DLKU)

2   Taiwo, I (2024) Hospitality operator Bob W and Osborne+Co to build £400m serviced apartments portfolio, Hospitality Investor, 19 July, www.hospitalityinvestor.com/serviced-apartments/hospitality-operator-bob-w-and-osborneco-build-ps400m-serviced-apartments (archived at https://perma.cc/7ERK-JW59)

2

The great technology divide

The hospitality industry stands at a crossroads. There is a great divide between operators who embrace being 'tech-enabled' and those who are not there – or at least not there yet. As the rest of the book will show, technology adoption is increasingly shaping guest experience and operational efficiency for hoteliers and short-term rental (STR) managers. Tech is changing how hospitality is delivered. Yet, a stark divide remains between hotels that have fully embraced modern digital solutions and those that continue to rely on legacy systems or even manual processes.

This divide has nothing to do with budget or property size – it concerns mindset, strategic vision and an organization's willingness to evolve. Hotels with just a few rooms have invested in cloud-based platforms, AI-driven guest services and data analytics to optimize their operations. Others hesitate, weighed down by outdated systems, budget constraints and an aversion to taking risks or making change.

The question is, why do some hotels embrace technology while others struggle to understand its benefits or make the leaps needed to implement it? More importantly, what are the long-term consequences of this divide for operators and their guests? This chapter will explore the key factors determining whether a hotel is a technology leader or tech laggard. Operators will be able to place themselves within the chapters of the rest of the book and determine whether they are on the road to providing 'tech-enabled' hospitality or are beginning to look like the vintage record player in a world of streaming services.

It seems that the divide also exists in how operators view tech investment on the bottom line. Some see tech adoption as a strategic move to improve the business, as an investment in longer-term growth and greater profit, while others view tech stacks as a cost.

REAL-WORLD EXAMPLE

HUSWELL leverages technology to accelerate growth

HUSWELL is a leading hospitality solution provider in Europe for short- and mid-term rentals. It offers a frictionless and effortless platform with an integrated marketplace of local service providers.

Positioned as a platform as a service (PaaS) company, HUSWELL combines its platform, technology, big data and AI with comprehensive services to maximize hosts' returns and ensure exceptional guest experiences.

For example, it connects to the likes of Airbnb and Booking.com to advertise the properties and drive bookings; offers cleaning, maintenance and repairs if required; and provides guests with 24/7 support, including check-in and check-out.

It currently has 32 office employees, 30 to 40 external supporting roles and offshore assistance to provide first-line support from locations including Madagascar (with a focus on the French language), Pakistan, the United States and the Philippines. 'Eighty per cent of our communication is answered within 10 minutes, 24/7, so all of the messages are being answered very quickly,' says founder and CEO Jean-Paul Godfroy.

He embraces what he calls extensive digitization: 'We have developed an online guest portal with all information about the reservation and the property. We digitize every home to keep energy bills as low as possible, and to guarantee security through electronic locks. An owner can also track all of this within the owner portal. From revenue to reviews, transparency is one of our core values.'

HUSWELL can also cover aspects including security deposits, rental agreements, regulatory reporting, guest verification, disturbance monitoring and damage protection. It is also a preferred partner of Salto Systems, which allows it to test different locks.

From its beginnings in Belgium, it has since expanded operations through acquisitions into France and Spain, as well as Scotland and England. 'We started to grow, focusing on the counter-seasonal areas to flatten out the seasonality curve,' Godfroy adds.

Challenges and opportunities

HUSWELL has been leveraging technology to accelerate its own growth, but more importantly, it looks to help smaller hospitality companies manage their properties, as they may feel overwhelmed by technology designed for larger-scale operators.

Saying no to F&B

While HUSWELL provides a wide range of services, it draws the line at food and beverage options. That's because, like Netflix or Uber, they are already available on demand. And through its partnership with guest experience platform Duve, HUSWELL can add on partners. 'For example, we have people offering massages, we have people offering breakfast,' says Jean-Paul Godfroy. 'It's a request feature rather than a real food and beverage system.'

The solution

HUSWELL takes technology very seriously – for Godfroy, so much so that he advises that operators should consider the platforms and software they use as stakeholders within their business, not just external vendors.

The gap he's looking to fill revolves around his belief that smaller operators often buy software that's actually better suited to multiple properties. The net result? They're not using it to its full potential, and may then look to keep buying yet more technology to try to fill the perceived gaps.

'A lot of the time, people do not leverage all or enough capabilities of the systems they already use. So, for example, I've spoken to a lot of other operators using a well-known Property Management System (PMS), but if you go deeper, they are not leveraging 80 per cent of its capabilities; they only leverage 20 or 30 per cent of the platform. Then they start looking for that missing 50 per cent, unnecessarily, in other systems,' he says.

'But the more systems you add – and that was like a movement two or three years ago, where a lot of people said, I'm going to use as much software as possible – the more likely the tower will fall over,' he adds.

The founder also urges hospitality companies to consider their technology provider not just as any other supplier, but as a 'stakeholder'. When shopping around for a PMS, the advice is to select one that will help you expand. 'If your goal is growing, you need to find the stakeholders because you can almost call these platforms stakeholders that will grow with you.'

HUSWELL is developing a platform that is built on top of its own PMS. 'We are working with our partner on it, and by the end of the year we will enable hosting for the smaller hosts, who have one, two or three properties.'

As for its proprietary technology stack, HUSWELL has built its front office using HubSpot, while its back office is built on enterprise resource planning system Odoo. 'Those two are connected to each other, and with guests, of course, in between, which is an amazing structure for us to keep on growing.'

HUSWELL then uses the guest experience platform Duve. 'We have a very strong partnership with them. We are a design partner,' Godfroy says.

Conclusion

HUSWELL appears to have organically evolved from a tech-enabled hospitality company into an actual technology company, building on its deep collaborations with its tech providers. This is likely due to its studious discipline of adopting different technologies and passing those learnings on to others.

From here, HUSWELL will likely be better placed to identify more operational pain points, paving the way for more expansion across Europe.

Two paths: 'tech-enabled' vs traditional operations

Experience-driven approach

'Tech-enabled' hotels and STR operators tend to prioritize guest-facing technologies. These kinds of tech elevate convenience for their guests and create seamless, personalized experiences. Mobile check-in and check-out, digital room keys, AI-powered virtual concierges and real-time in-app service requests have become standard features in these tech-driven properties. The ability to communicate instantly via messaging apps, receive tailored recommendations based on past stays and control room settings through smart devices transforms the guest journey into a frictionless and engaging experience.

Beyond convenience, 'tech-enabled' operators are using software to enhance efficiency with automation, allowing staff to focus on high-touch service moments rather than routine administrative tasks. AI chatbots and voice-activated services ensure guests receive 24/7 assistance without long wait times. The key here is that these properties see technology not as a replacement for hospitality but as an enabler of enhanced guest service. An experience-driven approach also requires a solid back-end with a PMS, Central Reservation

System (CRS) and Customer Relationship Management (CRM). You cannot have the bells and whistles without the basics.

Conservative approach

Other hotels, still the majority, take a more traditional route, often viewing technology as an operational necessity and a cumbersome cost rather than a strategic advantage. Front desk check-ins, physical room keys and direct phone calls remain the primary communication channels in these properties. While these hotels may integrate digital features, such as an essential online booking engine or property management software, they reactively rather than proactively adopt new technology.

For some, this reluctance stems from concerns over disrupting well-established service models, while for others, budget constraints prevent them from making significant technological upgrades. In some cases, operators fear that digitization could erode the personal touch that defines hospitality.

Strategic investment approach

Hotels that view technology as a business enabler rather than a cost centre also take a proactive investment approach. These properties recognize that a robust IT infrastructure streamlines operations and drives revenue growth and guest satisfaction. They set up a culture of innovation, continuously testing and adopting emerging technologies such as AI-powered guest insights, Internet of Things (IoT)-enabled energy management and integrated CRM systems.

Operators who view their tech adoption through an investment lens also understand the power of an interconnected ecosystem.

Risk aversion and budget constraints

Conversely, many smaller or independently operated hotels with tighter budgets tend to be more risk-averse when investing in unproven technology. These properties have hesitated to upgrade legacy systems due to high initial costs, concerns about staff adoption or uncertainty over investment returns.

Budget limitations often lead to a piecemeal approach to technology adoption, with operators implementing individual solutions without an overarching strategy. This fragmented approach can create integration challenges, leading to inefficiencies rather than improvements. Without a clear roadmap, tech adoption will often not fully deliver on its cost.

Data-driven operations

Those who embrace modern technology place their businesses in a position to capitalize on the wealth of data generated across various guest touchpoints. From booking patterns and spending behaviours to service preferences and feedback, this data, which will only grow in depth and detail as more AI is implemented, can be analysed to refine operations, help operators make better decisions and create hyper-personalized guest experiences.

Advanced AI-powered analytics platforms help operators forecast demand, adjust dynamic pricing and optimize inventory management. Smart automation further enhances operational efficiency – predictive maintenance alerts ensure proactive room upkeep, while real-time occupancy monitoring allows for energy-efficient room management. AI-driven sentiment analysis tools help hotels address guest concerns before escalating them.

Fragmented data systems

With AI, hotels can do much more with unstructured and distributed data, and it can save a lot of work extracting, cleaning and consolidating data. However, hotels that do not fully embrace integrated technology solutions could still struggle with siloed data, making it difficult to derive actionable insights. Without a centralized system consolidating guest profiles, purchase history and service preferences, and without the use of AI tools, staff will continue to rely on manual processes, leading to inefficiencies and missed opportunities.

For instance, a lack of integration between the PMS and CRM means that returning guests are not recognized or that service preferences from previous stays are not accounted for. As guests, we all can relate to the frustration of continually having to provide our details and preferences, even if we've stayed at a property or chain before. Impersonal experiences mean missed upselling opportunities and slower response times. Furthermore, without advanced analytics, hotels that aren't embracing tech tools will rely on historical data rather than real-time insights, making it harder to adjust pricing or anticipate fluctuations in demand.

'We've built out certain snippets of code that are required to have the existing tech stacks do what we need them to do, as opposed to what they were designed to do.'

Jason Fudin, CEO, Placmakr

Strategies for bridging the divide

When adopting new technology, hospitality operators will need to decide between incremental adoption – making gradual improvements over time – or radical innovation, involving a complete overhaul of systems. Both approaches have their advantages and drawbacks, and the right choice depends on the business's readiness, existing infrastructure and strategic goals.

The case for incremental innovation

Incremental adoption allows businesses to integrate new technology step by step, minimizing disruption while maintaining continuity in operations. This approach is typically beneficial for:

- **smaller or legacy-driven businesses** that may not have the budget or technical expertise to undertake a full-scale transformation;
- **large brands** because they are too big to do everything at once – most have built a data integration layer so systems on both sides can be replaced over time without disrupting the ecosystem;

- **mitigating risks** by testing solutions before committing to full adoption;
- **ensuring staff adaptation** with a phased training approach.

A typical example of incremental innovation is gradually upgrading a PMS by first integrating a cloud-based booking engine, then layering in guest messaging platforms, and finally adopting AI-powered analytics for revenue optimization.

'I hope that in five years' time we're no longer talking about cloud versus on-premises systems, that by then everyone's on the cloud and everyone's benefiting from the capabilities.'

Wouter Geerts, Director of Research and Intelligence, Mews

The case for radical innovation

Radical innovation – completely overhauling outdated systems in favour of an advanced, integrated solution – can be a game-changer for businesses looking to leapfrog ahead of competitors. This approach works best when:

- **legacy systems are causing inefficiencies** that result in revenue loss or guest dissatisfaction;
- **a business has the financial resources** to invest in a new end-to-end solution;
- **competitive advantage requires a significant shift,** such as adopting AI-driven revenue management or smart room automation;
- **right at the beginning,** new hotels can begin the journey being 'tech-enabled' and tech-forward when they open.

For instance, some hospitality brands have embraced being fully automated by implementing app-based guest experiences, eliminating front desks and replacing them with digital check-ins. These effectively operate 'staffless', which has its pros and cons. No on-site staff means that any issues that do need resolving require a different approach.

The main point here is that the guest should be aware and intentional about their booking choice: that is, they have *chosen* to stay in a property that is fully automated. That way, there are no surprises if they require any assistance.

Decision frameworks for tech adoption

Before deciding on an incremental or radical approach, hospitality businesses can use decision trees or frameworks to assess readiness. Key questions include:

- **Operational need:** What business challenges does the technology solve?
- **Budget and ROI:** What is the cost of implementation versus the expected return?
- **Staff readiness:** Does the workforce have the skills and adaptability required?
- **Guest experience impact:** Will the change enhance or disrupt guest interactions?

A risk-mitigation strategy is also crucial. Whether incremental or radical, businesses should pilot-test solutions, collect data and iterate before rolling out at scale.

TECH LEADER INSIGHT

Attribute-based selling and changing mindsets – Ulrich Pillau, Co-founder and CEO, Apaleo

PMS Apaleo was designed from the outset to be API-first, giving hotel and apartment operators the flexibility to work with a range of different platforms and create a unique experience for both guests and staff.

So it's no surprise that Ulrich Pillau, its co-founder and CEO, predicts that a high level of customization will influence the way guests book their stays in the future.

He expects that attribute-based selling, where guests can dictate which features they want for their room, will eventually replace the current method.

'More than 95 per cent of hotels have a traditional way of selling rooms,' he says. 'It's a combination of: this is the room type you want, such as single room, double room suite, executive room; and this is the price for a certain period which is connected to that room type. That's the way pretty much everybody does it.'

Of course, this type of upselling allows hotels to generate more revenue. But the CEO believes that allowing hotel guests to determine what product they really want will lead to more revenue.

'For example, a guest might say they want a room which has a nice view, is quiet, is far away from the elevator, on the lower floor, or upper floor, and has a shower. The guest determines first the features for the room, and then the technology will allow the hotels to come up with a price for those features.'

He claims that more personalized offerings in other industries have led to 20 to 30 per cent more revenue for the same product, and that Nike is a good example.

'Nike started on their website a number of years ago where actually you could go there and design your own Nike shoes. You might say that I want this colour, I want this form, I want this name on it or whatever,' he says. 'I think the big shift will come when people go away from traditional sales towards attribute-based sales.'

However, one barrier to progression is the hospitality sector's collective mindset. Pillau thinks that many hotel companies and chains, even when recognizing the need to embrace new technology, fail to change their mindset when it comes to thinking of the guest first.

'It's not just about putting new technology into place; it's also about changing your mindset on how you run your business. And if you don't do that right, you'll run into issues,' he says.

'It has to be a strategic process. Everybody has to be onboard. You need to get the owners onboard, the management onboard, the staff, the employees, everybody. If you want to become more autonomous and efficient, you have to design the guest journey separately or differently. You have to look at every procedure you have in the back end to make this automated. There's a lot of resistance from people taking these steps. We've seen this again and again,' he adds.

The example of attribute-based selling is just one of many. There are lots of areas where technology can improve efficiency within the hospitality space. Improved online guest journeys to provide better automation and a great digital guest experience, automation of manual back-office procedures, new AI use cases reducing the time people spend on processes and many other areas are up for change.

'Technology should be removing points of friction, removing inconveniences, ultimately making guests have a much better experience.'

Terry Whyte, The Vacation Rental Software Guy

Partnering with tech providers

Technology adoption in hospitality is clearly related to selecting software – but at the same time it's about forming the right partnerships. The sheer complexity of today's hospitality operations demands a well-integrated, strategic tech stack, and choosing the right technology providers plays a crucial role in ensuring seamless operations. The available tools can be transformative, but only when integrated effectively into a hotel's broader operational strategy.

By carefully selecting technology partners, operators are in a better place and have a greater chance of overcoming integration challenges. A strong technology partnership should be more than just a vendor–client relationship – it needs to be a collaboration in which the provider actively works to optimize solutions and improve efficiency, and adapts to evolving industry trends. The best partnerships allow hospitality businesses to focus on what they do best – delivering exceptional guest experiences – while technology providers handle the complexity of innovation, security and performance.

'A major challenge is turning all the data we collect into actionable insights. It's one thing to gather data, but it's another to interpret it in a way that leads to better decisions. Right now, we're missing opportunities to improve both operations and the guest experience simply because the tech we have doesn't fully support the kind of data integration and analysis we need.'

Hans Meyer, Co-founder, Zoku

Key considerations when selecting technology partners

With a multitude of tech vendors offering solutions tailored to hospitality, choosing the right partner requires a considered approach.

Operators should examine the following five key factors before committing to a technology partnership:

1. SCALABILITY: PLANNING FOR GROWTH
A technology partner should provide scalable solutions that align with the business's growth trajectory. Whether a hotel is expanding its room inventory, opening new locations or diversifying its offerings (such as adding co-working spaces or serviced apartments), its tech stack must support expansion without excessive cost or technical friction.

A scalable PMS, for instance, should allow a small boutique hotel to grow into a multi-location hospitality brand without needing a complete system overhaul. Similarly, a guest communication platform should integrate seamlessly across multiple properties, enabling unified messaging, automation and AI-driven personalization at scale.

2. INTEGRATION CAPABILITIES: THE IMPORTANCE OF APIs
One of the biggest challenges in hospitality technology adoption is system integration. Many properties rely on a combination of PMS, CRM, channel managers, payment processors plus guest communication, guest experience and operation management tools.

Application Programming Interfaces (APIs) play a key role in making different systems 'talk' to each other. A PMS with open API architecture allows properties to connect third-party tools easily, from business intelligence dashboards to guest experience platforms.

When evaluating a technology partner, operators should consider: does the software integrate with our existing tech stack? Are APIs available for custom integrations? How easy is it to add or replace integrations without disrupting operations?

3. INDUSTRY-SPECIFIC EXPERTISE
Technology providers with hospitality-specific expertise understand the industry's unique challenges, regulations and operational workflows. Unlike generic software companies, hospitality-focused tech providers are better equipped to deliver solutions that align with guest expectations, revenue management strategies and compliance

standards. This also goes for providers that uniquely understand the challenges of STR property management or independent boutique hotels versus select service aparthotels.

Operators should look for tech vendors with a proven track record in hospitality. Many specialist providers offer real-world examples and client testimonials and it's even better if they have dedicated customer-led advisory boards.

4. SUPPORT AND TRAINING: BEYOND IMPLEMENTATION

Technology adoption, after installation, then requires ongoing support, training and troubleshooting to maximize effectiveness. The best technology providers offer 24/7 customer support, comprehensive training for staff and dedicated account managers for long-term success. In choosing a partner, hotels should assess if the vendor provides onboarding and training for employees, find out how quickly its support teams resolve issues, and determine if there is a dedicated success manager for long-term optimization. Even more importantly, having an interface that is self-explanatory and doesn't require much staff training is ideal.

5. REPUTATION AND RELIABILITY

Before committing to a technology partner, hospitality operators should conduct thorough research into peer reviews, industry reputation and customer satisfaction. Some due diligence steps include reading reviews on platforms like G2, HotelTechReport and Capterra, speaking to other hoteliers who have used the solution, and attending hospitality tech expos to see product demos and meet vendors.

A vendor with a well-established track record of reliability is crucial, as poor software performance can disrupt guest experiences, revenue management and operational workflows.

'We can create a five-star experience without having five-star staff, with overhead costs. That's what I'm hoping to see this grow and evolve into, with the tech a key component of that.'

Kent Hatcher, Director of Product, Mint House

KEY TAKEAWAYS

Investment or cost: Technology is either seen as an investment or a cost, with forward-thinking operators using it strategically while others hesitate due to budget concerns and risk aversion.

Incremental or radical innovation: Businesses must choose between incremental or radical innovation, balancing gradual tech adoption with full-scale transformation based on their goals and resources.

Strong tech partnerships: Strong tech partnerships and data integration are crucial, as disconnected systems create inefficiencies, while well-integrated solutions drive growth and personalization.

Risk aversion: This holds many operators back, leading to fragmented tech adoption that results in inefficiencies rather than improvements.

Data and competitive advantage: Data-driven decision making is a competitive advantage, as AI-powered analytics help predict demand, optimize pricing and enhance operational efficiency.

Real-World Example – HUSWELL: This Belgium operator exemplifies tech-driven hospitality, using AI, automation and integrated platforms to optimize operations and enhance guest experiences.

3

The foundation of tech-enabled hospitality

The global pandemic accelerated a shift in hospitality and the use of technology. Especially as a result of social distancing mandates, guests became used to doing things without the need for in-person human interaction. For example, contactless check-ins became more common as guests became used to doing certain things for themselves. Overall, guests adapted easily to this change in the hospitality industry, and many seemed to prefer a more digitized experience as it matched their digital expectations elsewhere. It was during 2020–21 that technology really began to take centre stage for a growing number of operators.

So what are the essential elements that form the bedrock of being or becoming a '*tech-enabled*' hospitality provider? How do hoteliers and property managers excel in a world of increased guest expectations, rising costs, staff shortages and constant change? From understanding your technology needs to balancing the digital with the personal, this book, the subsequent chapters, real-world examples and tech leader spotlights will explore how to create a robust infrastructure that not only supports current operations but also prepares for future growth. In the world of hospitality, as in life and business, a strong foundation is everything.

Being a 'tech-enabled' service provider means providing a product or service that carefully combines human interaction and expertise with technology so that a hotelier or property manager can deliver a guest experience more efficiently than through traditional models. It also means leveraging technological advancements to streamline processes, make the best use of data and reduce friction, time and errors. It doesn't mean running things without any human input or human touch, although it can mean that. The majority of 'tech-enabled' operators interviewed as part of this book's research believe that tech adoption enhances human interaction and the ability to provide 'hospitality' rather than diminish it.

Being tech-enabled means still providing guests with exceptional hospitality service while benefiting the business through reduced time and resources. This ultimately reduces costs and adds to the bottom line. Being tech-enabled is the future for all hospitality businesses. Hospitality may well always be about hospitality, but it is also about running a profitable business.

'Hospitality is the future of hospitality.'

Ryan Killeen, Co-founder and CEO, The Annex

For today's hospitality provider, technology is more than the management of various software platforms. It is there to help them stay competitive in a market where guest expectations are higher than ever. However, any operator developing and maintaining a tech stack must be strategic and carefully plan their business needs right from the get-go. They must also ensure that their team is fully onboard with any change, adoption or development.

Bringing the team on the journey

One of the biggest barriers to any operator's successful 'tech adoption journey' is its team. This applies to those running both hotels and short-term rental (STR) operations. The team is the most important aspect of any business, especially a hotel or property management company that provides service and experiences. So, making sure the team has effectively been brought on the digital adoption journey is, perhaps, the single most important element of building a 'tech-enabled' hotel or STR property management business from scratch, or transforming an already established business. The team needs to be fully onboarded, and provided with sufficient training, as even the most advanced tools can fail, leaving a business with a fragmented and inefficient operation.

Hoteliers can overcome resistance to change from middle management and employees by implementing and sticking with certain values and strategies, such as building a 'change mindset' into the company's foundation from the bottom up and involving middle management in the planning phase of tech adoption. They shouldn't just choose a new software because it is shiny and new, and everyone else seems to be using it. They must ensure that anything they purchase has gone through a rigorous planning stage with the entire team. They should collectively ask questions such as 'What pain point are we looking for this software to solve?' and 'Will this tech require the team to do things fundamentally differently, and if so, in what ways?'

Other things to consider include ensuring time and resources are allocated to training, development and staff support. Is there a clear internal communications plan in place and an effective feedback loop?

Steps to consider when bringing a team along on the journey to 'tech-enabled'

Conduct a pilot: Wherever possible, a hotelier should start with pilot programmes that allow employees to experience the new systems on a smaller scale. Positive experiences can help alleviate concerns and build enthusiasm for broader implementation.

Create a change mindset: A team should be encouraged, from leadership to front-line staff, to adopt a shift in mindset about how the business is run. This involves educating staff on the benefits of automation and new technologies, emphasizing that these changes are meant to enhance, not replace, their roles. Often tech will replace human roles; in that case, it's important that the company is transparent and fair about it. If not, rumours could kill motivation and the project.

Embed feedback mechanisms: Establishing feedback mechanisms and feedback loops where employees can voice their concerns and suggestions is imperative. These can be posted either on open forums or anonymously. Actively listening to teams' input encourages a sense of ownership and collaboration. And leaders might also learn something!

Focus on internal communication: Maintaining open lines of communication regarding the reasons for the changes, the expected benefits and how these changes will impact a team in their roles is also required. Transparency reduces anxiety and resistance, and clarity can encourage a change in mindset.

Involve those impacted in planning: Middle management and front-line employees impacted by change in the planning and decision-making processes must be involved as a hotel explores adding new tools. This inclusion can help them feel valued and more invested in the changes being implemented. They may also have good insights to bring to the table.

Provide suitable training and support: Providing comprehensive training and support to help staff adapt to new technologies and processes is essential. This can alleviate fears about their ability to perform their jobs effectively and will ensure they are using the tools in the most effective way.

Recognize success and reward behaviours: It's critical to recognize and reward employees who embrace change and contribute to a transition. It may encourage others to embrace change and contribute as well.

By focusing on these change management strategies, hoteliers and property managers can create a more receptive environment for change, ensuring they are bringing their entire company with them on the journey to become 'tech-enabled'. This will ultimately lead to a smoother transition to new technologies and processes.

'It's not about putting new technology into place only. It's also about changing your mindset on how you run your business. And if you don't do that right, you'll run into issues.'

Ulrich Pillau, Co-founder and CEO, Apaleo

Creating a strategic roadmap

The first step a hotel needs to take is to assess its current technological capabilities and identify gaps. Is it in the area of revenue management that it is falling down, or is it guest services? Are team service levels disjointed, or does the hotel need a Property Management System (PMS) change? Undertake a thorough audit of the existing tech stack, evaluating what works well and where improvements may be needed. Understanding the starting point is key to understanding any goals.

Clearly defined business objectives should also drive the roadmap. Is the aim to enhance guest satisfaction, improve operational efficiency or expand market reach? It might seem obvious that each objective will require different technological solutions, but prioritizing needs is equally important. Not all tech upgrades need to happen at once. Prioritizing will also ensure that possible future initiatives are chosen based on their potential impact and feasibility. A phased approach also allows for smoother implementation, giving a team time to adapt, minimizing disruptions to operations.

Any roadmap should also account for any future growth, ensuring selected technologies can scale with the business. This might be to allow for increased guest numbers, to add new locations or develop additional services. Scalability ensures that tech investments continue to deliver value as the business evolves.

Doing more with less

As is clear, a team is pivotal to a successful hospitality business. Still, there are serious challenges many operators face today because of staffing shortages and what can feel like an ever-diminishing talent pool. Operators' concerns around talent acquisition, quality and employee churn are too real. As resources are often stretched thin, the ability to do more with less can be a game-changer. With razor-thin margins and high operational costs, the hospitality industry stands to benefit immensely from technology that boosts efficiency without sacrificing quality.

Using data to analyse guest behaviour and preferences, hotels and STR managers can optimize everything from room pricing to inventory management to guest communications, ensuring that resources are allocated where they're most needed. Targeted decision making cuts costs and provides the best service possible for the end user.

Automating routine tasks is another area where technology can seriously impact how a hospitality business allocates staff. For example, mobile check-ins reduce the workload for front desk staff, and smart room controls and mobile apps allow guests to adjust lighting and temperature and even select entertainment and housekeeping options from their devices, reducing the need for in-room staff interventions.

TECH LEADER INSIGHT

When software evolves in response to hotel challenges – Leah Rankin, Chief Product Officer, SiteMinder

The hospitality software market is a multi-billion dollar industry. This is in part because the accommodation sector itself is highly fragmented and extremely low-margin, with business owners looking to technology to give them an edge and the ability to carve out extra revenue where possible.

Software companies are constantly responding to new needs from operators, and the sector appears to be growing in tandem with operational trends. Today's most successful hospitality technology brands have not dictated the direction of solutions in the marketplace but instead listened carefully to their customers.

A case in point is SiteMinder. The Australia-headquartered global company was founded in 2006 and began life as a hotel channel manager, which is a technology that allows hotels to essentially sell and manage rooms online via third-party and direct booking channels. Over the past 18 years, SiteMinder has evolved into what it describes as an 'online hotel commerce software provider' that now specializes in helping hotels to optimize their critical revenue streams.

In the early 2000s, distribution was difficult for hotels, as they used mostly manual processes to get their inventory out to the fast-growing online travel agencies (OTAs). The lack of automation led to errors such as double bookings or overbookings, which were an operational headache and also often meant a poor guest experience.

But easing this challenge for the hotel manager and building a solution that allowed for 'one communal place' for the management and distribution of rooms and rates, and connecting a hotel room inventory to a multitude of OTAs, was where the channel manager stepped in.

'The channel manager took the pain away from the double bookings, but it also created an opportunity for hotels because all of a sudden they weren't limited to the number of channels they could be connected to,' says Leah Rankin, SiteMinder's Chief Product Officer. 'It took their world from being static to dynamic, because they could change prices in real time in response to market demands.'

Once embedded into a hotel's ecosystem, software companies could explore the other operational challenges faced by hotel operators. Smaller, independent hotel groups, in particular, did not have sufficient technology resources to manage other areas of marketing such as developing their own website to capture direct bookings or accept online payments.

This need spurred the rise of the platform, and early on SiteMinder spotted an opportunity to build this holistic solution for its customers. 'Often it's an owner operator, or it's a small team that's wearing many hats and delivering great guest experiences, which is the core of what they're trying to do,' Rankin says. For example, the software went on to offer pre- and post-stay guest engagement and communication solutions, and modules that help brands upsell. 'It's less about just the room, it's more about the experience,' Rankin adds.

SiteMinder also created a booking solution for its customers to generate traffic directly so hoteliers could better 'own' the guest experience, while also recognizing that its channel partners were key to the success of its hotel clients.

For example, with the advent of hotel metasearch websites (such as Trivago, Kayak and even Google) that aggregate results from other hotel search platforms, SiteMinder developed new connections to again help hotels generate more traffic. 'Ultimately, it's all about connecting the hotel with the right guest at the right time through the right channel,' Rankin said.

Despite the expansion in services, SiteMinder's distribution and revenue software ultimately aims to focus on servicing the commercial needs of the hotel so the PMS can focus on a hotel's day-to-day operations. It's for this reason that companies like SiteMinder, which has around 44,500 hotel customers globally, collaborate closely with a hotel's PMS while using the large and deep set of data that runs through its platform to create unique reports and insights for hotels to make more informed decisions around revenue.

Looking to the future, Rankin predicts AI will provide hospitality businesses with insights on their next best steps to take, analysing data to advise on the areas that the hotel should focus on.

'Gone are the days where you needed to have a real understanding of the hotel industry and Revenue Management 101,' she says. 'You needed to know what you were doing with these tools. AI is changing the game in the revenue management space.'

Indeed, SiteMinder recently introduced hybrid technology that leverages AI and machine learning to bring together big data to predict future demand for hotels, make recommendations on actions that best respond to that demand, and let hotels take action within their distribution platform in real time. The technology is designed to simplify revenue management and make it accessible to every hotel rather than the limited few who have the required budget and resources to invest in a Revenue Management System and dedicated revenue management teams.

Overall, it will further accelerate the convergence of distribution, revenue optimization and market intelligence that SiteMinder says it has been witnessing in the industry in recent times. 'I'm excited about AI, and what it can do for the future. As an industry, we're a little bit behind some of the other industries out there in their adoption and use, but it's really emerging and it's changing quickly,' adds Rankin.

Is all tech created equal?

In the rush to embrace new technology, it's easy for operators to get caught up in the hype of the latest AI tools, keyless door software, guest messaging apps or digital concierges. It's not uncommon to be seduced by vendors who promise that their platform or tool will revolutionize operations.

However, not all tech is created equal, and adopting the wrong software will often do more harm than good. Poor choices can be cumbersome, become very expensive, and may even require a great deal of time and money to fix. The key to being strategic about tech stack decisions is selecting technology that aligns with the business's specific needs and goals rather than simply chasing the latest trends.

All hotels should endeavour to purchase software that actually solves a pain point or leverages an opportunity. It needs to be compatible too with the other tech currently in use. They also need to check that the pain point isn't easily solved by the existing software. All hospitality operators will understand and be familiar with the rising monthly costs of their various Software as a Service tools. Reducing these costs, or at least not necessarily adding to them, should always be a consideration.

For smaller independent operators, purchasing an all-in-one PMS might be all they need to begin the journey. These cloud-based software platforms typically offer a suite of tools designed to handle everything from reservations to guest communications in a streamlined package. On the other hand, larger businesses with more complex operations or ambitious growth plans may require a more customizable PMS that can be tailored to their unique needs. Refer to Chapter 4, which covers PMSs, for more details about these choices.

When building from the foundations, it's also essential to consider the scalability of tech solutions. What works for a boutique hotel might not be suitable for a large resort or a chain with properties in multiple locations. The ability to integrate new tools as the business grows is essential.

Ultimately, the best technology solutions support a business's strategic objectives. A hotel can ensure an investment pays off by carefully evaluating *all* the options and choosing the right tools.

Balancing technology and the human touch

While technology can automate many aspects of the guest experience, guests often remember the personal interactions. The challenge is finding the right balance – leveraging technology to enhance service without losing the personal connections that define hospitality.

Technology should be seen as a tool that empowers staff, not as a replacement for them. For example, AI can handle routine inquiries and tasks, but it's member of staff's warmth and empathy that will make a lasting impression on guests. A well-timed personal interaction – whether it's a friendly greeting, a thoughtful recommendation or a simple gesture of kindness – can turn a good stay into a great one.

'At the end of the day in the hospitality business, you need to make amazing experiences for people that are coming to create memories, and that's what we are here for.'

Shahar Goldboim, Co-founder and CEO, Boom

Moreover, technology can actually enhance these human interactions by providing staff with the information they need to deliver personalized service. For instance, a Customer Relationship Management (CRM) system that tracks guest preferences can alert staff to special requests or previous issues, allowing them to tailor their service accordingly.

The goal is to use technology to create a seamless, efficient experience that still feels personal and human. By striking this balance, guests receive the best of both worlds – the convenience of modern technology and the warmth of traditional hospitality.

Understanding unique technology needs

Every hospitality business is unique, with its own set of challenges, goals and customer expectations. Understanding specific technology needs helps the business and its team pick the right tools and most suitable strategy.

Assessing exact needs requires a lot of front-ended questioning and some deep thought. A property's tech needs will also vary depending on the business model and the size of operations. For example, a boutique hotel may prioritize personalized guest experiences and need a sophisticated CRM system, while a large chain may focus on operational efficiency, requiring robust PMS and integration capabilities. STR operators with unique units in multiple locations will have very complex needs that are different from a hotel with standard rooms and one building to manage, or even aparthotels with multiple units across a couple of buildings. Equally, operating across borders can impact tech stack requirements.

The key components for building a tech stack

The cornerstone of any hospitality operator's tech stack includes several critical components that together form the backbone of efficient, guest-centric operations. Table 3.1 illustrates each component, its role in a hospitality manager's tech stack and some context on why it's important. By integrating these components, a hospitality operator can create a system that supports day-to-day operations and enhances guest experiences.

There can be a diverse range of systems and platforms within a technology stack. Here are some of the basics.

TABLE 3.1 The foundations of a tech stack

Component	Role	Importance
Artificial intelligence (AI) and automation tools	AI-driven tools such as chatbots, virtual concierges and automated check-in/check-out systems streamline operations and enhance guest service (see Chapter 12).	AI and automation reduce manual workload, allowing staff to focus on more personalized guest interactions and complex tasks.
Booking engine	The booking engine is a software application that allows guests to book rooms directly from a hotel's website.	Direct bookings are crucial for reducing dependency on third-party booking platforms and increasing profit margins. A good booking engine is integrated with the PMS to manage availability and pricing dynamically.
Business intelligence tools	Analytics and reporting tools provide insights into operational performance, guest behaviour and financial metrics through dashboards and reports.	Data-driven decision making is critical for optimizing operations, improving guest experiences and increasing revenue.

(continued)

TABLE 3.1 (Continued)

Component	Role	Importance
Central Reservation System (CRS)	The CRS serves as the central hub for managing room inventory, rates and bookings across multiple distribution channels, including direct websites, OTAs and Global Distribution Systems.	Its importance lies in its ability to streamline operations, prevent overbookings and optimize revenue by ensuring real-time synchronization of availability and pricing across all sales channels.
Channel manager	A channel manager connects a hotel's inventory to various OTAs such as Booking, Expedia, Airbnb, Agoda or any number of small specialist channels. The channel manager controls availability, rates and bookings across the multiple platforms.	It prevents overbooking and optimizes distribution, ensuring that the property is visible on the most relevant channels.
Customer Relationship Management (CRM) system	A CRM system helps manage guest interactions and relationships, storing detailed guest profiles, preferences and history. It looks after all the data that forms part of the guest journey and guest profile with the hotelier or property manager. There can be overlaps in functionality between the PMS and the CRM (see Chapter 9).	It enables personalized service and targeted marketing, enhancing guest satisfaction and loyalty.
Guest experience platforms	These platforms include tools for guest communication (like messaging apps), self-service check-in/check-out kiosks and mobile apps that allow guests to control their stay, including aspects like room service and room settings (see Chapter 11).	Enhancing guest satisfaction through personalized and convenient services, these platforms are vital for modern guest engagement.
Internet of Things (IoT) devices	IoT devices such as smart thermostats, lighting systems and keyless entry locks are increasingly being integrated into hotel rooms (see Chapter 7).	These technologies enhance guest comfort and energy efficiency while providing valuable data on guest preferences and usage patterns.

(continued)

TABLE 3.1 (Continued)

Component	Role	Importance
Operations management platforms	This system manages the scheduling and monitoring of housekeeping tasks, ensuring rooms are cleaned and ready for guests on time (see Chapter 8).	Efficient housekeeping management is crucial for operational efficiency and maintaining high standards of cleanliness.
Point-of-Sale (POS) system	POS systems handle all transactions within the property, including restaurants, bars and other outlets. These are more typical for hotels than STR operations that don't have these options for guests. The same applies for select or limited-service hotels.	Integration with the PMS allows for seamless billing and reporting, and ensures that all guest charges are accurately reflected in their final bill.
Property Management System (PMS)	The PMS is the central hub of a hospitality operation, managing all core functions such as reservations, check-ins, check-outs, billing and room assignments (see Chapter 4).	A robust PMS integrates with other systems in the tech stack, ensuring seamless operations and providing real-time data across various departments. The most important function of a PMS is holding inventory, rates and guest profiles.
Revenue Management System (RMS)	An RMS uses algorithms to analyse market demand, competition and booking patterns to optimize pricing and inventory allocation (see Chapter 6).	Dynamic pricing strategies powered by an RMS can significantly increase revenue by ensuring that room rates are competitive and reflect real-time market conditions.
Security and compliance solutions	These are systems that ensure data security, such as GDPR compliance tools, and technologies like surveillance and access control systems.	Protecting guest data and ensuring physical security are non-negotiable aspects of hospitality management.

REAL-WORLD EXAMPLE

How The Annex transitioned from tech focus to guest focus

Ryan Killeen co-founded The Annex, a hotel named after the Toronto neighbourhood where it's located, in 2018 after a career path that included roles at Airbnb and STR apartment management company Sonder.

He recalls that when the brand launched six years ago, it emphasized a technology-enabled hospitality approach, focusing on aspects such as contactless check-in.

That technology was put to the test during the pandemic, as the hotel managed to operate fully remotely while hosting front-line healthcare workers. 'The technology allowed the workers to gain access to the building and to go in and out of the rooms without the need for staff on-site. These front-line workers were able to make requests, and the hotel was able to fulfil anything that would typically be done with someone on-site,' Killeen says.

Fast-forward to the present day, and the CEO claims that hotel operations have reached a point where, technically, people aren't needed on-site. However, that's not the case for The Annex today, as Killeen opts for human connection, with travel and experience to animate and add to the technology: 'We ensure our team is on-site 24/7 to really enhance the guest experience.'

Killeen also says the company is focusing on language that's more hospitality-centric – but believes the technology is currently better than it's ever been.

'We have started to better understand how to utilize technology as our back-end secret and repurpose our team to focus on the guest experience,' he says, adding that it's in part helping secure glowing reviews, with 4.8 stars on Google and 800+ reviews and counting.

The fast pace of new developments in hotel technology, notwithstanding AI, can prove a frustration, but The Annex is able to overcome this and will lean on technology further in the future as it looks to expand.

Challenges and opportunities

One of the main challenges with hospitality technology is that it is attracting a lot of attention from venture capital. More cash is being injected into the space and, at the same time, software providers are continuously changing or adding new software to compete.

For Killeen, that means real-time adjustments as his team can learn something one week, and the next week, it doesn't exist, or it changes. The Annex has a varied tech stack, with different platforms for everything from access management to guest messaging, housekeeping and reviews, and from revenue management to channel management.

'Another challenge when using third-party software outside of the PMS is that you typically have to have five, six tabs open on your computer, flipping back and forth,' he says.

Branding challenges for STR and independent hotel operators

Branding is another challenge, particularly for operators in the STR sector. Larger hotel groups may not have the agility of independent hotel brands and STR operators, as they're limited by how far they can play around with technology and make decisions due to a level of bureaucracy, argues Killeen.

But STR companies don't have the brand power that hotels have, limiting their appeal to price-driven consumers.

'There's one thing that can't be done with technology that takes time, which is building a brand. It's not a website and a logo. It goes far beyond that. And even the most experienced STR operators are in the first decade of their operations,' he says.

The solution

One way to overcome the constant cycle of change is to have an agile mindset, and Killeen says that hoteliers need to accept that technology, like medicine, is ever-evolving.

'We have an ethos of accepting change and working with it,' he says. 'It's an ongoing challenge. Technology is never going to be "finished".'

As an example, he highlights the 'old-world hospitality' of some hotel brands. These hotels may offer a definitive experience through standard operating procedures that have been done the same way for more than 40 years. 'Those are never going to change, but technology is never going to be set in stone,' he says.

To cope with the plethora of new platforms, Killeen insists on testing new software in a sandbox environment.

'Most software companies run an incredible sales process, so it's easy to find yourself signing the contract before even actually really testing the software,' he notes. 'We've set up a demo environment that replicates our hotel, and anything we have come across or that we're interested in, we're happy to try once, but we'll actually put it into the flow of a day-to-day operation.'

The CEO also says that he checks what stage the vendor company is at from a funding perspective. Again, as more venture capital pours into the hospitality technology space, he warns that he's now starting to see a lot of companies emerge and disappear overnight.

'We're targeting Series A and B companies to ensure anything we add to our ecosystem is here for at least a 12- to 24-month period,' he adds.

Killeen also says the company challenges itself on a quarterly basis, to see if it can do things better with the software. 'Where can we eliminate and consolidate?' he asks.

The wave of new entrants to the tech scene means there's a stronger case for consolidation in the sector. For example, the CEO cites PMS Mews as one to watch because it has taken the Shopify approach of allowing third-party developers to come onto its platform and build out a marketplace.

From The Annex's perspective, Killeen says, Mews will soon be able to 'completely eliminate' some platforms, so he is already starting to see the reality of consolidation. 'I would love to see everything in a consolidated dashboard that doesn't require the team to function outside of that singular dashboard,' he adds.

The Annex on AI

Ryan Killeen urges caution when it comes to any technology providers that talk up their AI.

For example, The Annex uses its guest messaging platform to automatically generate guest review requests. Questions include 'How was your stay at The Annex? Please give us a rating from one to five.' If the guest clicks five, it automatically sends them a link to Google. For anything lower, it advises that management will be in contact.

'We're not using a review management platform. There's a lot of tech vendors that have come out to say we're AI and we learn how you speak and all this,' Killeen says. 'Responding by putting a personal touch, when you can, on some things, like reviews, makes a big difference to me. If you look at Google and look at our reviews, the way we respond is very human. It doesn't feel robotic whatsoever.'

However, he says, The Annex uses AI in ID verification. That means it's scraping the internet faster than ever, looking for things that match or don't match.

'The biggest thing for hospitality, and for us, will be the communication aspect, when we're messaging people. Now a lot of the communication is pre-automated and facilitated through AI. If you're asking specific questions, we've loaded the machine up, for lack of a better explanation, with keywords, examples and recommendations, and it's now starting to auto-populate recommendations that are on the mark. I'd give it a 7 out of 10. There are still times where it'll do something hilariously wrong, but people get it pretty quickly.'

Conclusion

Although currently a single property, The Annex encapsulates much of what is happening in the wider hospitality industry. It potentially offers a blueprint for other independent, 'tech-enabled' hoteliers who are assessing how to leverage technology without being overwhelmed.

The Annex's future pathway involves an ambition to expand, with multiple locations in the pipeline.

'If we continue to have one property for any longer than 18 months from today, I'll believe that I've failed miserably. Our ambitions are to expand beyond Toronto. The Annex is a brand that I think would resonate really well in major markets across North America, Europe and to some extent Asia,' Killeen says.

Having built up an ethos of 'brand power and technology' over the last six years, the CEO believes in the brand's potential. But Killeen is committed to putting the human touch first, backed by technology.

'Where do I see hospitality and technology going in the future? Hospitality is the future of hospitality,' he says.

Meeting guests where they are

We've talked a lot about technology and how it can help a hospitality business, but let's never forget the most fundamental element of running a hotel or a STR operation, and that is the guests. Never forget that no matter how much a piece of software will run something efficiently and cost-effectively, at the end of the day, if it doesn't have either a positive or neutral impact on guests, then it is not worthy of being included in a tech stack.

'The efficiencies that you're getting from technology can be amazing. If you just think about all of the emails that are being sent with sales quotes, event discussions, or the communication between different departments like the front desk and housekeeping or maintenance; the technology is there to automate a lot of that and make everything much more efficient.'

Wouter Geerts, Director of Research and Intelligence, Mews

KEY TAKEAWAYS

Strategic planning is crucial: Creating a well-thought-out strategic roadmap is essential for successfully integrating technology into hospitality operations. Flexibility and scalability must be built into the plan to adapt to future growth and changes in the industry.

Select technology for unique needs: Identifying unique pain points and selecting technology solutions that address those issues effectively are important for any hotel operator. Consideration should also be given to the size and complexity of operations.

Balancing tech with humans: While technology can enhance efficiency and automate many tasks, some 'tech-enabled' operations use technology to empower staff to provide more personalized and memorable guest experiences, not replace human connection.

It's a journey, not an endpoint: Hospitality technology is constantly evolving. Regularly reviewing and updating a strategy ensures that operations remain competitive and aligned with current trends and guest expectations. An agile mindset and a willingness to adapt are crucial for long-term success.

Not all tech is created equal: It's essential to select technology that addresses specific needs and goals, rather than chasing the latest trends.

Consolidation shift: The hospitality industry is seeing a shift towards consolidation in tech solutions, with some providers offering comprehensive platforms that can replace multiple separate tools.

Real-World Example – The Annex: This Toronto boutique hotel has created a tech strategy that is mindful and flexible, ultimately putting the guest experience at the forefront of operations.

4

Property management:
The hub of hospitality

For hoteliers and short-term rental (STR) property managers, the Property Management System (PMS) is the beating heart of operations. It's the hub connecting every aspect of the business, from reservations to housekeeping, guest communications to financial transactions. The evolution of PMS technology over the last few years has transformed how hospitality businesses operate, making them more efficient, responsive *and* guest-centric.

Today's cloud-based PMS platforms are a far cry from their predecessors. Gone are the days when a PMS was just a glorified booking system. Today's solutions are sophisticated ecosystems designed to handle the multifaceted demands of running a complex hospitality business. They integrate (almost) seamlessly with other technologies, providing a unified interface that simplifies management tasks and enhances the guest experience. Key vendors in the space have referred to themselves as the Salesforce or Hubspot of hospitality – giving an insight into both the capabilities and the ambitions of the current PMS market.

A big difference between 'modern' PMSs and legacy models is how they were originally designed and the purpose that they were originally serving. Many of the legacy PMS platforms built 20–30 years ago were based on the business requirements at that time, which were most certainly different from what a hospitality operator is looking to achieve today. Back then, hotel stays or STR bookings were not made online but through call centres or travel agents. Guests would either pick up the phone or literally walk into an office or retail store to book their next trip. The 'connected trip' was also more standard as travel agents packaged up hotel stays with flights, car rental and tours. This meant that bookings were often centralized through one source.

There were also far fewer other technologies being used by hoteliers and managers. Many of hospitality back-end and front-end operations were still manual, and especially so for smaller and mid-sized operators. The larger brands may have had limited systems in place, but these were still largely unrecognizable compared to those used today. Tech stacks in the past tended to be cumbersome, expensive and not connected to each other at all. When the first iteration of the PMS was developed, the key missing ingredients were a live connection to the online/digital world and the ability to connect seamlessly to other software. The old guard of PMS simply didn't need to develop that functionality. So they didn't. As the world moved online, so too have property management software options adapted and developed.

Cloud-native PMS platforms, based on Software as a Service (SaaS) models, have disrupted the ecosystem. They are easier to integrate, more cost-effective and have the ability to be constantly (or at least very often) updated through a robust API (Application Programming Interface) connection.

Newer versions of property management software were created to be 'cloud-first' and with open APIs so that operators would have access to real-time integration. Many SaaS models also require less time to install and get running. This makes them a much more viable option and cost-effective for almost every operator, no matter the size or scale of the business.

The role of interfaces

APIs play a crucial role in the hospitality industry by enabling seamless communication and integration between various software systems. In the context of hospitality technology, APIs act as intermediaries that allow different applications to interact and share data efficiently. This, in turn, enhances operational efficiency, staffing utilization and the customer experience. With the PMS at the heart of connections for hospitality businesses and with APIs acting as connectors that link different departments and systems together within a unified interface, streamlining operations and enhancing the guest experience become easier.

Another way to envisage a PMS with APIs is to think of a spider's web with thousands of invisible threads connecting and transporting data, making it strong, malleable, extremely efficient and fit for purpose. At a fundamental level, APIs are a communication tool or gateway. They allow the PMS to communicate with booking engines, channel managers, Customer Relationship Management (CRM) tools and other essential hotel software.

In the past, hospitality operators would have relied on multiple disconnected systems, which often led to inefficiencies and operational challenges. Interfaces always existed but they were point-to-point (often with a physical cable), closed and proprietary, which made them difficult to manage and maintain. If one system was updated all the connected systems had to be updated too. If there was an issue, it was hard to find its source. Hoteliers and managers were forced to purchase several separate and disconnected tools for different functions, such as revenue management, guest communications, channel management (distribution) and similar. This could lead to integration issues and blame shifting among vendors when problems arose.

The hub-and-spoke model: all-in-one versus marketplace

Today's modern PMS market is typically split between a 'marketplace model,' a hub with many spokes, and the 'all-in-one' approach, which considers the wheel as a whole. For many hoteliers and property managers, choosing between the two approaches is akin to comparing apples and oranges and realizing that there are 'different strokes for different folks'. One system is not better than the other. They are just different. Hospitality operators will choose one or the other based on their priorities, future plans and current needs.

The debate between all-in-one PMS solutions and marketplace models is a central theme in the evolution of property management technology. Both approaches have merits and can significantly impact a business's operations. However, they also have some disadvantages, and neither is necessarily the perfect answer to a hotelier or property manager's significant needs when it comes to running a business.

All-in-one systems: simplicity and integration

Put simply, all-in-one systems offer a cohesive solution where all functionalities are integrated into a single platform. This approach simplifies operations by providing a unified interface for managing every aspect of the property. In theory, they mean that an operator needs only one solution, one 'source of truth' for managing and operating its business. Operators may still choose to bolt on and use very specialist 'point solutions' for the delivery of very specialist services such as door locks, business intelligence or guest messaging. However, the essential theory is that the PMS partner has developed everything that they could need to run their business. These solutions tend to be suited to operators that are on a smaller scale or have simpler needs.

> 'The Property Management System must transcend its origins as merely a reservation tool and plug and play. It must evolve into the central hub of a comprehensive tech stack, integrating deeply with other systems to drive operational efficiency and innovation, setting the foundation for future success in the hospitality industry.'
>
> **Terry Whyte, The Vacation Rental Software Guy**

The key advantages to an all-in-one PMS include:

Data consistency: An integrated system ensures that all data is consistent across the platform. This is crucial for accurate reporting and analytics, which in turn supports better decision making.

Easier to use: A unified system tends to have a more intuitive user interface, as all modules are designed to work together seamlessly. This can enhance the user experience for staff, leading to increased productivity, fewer training hours and, in turn, greater efficiency.

One source of truth: In theory, having just one main technology partner means that you have only one point of contact, one billing system and one entity to blame when things go wrong. Ideally, having an all-in-one PMS partner would eliminate all of the hassle and pain points of finding the right software partner to take responsibility and fix things should an issue arise.

Streamlining operations: With all features under one roof, staff can, in theory, manage reservations, check-ins, housekeeping, guest communications and billing from a single dashboard. This reduces the need for multiple logins and systems, thereby minimizing errors and training time.

For many, the transition to an all-in-one solution addresses connectivity pain points by providing a single, cohesive system where all functionalities across the hospitality business are integrated. This approach not only simplifies operations but also ensures accountability.

There are significant advantages of all-in-one systems and they can be best compared to the evolution of the smartphone. Just as smartphones have consolidated multiple devices such as payment, camera and apps into one, the all-in-one PMS solution brings together various functionalities under a single platform, offering value that is far beyond just cost savings. This integration reduces training time for staff, enhances connectivity and ensures a more coherent operation.

But even if it's not cheaper, proponents of all-in-one solutions argue that the connectivity, the fact that everything is in a single ecosystem, is valuable. It's more coherent. You don't have connectivity issues and, crucially, you know who to blame and who to contact when things go wrong.

However, the all-in-one approach is not without drawbacks. The primary concern is the potential for limited functionality in specific areas. While the system may cover all bases, it might not excel in every aspect. This can be a critical issue for businesses with unique or highly specialized needs.

Marketplace models: flexibility and customization

On the other hand, the marketplace PMS model for property management allows businesses to pick and choose from a variety of best-of-breed solutions covering everything from revenue and pricing to AI tools, specialist guest journey platforms and property access. This modular approach offers significant flexibility and customization, which can be a game-changer for many operators. It's particularly suitable and popular with hospitality brands that have good tech resources in-house or have reached a size where needs can become far more complex and require specialist technology to perform certain tasks. These would be beyond the scope of the average all-in-one PMS.

> 'As technology becomes more advanced, integration between various systems, like PMS and guest services, is essential for providing a seamless guest experience.'
>
> **Steve Davis, CEO, Operto**

The benefits of a marketplace PMS include:

Champions innovation: The marketplace approach encourages innovation, as software providers constantly compete to offer the best solutions. This results in a dynamic ecosystem where businesses can benefit from the latest advancements.

Increasing scalability: As a business grows, it can add or upgrade individual components without overhauling the entire system. This makes the marketplace model highly scalable and adaptable to changing needs.

Tailoring solutions to needs: Businesses can select the best tools for their specific needs, whether that involves a superior booking engine, advanced CRM capabilities or cutting-edge revenue management software. Tailored solutions ensure that each component of the PMS is best suited to the business's unique requirements.

Proponents of the marketplace PMS say that investing in a PMS with an API-first approach is akin to installing virtual doors that allow data to move freely between the PMS and other integrated systems. This requires significant investment and resources to build and, importantly, maintain API connections. The beauty of standard APIs is that they don't require investment or custom development and they are very low maintenance. But the available tools give operators wider choices to add, install and use any kind of connected software to enhance their operational efficiency and add to the guest experience.

A downside of the marketplace model is the potential for integration challenges. Ensuring that all chosen components work together seamlessly can be complex and may require ongoing IT support. Additionally, managing multiple vendors can be time-consuming and may complicate troubleshooting. There is no single 'source of truth' to blame when things go wrong. There may also be varying degrees of maintenance for each vendor the hotel works with, and they will all likely innovate at different paces.

TECH LEADER INSIGHT

A historical perspective of the vacation rental Property Management System – Saber Kordestanchi, Co-founder and Chief Strategy Officer, Hostaway

Both vacation rental and hotel PMSs help streamline operations and enhance the guest experience, but they are actually disparate platforms.

A vacation rental PMS needs to cater to unique properties with a significant focus on guest communications to reflect the lack of a front desk and the fact that guests aren't checking in to standard hotel rooms. A high degree of integration with third-party services, such as cleaning and maintenance for remote property management, is also critical.

Perhaps most importantly, the evolution of the vacation rental PMS has been shaped by online travel agencies (OTAs) and later Airbnb, according to Saber Kordestanchi, co-founder and Chief Strategy Officer at Hostaway.

'A lot of solutions available for vacation rentals were built 30 years ago. They were based on the business requirements at the time, which usually involved in-person offices, and you would likely have a rental office in a beach town, and as a guest you went there to pick up your keys,' he says.

At that time, most vacation rental bookings were generated through referrals and repeat customers. With the development of the internet, rental websites eventually included pictures and a phone number for making a booking.

In the early 2000s, OTAs began gaining substantial market share in the travel industry. Travellers were now booking their plane tickets, hotels and vacation rentals online. This is where Airbnb saw an opportunity, Kordestanchi argues, and created a new marketplace for vacation rentals in traditionally non-vacation rental locations.

'The old tools were no longer applicable because the people who were booking on Airbnb didn't phone, they didn't show up in person to an office – they booked online,' Kordestanchi says. 'PMSs were missing this live, real-time connection to properties advertised online: who was booking where, and at what price.'

Since then, numerous platforms have been developed to cater to the unique characteristics of the STR sector, and these continue to enhance processes, operations and, ultimately, the guest experience.

However, the journey hasn't been easy. In the early days, many different connections were needed. A property manager needed to buy a separate PMS and a channel manager and connect them together if they wanted to communicate with the guests. They also needed to buy a separate tool to manage finances and maintain their website.

'You needed to buy 10 pieces of software just to run your business. You spent a lot of time vetting the software. It was like a network and you had to map the entire landscape,' Kordestanchi continues. Often, connections would break and it wasn't uncommon for the various providers to blame each other. Owners and operators were, therefore, caught in the crossfire and even ended up losing money.

Advancements in technology have spurred the creation of all-in-one PMS solutions – similar to the hotel industry. From a business perspective, the risk of having a major single point of failure outweighs the complexities and inefficiencies of buying multiple pieces of software.

The ongoing movement towards all-in-one solutions is behind the current wave of industry consolidation, but the Hostaway co-founder says he believes there is also value in having an open marketplace.

Fully tech-enabled: building your own PMS

For some ambitious, smaller hospitality operators, developing their own PMS that will meet their specific operational needs is sometimes a choice they make. However, most large hotel chains have abandoned their homegrown PMSs and are going off the shelf.

These custom-built systems require significant upfront investment and ongoing development costs, but they also allow for unparalleled flexibility and scalability. A purpose-built, proprietary PMS ensures that every aspect of a hotelier or property manager's operations – from booking to guest communications – is finely tuned to *their* business model and future ambitions.

By building their own PMS, operators hope to streamline their operations and gain a competitive edge through enhanced data management, improved customer service and greater operational control.

REAL-WORLD EXAMPLE

Cocoonr sees benefits in building technology from scratch

Cocoonr, founded in 2015, specializes in short- and mid-term rental property management and concierge services for a range of accommodation types, including apartments, villas, houses and chalets across France. Overall, it manages more than 3,500 properties.

The company launched Book&Pay in 2019. This digital platform helps second-home owners in the French market rent their properties for short stays through OTAs. Book&Pay also facilitates revenue management and guest communications for the owners or agents.

At the same time, Cocoonr works with 200 local concierge partners who carry out logistical services, such as accommodation preparation and maintenance, laundry and guest check-ins and check-outs.

While the Cocoonr brand covers cities like Strasbourg, Bordeaux, Nancy, Lyon, Marseille and Toulouse as well as the French leisure markets (Arcachon, Saint-Malo, Dinard), Book&Pay has wider coverage with a presence all over France, in all types of market (urban, leisure, mountain) and in the French Caribbean islands (including Guadeloupe and Martinique).

Cocoonr is very selective about the owners it accepts onto the platform, and its portfolio is constantly curated. That makes the difference in terms of performance (average daily rate, occupancy rate) and guest satisfaction.

Understandably, given its French and Francophone background, 70 per cent of guests staying with Cocoonr come from France. Other inbound markets include the UK, Germany, Belgium, Switzerland, Spain, Italy and the United States.

The Cocoonr.fr website represents an average of 20 per cent of the company revenues. In some markets, it's above 30 per cent. There is no marketing investment on sales; its direct revenues are coming from the loyalty of guests who have had a nice experience and want to repeat it in another location.

Challenges and opportunities

What makes Cocoonr stand out as a hospitality provider is that it decided from the outset to invest in building its own hospitality tech stack.

'We built it from zero because nine years ago we weren't very happy with the technology on the market, and we thought it maybe wasn't so difficult to build our own custom stack starting with a PMS,' says Antoine Serrurier, CEO and co-founder, Cocoonr and Book&Pay. 'That was one of the most important and best decisions we made.'

It was also a bold decision. Serrurier admits there was a high initial cost to develop the PMS, but recalls that, at the time, there was an ambition to grow the company, and this was felt strategically as the best and most efficient long-term way to do this.

'That was our bet at the beginning. But for hospitality businesses that are too small and don't have a growth and scale plan, it could become just a cost,' he says. 'If we only wanted to stay in one or two cities, we would have taken all the good tools already designed and developed that were on the market like everybody else. But as we wanted to be all over France, it was the right decision to build our own technology.'

Today, the company has 120 employees and gains are being realized in terms of profit margin and efficiency.

That's not to say the company isn't challenged by some aspects. Like many brands, it wants to enhance guest communication, particularly messaging speed.

'We can improve our efficiency in terms of guest relations and guest messaging,' Serrurier notes. 'We already have all the messages from all the OTAs in our PMS, but we need to improve this part to be more efficient, to not miss urgent messages or requests we need to deal with. It's a pain point that technology can solve quickly.'

Leaning into local knowledge to grow revenue

Cocoonr wears many hats. On top of developing the digital platform Book&Pay, it acts as a real estate agency that helps investors. This is thanks in part to its

14-agency footprint spread across France, meaning it possesses a lot of local knowledge.

As a result it can offer a range of ancillary services, such as exploring an investment's rental potential, looking at local regulations and advising on adapting accommodation to seasonal trends. It's a smart move as it's effectively recycling its expertise and know-how, feeding data back into developers, leading to more available rentals and ultimately increasing turnover.

The solution

Keeping it simple lies at the heart of building your own tech stack. The PMS that Cocoonr has built has many of the functionalities of other systems – and the CEO admits, 'It's not a revolution; it works well to welcome 2,000 or 3,000 people a week. It works perfectly.'

However, for channel management it has a long-standing partnership with Rentals United, where it leverages its many connections to the major players for distribution such as Booking.com and Airbnb.

Serrurier describes Cocoonr's proprietary tech as 'deep' PMS, as it can do everything it wants with the guest, the host, its own teams in the headquarters or the teams sitting in its local agencies, on top of connecting into its concierge partners.

One key advantage of building its own technology is that if the company needs to improve a feature or function, it can do it itself. Feedback from users, including hosts, is encouraged and new feature requests are set in a workflow, so the team is able to see the improvements lined up for the PMS over the next six months. Cocoonr has five internal developers and a Chief Technology Officer overseeing this.

'We make our own decisions on what needs to be developed in terms of new features or what needs to be fixed in terms of problems, and that's comforting,' Serrurier says.

As for upping its guest communication game, Cocoonr is utilizing OpenAI, with integrations also set to improve time saving and efficiency for its dispersed teams. 'We integrate AI where we think we can do a better job for our guests or for our teams, without decreasing the quality of what we are doing. We are integrating it slowly but surely,' the CEO adds.

Conclusion

Despite an incredible array of technology providers in the marketplace today that can home in on specific pain points within the hospitality sector, Cocoonr has decided to go its own way. It saves time and money, but such a technology play isn't for the faint-hearted. Any hospitality company considering following suit would need to be highly ambitious, with a serious growth strategy in place.

But as Cocoonr has demonstrated with complementary spin-off Book&Pay, there's scope for natural evolution. Its success should inspire other tech-focused hospitality startups to look beyond their own businesses.

Cocoonr secured backing from private equity firm UNEXO Crédit Agricole Ille, and Vilaine Expansion, the investment arm of French banking group Crédit Agricole, in 2023, indicating that more technology expansion could be on the way.

Is there another way?

At the moment, you can't realistically run a hospitality business with more than a handful of rooms without a PMS. But is there a future where the PMS is not quite so central to operations? Could there be a world where the PMS may well still remain the scaffolding of operations, the core structure, but one of a number of guest-facing tools takes the lion's share of the guest management side of running a hotel or STR business and either eclipses the role of the PMS or at the very least matches it?

The guest management tools, in essence, become the hub, with the PMS as one of the spokes. With the rate of innovation in the guest management side of operations flourishing, this is a real possibility. The future of AI as a fundamental structure for layering over current PMSs is also an interesting development to watch. This could be where PMSs deepen the development of their own AI capabilities, or 'AI-first' platforms start to shake up how hoteliers and managers use their current PMS solutions by adding that AI layer.

'The Property Management System is the backbone of operational efficiency in hospitality. It must connect the dots across data and technology, making information accessible and actionable in real time to truly enhance the guest experience and drive consistency across the brand.'

David Peller, former Global Managing Director, Amazon Web Services Travel and Hospitality

Choosing the right PMS

The decision between an all-in-one system and a marketplace model, or building your own, ultimately depends on the specific needs and resources of the business. Here are a few considerations:

Budget: All-in-one systems often have predictable pricing structures, whereas marketplace models might incur additional costs for integrating and maintaining multiple solutions.

Business size and complexity: Smaller businesses with straightforward operations might benefit more from the simplicity of an all-in-one system. Larger enterprises with complex needs may find the flexibility of a marketplace model more advantageous.

Growth plans: Consider the long-term growth strategy. If significant expansion or diversification is anticipated, a scalable marketplace model might offer better long-term benefits over an all-in-one system. Moving PMS can be clunky and expensive.

Technical expertise: Businesses with limited IT resources might prefer an all-in-one system for its ease of use. Those with strong technical capabilities might leverage the customization potential of a marketplace model. Those with significant time and money to invest in building their own proprietary systems may look to that solution.

In addition, when a business is choosing a PMS partner, it needs to focus on having the right APIs rather than endpoints or connections to gauge integration robustness. Ensuring the PMS has reliable uptime to avoid disruptions in service and data access is critical. It's a good idea to test the PMS in a live environment before purchase to evaluate its performance and compatibility with third-party apps – especially when opting for a marketplace model.

'Many companies struggle to maximize the potential of technology due to limited human resources and expertise. Without dedicated personnel to manage and analyse tech tools, companies often fail to leverage the full capabilities of their systems, leading to underutilization.'

James Cornwell, Founder and CEO, Curated Property

Innovations shaping the future of property management

As technology continues to evolve and hospitality operators' needs continue to deepen, PMS capabilities will also change.

Here are a few innovations in the PMS space to watch:

Accessibility for smaller operators: For smaller independent hotels, there is a trend towards creating 'light' PMS solutions that are user-friendly, with simplified interfaces and features tailored to operators who may not have extensive experience in the hospitality industry. These solutions make it easier for smaller hotels to manage their operations without needing technical expertise.

Artificial intelligence (AI): AI-driven tools are enhancing everything from revenue management to personalized guest experiences. Machine learning algorithms can predict booking trends, optimize pricing and even anticipate maintenance needs. The PMS market is also being positively impacted by AI innovation because of further automation and interaction with other systems.

Internet of Things (IoT): IoT devices are becoming increasingly integrated with PMS platforms. Smart thermostats, keyless entry systems and connected appliances offer an elevated, seamless experience for guests while providing valuable data for operators.

Mobile functionality: Mobile and web apps for PMS platforms are transforming how staff interact with the system. On-the-go access to information and the ability to perform tasks remotely can significantly enhance operational efficiency. What is key is to ensure that a PMS partner has the foresight and vision to develop according to the needs of a hotel, such as a mobile app and a unified inbox accessed in one place that show all messages and emails, whatever platform they are connected to.

The PMS is the central hub that can make or break the efficiency and guest experience in the hospitality industry. Whether a company opts for an all-in-one solution or a marketplace model, the key is to choose a system that aligns with operational needs and growth ambitions. Embracing the latest innovations in PMS technology can set a business apart.

'Investments into tech have always been considered as hard, such as I need to put a new system in there and it will cost me so much, instead of looking at the returns you get from deploying new technology in a good way.'

Ulrich Pillau, Co-founder and CEO, Apaleo

However, remember that onboarding a new platform is not always as simple as the vendors would often like to make out. Changing PMS can be costly and time-consuming and can create any number of headaches for your team. As one of the tech leaders I spoke with in researching this chapter said to me, 'Changing PMS can be akin to doing open heart surgery with a fork!' With that in mind, a business should choose a PMS that it envisages being with for the long game. That might be because of the functionality it affords, the stability of its investments, its customer service record or its partnerships. However, it is equally important to determine how needs might change over a period of time.

KEY TAKEAWAYS

Central role of a PMS: Modern PMS platforms are essential for integrating various aspects of hospitality management, including reservations, housekeeping, guest communications and financial transactions.

Evolution of a PMS: Today's cloud-based PMS platforms have evolved significantly from their legacy counterparts. They are now sophisticated ecosystems that integrate seamlessly with other technologies. Application Programming Interfaces (APIs) play a crucial role in enabling seamless communication and integration between various software systems in the hospitality industry.

All-in-one systems vs marketplace models: The chapter discusses two main approaches to PMS solutions. All-in-one systems offer simplicity and integration by consolidating all functionalities into a single platform, while marketplace models provide flexibility and customization by allowing businesses to choose from a variety of best-of-breed solutions.

Technological advancements: Innovations such as AI, the IoT and mobile functionality are transforming PMS capabilities. These advancements improve operational efficiency, add more to the guest experience and allow for adaptability to future developments.

Building a custom PMS: Some 'tech-enabled' hospitality operators are developing their own PMS to meet specific operational needs. This approach allows for unparalleled flexibility, enhanced data management and improved customer service.

Challenges of integration: While marketplace models offer flexibility, they can also present integration challenges. Ensuring that all chosen components work together seamlessly can be complex.

Rise of guest management tools: There is potential for guest management tools to become more central in hospitality operations, possibly eclipsing the role of the PMS. The integration of AI could further transform how PMS solutions are used.

Real-World Example – Cocoonr: This property management company built its own PMS, which has led to significant benefits such as streamlined operations, better compliance with local regulations and the ability to quickly adapt to new technological needs and guest expectations.

5

Marketing and personalization in hospitality

A whopping 71 per cent of consumers now expect personalization when it comes to experiencing a product or service, with 76 per cent getting frustrated when it doesn't happen, according to McKinsey and Company's 'Next in Personalization 2021 Report'.[1] We all know how great it feels when we experience being seen and heard and our preferences are met, seemingly with little effort. If I go into a hotel room and there is Earl Grey tea, shortbread cookies and a window that opens, then I'll be a loyal customer for life. But personalization at its best happens way before the stay. It starts in the early search, planning and dreaming stage and then comes into its own in the booking part of a guest journey.

However, true personalization can only happen using collected data. The hospitality industry and its unique operators can only really provide personalized touchpoints if they know who their customers are. This needs to go beyond just understanding a persona or demographic likely to book your property.

The McKinsey report revealed that companies that excel at demonstrating customer intimacy generate faster rates of revenue growth than their peers. The closer organizations get to the consumer, the bigger the gains. This makes total sense, but it's easier said than done for many operators.

True personalization means you actually *know* the individual guest and their preferences. This, of course, is the problem. Getting data in the first place is hard, but what is harder is ensuring that the known information about a guest connects with all touchpoints across both guest-facing and internal operational tech.

We all know the frustration of booking a hotel room via an online travel agency (OTA), only to have emails sent from the operator with seemingly no knowledge of who you are and therefore needing to reaffirm your email, address and reasons for travel. We also all know what it's like to spend a second, third or fourth visit to a brand or even a property, and they still don't get that you don't want a smoking room, let alone anticipating that you like hard pillows and an extra blanket. Data silos are one of the fundamental pain points of the hospitality industry and what holds it back from truly performing personalization.

Marketing in a privacy-first world

Fundamentally, collecting and using data comes with privacy issues. While consumers certainly care about privacy, what they really want is value for their information and transparency about how companies are using it.

Consumers today are generally aware that marketers track their online activities. Many accept this practice, understanding that it can lead to more tailored experiences. In fact, some consumers deliberately opt into cookies on brand websites, recognizing that this allows companies to provide more relevant content and offers. Data collection can benefit both parties when used responsibly: customers enjoy improved experiences, while businesses see significant gains.

Getting the basics right

When it comes to marketing and personalization, a shift needs to happen. Data collection and data use need to become more sophisticated so operators and marketeers can move along the journey from marketing to *all*, to marketing to *many*, to marketing to *some*, to marketing to a *few*, to marketing *one to one*.

For example, the holy grail of such a marketing journey could look like the following. A small independent hotelier with a riad – a traditional Moroccan house or palace with a garden and courtyard – in

Marrakech starts off with a website and is listed on an OTA. With this strategy alone, she is marketing to *all*. To refine her marketing, the riad owner starts to use search engine optimization and creates tailored content aimed at attracting those who might be looking to visit North Africa. That signifies a shift from *one to the world*, to *one to many*. She soon realizes that she'd be better off focusing her resources and efforts on only those who are interested in staying in a riad in a medina (historical district) of Marrakech this coming season.

So, she shifts to ensuring her listings and owned content specifically refer to the medina and staying in a riad over winter. She sets prices accordingly and uses revenue management to maximize bookings. This is marketing to *some*.

Digging deeper, she realizes that it is just couples that she wants to attract, so she further focuses on the romantic aspects of the property, providing content related to intimate dining choices and experiences. She has now shifted to marketing to a *few*. From here, it's a big leap to marketing *one to one*. Marketing to one means knowing that Mr and Mr Jones are currently looking for a romantic stay in a riad in the medina. They are searching online right now, and our small independent hotelier knows that they are looking as she is tracking their progress and has a digital relationship with them.

The role of the OTAs

For many operators, scaling personalization is where it gets really tricky. If you are looking to welcome more than a few hundred guests each year, then having the skills and tools for personalization that can scale is challenging. This is where the OTAs come in. At their core, platforms such as Expedia, Booking.com, Airbnb, Trip.com, Agoda and Mr & Mrs Smith have poured billions of dollars into marketing, search and personalization. They are marketing machines providing leads (at a price, of course) to operators.

By collecting and analysing user data, OTAs offer tailored recommendations, implement dynamic pricing and deliver targeted marketing campaigns. They optimize user interfaces, suggest complementary products and use personalized communication to boost customer retention. OTAs also employ mobile personalization and harness AI and machine learning to refine their offerings.

This data-driven approach allows them to identify travel trends, improve user experiences and increase revenue through cross-selling and upselling. Ultimately, OTAs aim to provide a seamless, personalized journey for travellers while maximizing their own business potential in the competitive travel market.

'In the past everything has been reservation focused. The movement is set to become more customer focused. So where hotels in the past talked about RevPAR, we talk about customer lifetime value.'

Willem Rabsztyn, Co-founder and CEO, Bookboost

The changing world of search

It's the changing world of search marketing that really has the potential to impact travel and hospitality. Both OTAs and some of the more digital-first hospitality brands already leverage data analytics and AI to deliver tailored search results and recommendations based on a user's past behaviour, preferences and current context. 'Lookalike' marketing, which is based on the preferences of others that look like you, is also used. This personalized approach also extends to retargeting campaigns and email marketing, creating a more engaging and relevant experience for potential guests.

Of course, for a number of years now, we've seen the rising importance of visual content in search marketing. With the integration of visual search capabilities in major search engines, hotels are optimizing their image and video content to appear in the visual search results. This includes using high-quality photos, virtual tours and AI- and user-generated content to showcase their properties and amenities.

What's still at the beginning of the journey is using generative AI and machine learning to serve up hotels and short-term rentals (STRs) with prospective guests through 'matching'. And today voice search is growing. We're likely moving towards a predominantly voice-based interface, where users will interact with their devices through natural conversation. Imagine simply speaking to your smartphone, saying something like, 'I'm considering a vacation. What are the top 10 destinations that would suit me?' This shift represents a move away from traditional text-based searches towards a more intuitive, AI-driven approach that can interpret context and preferences, and deliver more relevant results through verbal communication.

Imagine being offered options for stays and destinations that are perfect for you, but you didn't even know existed or had no idea would be the perfect fit for your wants and needs. Brian Chesky, Airbnb co-founder and CEO, said in a Skift Global Forum interview in 2024 that Airbnb lists homes in 100,000 destinations but most of us only ever think of just 100 places max.[2] We need our minds to be expanded with new options and the transformation of search is that vehicle. Imagine also the positive impact on reducing over-tourism when the industry can redistribute travel by providing options that are just right for a traveller and not just the most popular.

The rise of the omnichannel

The rise of the omnichannel refers to the evolution of marketing and customer service strategies to provide a seamless, integrated experience across multiple platforms and touchpoints. It's an approach that recognizes that modern consumers interact with brands through various channels – websites, mobile apps, social media, physical locations, user groups, publications, communication tools and even direct mail. What it really means is that you are meeting your prospective customers where they *actually are*. We all know that booking travel requires a lot of different touchpoints, lots of deliberation and time spent researching.

Long gone are the days when you could reach your prospective customers through just a couple of channels, such as a website and maybe some Facebook ads. Today's consumer is both flighty and disloyal when it comes to where they get their information and so you need to be at the forefront of a prospect's mind, with a consistent message in all the channels they frequent. In essence, an omnichannel marketing approach aims to create a cohesive customer journey across all these touchpoints.

The rise of omnichannel marketing is driven by the need to connect with customers on their terms, empowering them to engage with brands seamlessly across all touchpoints. Successful implementation requires consistent content and interactions across channels and optimized data-driven decision making. As technology continues to blur the lines between online and offline interactions, omnichannel marketing aims to enhance consumer experiences across all physical and digital channels customers use to interact with brands.

> 'When you look at the big brands, they are totally famous. You will always have room for the five-star. This type of chain will always have a justification to exist, and will always have sufficient customers that would like to have this personal service which is supported by technology.'
>
> **Ulrich Pillau, Co-founder and CEO, Apaleo**

Is there a future for direct bookings?

With all this talk of omnichannel, data collection, data silos, personalization and knowing your customers, there is also a significant cost to marketing and personalization. A good question is whether there is really a realistic future for most of the hospitality sector to invest in marketing themselves to grow their direct bookings or just rely on the OTAs to deliver qualified marketing leads for a relatively 'good' price paid only on commission.

A hotelier or STR operator may well decide that building a significant direct booking strategy just isn't worth the hassle and cost, but that does leave them vulnerable to keeping all their eggs in just one basket with all the *power* of their business in the hands of others. So, it's generally assumed that a mixed distribution strategy is best, with the OTAs utilized as lead generators. The first booking can be on them, and then it's up to the hotelier to build a relationship (one to one) with the guest to maximize any future stays.

Guests often develop stronger connections to the hotels where they stay rather than the platforms they use to book. This loyalty stems from positive experiences, such as good service, comfortable rooms and convenient locations. While OTAs offer a wide range of options, they mostly lack the personal touch that hotels can provide directly. However, hotels and STR brands can compete effectively against OTAs by focusing on creating exceptional guest experiences, offering the right promotions and implementing effective marketing strategies. These efforts can encourage guests to book directly, nurturing stronger relationships and repeat business despite the convenience of OTA platforms.

'At the end of the day, operators are gunning for five-star reviews, repeat bookings and word-of-mouth recommendations.'

Steve Davis, CEO, Operto

Attribute-based selling

Attribute-based selling (ABS) is a very new approach to selling in the hotel industry. ABS essentially allows guests to customize their room selection based on specific features or, more specifically, the attributes they value, rather than choosing from predefined room types. So I might be willing to pay more for a balcony because I like having my tea outside first thing in the morning, but my neighbour might just be using his room as a convenient stop-over, so wouldn't consider a balcony a plus.

For those new to ABS, here's a summary of the key aspects:

Challenges: Implementing ABS can be complex, requiring changes to inventory management systems and distribution channels. Many third-party booking platforms don't yet fully support ABS, although this is coming.

Customization: Instead of offering traditional room categories like 'standard double' or 'deluxe king', ABS lets guests choose specific attributes such as bed type, room size, view, floor level or proximity to elevators.

Definition: ABS enables hoteliers to sell individual room attributes separately, allowing guests to build their ideal room by selecting only the features they desire and paying more for them.

Enhanced guest experience: ABS provides guests with more control over their stay, potentially increasing satisfaction by allowing them to pay only for the features they want and also giving them the exact room configuration that they value.

Revenue optimization: The ABS approach can increase hotel revenue by allowing properties to charge for individual attributes that guests value, rather than bundling them into fixed room types.

Technology requirements: Successful implementation of ABS requires integrated data systems, flexible booking platforms and often AI-powered pricing and inventory management tools. This is still in its infancy.

While ABS is still in its early stages in the hotel industry, it represents a significant shift in how rooms are sold and how guests can customize their stay experiences. Some hotel brands are already experimenting with it, and it certainly gives hoteliers the opportunity to also position themselves uniquely across various platforms. For instance, a hotel might present itself differently on Booking.com, Airbnb and Secret Escapes, optimizing its appeal for each platform's audience.

As OTAs evolve to allow more customization options, hotels will be able to push more detailed, attribute-based offerings through these channels. This enables greater personalization and control over how rooms and services are presented and sold across different platforms. As technology advances and consumer expectations evolve, ABS will likely become an increasingly important strategy for hotels looking to differentiate themselves and maximize revenue from more than just the rooms. For example, if there is a high demand for balconies, the systems can price these accordingly, even if the hotel itself has low occupancy.

TECH LEADER INSIGHT

The evolution of the digital marketer – Steve Collins, VP of Digital Marketing, SHR, Access Hospitality

Close your eyes. Imagine you own a beautiful hotel, but your hotel doesn't have an equally beautiful website. It stands to reason the only people who are going to see your hotel are the people walking past it on the street, argues Steve Collins. In the online world, they're probably going to bypass you for your competitor – because your competitor has a beautiful website and you don't.

This rationale from the Vice President of Digital Marketing at SHR, a company that provides a suite of hotel technology applications, is drawn from a decade of experience.

Collins joined SHR's digital team in 2015, and has worked across various senior roles across digital marketing, paid search, SEO, social media advertising and more – with the overriding goal of helping hotels secure direct web traffic to the booking engines housed on their own websites.

As well as needing a cutting-edge website with a booking engine, hotels need a comprehensive digital marketing strategy in place to make those bookings happen.

A question of timing

'We have been in this never-ending dog fight with OTAs to capture the existing demand, which is always way down the marketing funnel. It's so far beyond when someone started looking for their travel. This is the end bit, this is the booking bit,' he says.

He encourages a broad, multi-modal perspective on digital marketing, and says the online journey for a person booking a hotel or airline ticket is anything but linear.

'There is no direct line. It's an absolute mess of engagement and touchpoints and every single journey is personal,' Collins says. As a result, it's a digital marketer's task to influence and impact, ultimately providing a means to book at the perfect moment.

'As a hotelier, what you really can do is be present. If you're planning to go to New York in a few months' time and you've started doing your research, you're probably going to book your flights first. That's the trigger for when a hotel knows and understands its audience and should start showing up and being present within that conversation,' he says.

And the way a hotel can display an advert at that 'perfect recall moment' needn't be a big, flashy message, he argues, but a simple prompt to book directly straight away.

'It just needs to solve the problem for them coming to a New York hotel near Manhattan or near Central Station,' he adds. 'Get that message out there because when that flight is booked, something will trigger with the hotel. And when they're actually on Booking.com or Expedia later on with the flight booked, they will have a visual of the image, or the hotel name they have already seen.'

Bigger picture

Meanwhile, today's digital tactics have evolved significantly over the past 10 years. Attribution, which is how advertisers determine how those tactics and subsequent customer interactions contribute to sales or conversions, used to be mostly based on whether an online advert was clicked and eventually booked by the same person.

But Collins says the nuance around the 12 organic clicks the website received from that same user, any social media impressions, and perhaps a video or image advert that got an impression six months prior, was missing when it came to attribution.

'The tools for us to actually be able to engage with early-stage travellers have come an awfully long way, and the measurement has come along with it,' he says.

But at the same time, he likens the process to billboards: they have an impact but it's hard to measure exactly how many clicks would come to your website from them. 'You can't measure the revenue that's come through those clicks, but you can absolutely see the pace of revenue, the pace of traffic, the overall impact on your sales, flowing through the business from the milestone of you putting the billboard up,' he says.

The key takeaway? A hotel needs to be active on social media, Google Ads and other advertising platforms, as well as have strong SEO. 'If you don't have access points set up off-site across the internet, no one can get to your website,' Collins warns.

Future-proof strategies

A multi-pronged marketing strategy also includes 'digital PR', website personalization and awareness of how the new generation of AI-based search will evolve.

Digital PR, according to Collins, is the new name for 'backlinks', which are links on other websites, such as an online review on a leading travel blog, but point back to the hotel's website. 'It's a better name for it because if you are doing backlinks, it sounds boring and laborious,' he jokes. 'But if you're doing digital PR, there's positivity around that.'

And it's a practice that provides a hospitality brand with credibility. 'We think that's going to be a big part of what SEO for hotels is about, particularly the high-end, luxury properties,' Collins adds.

'Smart content' is another key strand, and a hotel website can incorporate personalization to such an extent that a homepage will look different depending on the visitor, all based on their previous engagements.

One visitor might be welcomed with a video of the golf course, while another is greeted by an image of the hotel's spa. And each return would continue to adapt based on the individual's previous website visits, or other trackable online activity.

'You visited the spa section on the last visit to the hotel website, so when you come back, it's actually the text on the homepage, the heading has changed and the image on the website has actually changed to a spa. And it's remembering your dates and the offer you looked at,' says Collins.

'It's the same website, but a completely different experience. It's not forcing us into different landing pages or anything like that. You're on the homepage, it's just changing based on the cookies that you've dropped along the way. That to us is the future of personalization,' he adds.

And as expected, the digital expert advises hotels to prepare for the arrival of generative AI search, where longer, more conversation-like 'prompts' can be asked, so a user can request hotel suggestions as well as tips for a multi-day vacation itinerary.

'They are essentially getting rid of the 10 blue links and changing the experience of what you're actually seeing when you put a search in,' says Collins. 'It's no longer just "hotel in London" or "best hotel in London" or "hotel near me". Someone instead will type that they need a hotel with meeting rooms, and a bar and somewhere to go for a swim.'

Digital marketers now face the situation that suddenly the 'hotel in London' search has just expanded out to a sentence with four or five key triggers that need to be met for Google or another search engine to deliver back that result. Traditionally, marketers would have been bidding on a brand name, or the hotel, or 'hotel with spa' or 'best hotel with spa'.

'That is going to change everything,' says Collins.

The battle to gain more direct bookings looks likely to ramp up, with Collins believing that hotels are conscious that they have let OTAs do their brand marketing for them for too long.

Key components of marketing personalization

There's a great deal to think about and a lot of information to process when it comes to implementing a marketing strategy and truly offering customers a personalized experience when marketing to them. Below is a summary of the main core components:

Advanced analytics and machine learning: Using sophisticated tools and predicting guest preferences and behaviours for more accurate personalization and then using automation to implement.

Attribute-based selling (ABS): This growing segment of selling allows guests to select and pay for specific room features and amenities that matter most to them. Would you pay more for a balcony, a room on the first floor or a king-size bed?

Comprehensive guest profiles: Hospitality operators need to start with knowing their guest profiles, so implementing a Customer Relationship Management (CRM) system that aggregates data from various sources, creating a centralized database of guest information, is vital.

Granular inventory: Having a granular inventory means breaking down room types and amenities into more specific attributes, allowing for more detailed customization options.

Omnichannel approach: The means of delivering consistent personalized experiences across various channels, including email, website, mobile app and on-property interactions. Being in all the places where your customers are.

Personalized pricing: Can you adjust rates based on individual guest preferences, willingness to pay and the specific attributes they value?

Real-time data utilization and unified data systems: Incorporating up-to-date information about the guest and their current trip to provide timely and relevant personalization while integrating data across various touchpoints and systems to create a cohesive view of the guest and their interactions with a brand.

Tailored recommendations: This means offering only a limited number of highly relevant choices based on guest preferences and behaviour patterns, rather than overwhelming them with too many options.

Trip context: This means that you need to consider the purpose, timing and circumstances of each individual stay to provide relevant offerings. Is it a honeymoon, business trip, a family reunion or a visit for a graduation?

Bringing these components together creates a more individualized and relevant experience for guests throughout their customer journey, from initial booking to post-stay engagement, which leads to more effective marketing in the long run.

'Personalization continues to be one of the hottest topics in the industry and it impacts everything from managing top-of-funnel awareness and demand all the way through to driving conversions, sales, and driving loyalty and long-term value at the customer level.'

David Peller, former Global Managing Director, Amazon Web Services Travel and Hospitality

The role of data in marketing and personalization

At the heart of effective personalization lies data. Lots and lots of data. But rather than just collecting information, a more intelligent approach is needed to create comprehensive guest profiles that inform every interaction.

These profiles go far beyond basic information like name and contact details. They encompass a guest's booking history, preferences for room types and amenities, dining choices, use of hotel services, feedback from previous stays, 'look-a-like' data and even data from external sources like social media (with appropriate permissions, of course).

But data alone isn't enough. The magic happens when this information is processed and analysed using sophisticated CRM systems, data analytics tools and AI. These technologies can identify patterns, predict preferences and generate insights that enable tailor-made experiences.

For example, a hotel might use AI to analyse a guest's booking history and notice that they always book spa treatments during their stays. The system could then automatically offer a discounted spa package the next time that guest makes a reservation. Or it might notice that a guest always requests extra pillows and automatically adds that to their room setup for future stays.

As the industry collects more and more information about guests, it has a responsibility to handle that data ethically and securely. Regulations like General Data Protection Regulation in Europe, the California Consumer Privacy Act in the United States or China's PIPL regulation have raised the bar for data protection, and hospitality businesses need to be on top of their game.

As well as avoiding fines (which can be hefty), businesses will also build trust with guests. People are increasingly aware of the value of their personal data, and they want to know if it's being used responsibly.

But collecting and protecting data is only half the battle. The real challenge often lies in making that data accessible and useful across an organization. Many hospitality businesses struggle with data silos – pockets of information trapped in different systems that don't talk to each other.

Imagine a scenario where a guest's preference for hypoallergenic bedding is noted in the PMS, but that information never makes it to the housekeeping system. Or where a guest's complaint about slow room service is logged by the front desk but never reaches the food and beverage team. These disconnects can lead to missed opportunities for improved service.

The solution? Integration. Creating a 'single source of truth' for guest data that feeds into all relevant systems. This is easier said than done, especially for larger organizations with legacy systems. But it's a crucial step in leveraging data for effective personalization.

REAL-WORLD EXAMPLE

Forge Holiday Group blends marketing strategies to drive direct bookings

The Forge Holiday Group has four holiday divisions: Sykes Holiday Cottages, Forest Holidays and UKCaravans4Hire in the UK and Bachcare, a short-let rental company in New Zealand. It also has about 20 additional regional brands in the UK. Overall, the group offers more than 31,000 properties across the UK, Ireland and New Zealand to guests and holidaymakers. Sykes Holiday Cottages and Forest Holidays are also certified B Corporations in recognition of their positive environmental and social impact.

Challenges and opportunities

Predominantly UK-focused (excluding international brand Bachcare), Forge Holiday Group wants to grow the number of direct and repeat bookings. That's not unusual, because almost all hospitality brands want loyal guests in order to increase their 'lifetime value', which means lower marketing costs associated with attracting new customers. But Forge Holiday Group isn't a typical hospitality brand; it has a number of niche businesses, most notably Forest Holidays, which operates and markets log cabins across 13 locations, and which recently received significant investment to expand.

'The single biggest problem we have in that business is brand awareness, so the way we look at our media spend is very different,' notes Graham Donoghue, Group CEO, Forge Holiday Group. 'We tend to spend more money on creating awareness of the brand because it's one of the best things that people haven't yet heard of.'

The so-called staycation market boomed during and after Covid, as many people couldn't fly, or preferred to avoid flying, but the CEO is tackling what he perceives to be a key misunderstanding. 'When some people go on a forest holiday, they think they've done it,' he says. 'But every location is different. So, a different type of education is required, and you may spend more money on "above the line" advertising, partnerships or brand campaigns for awareness creation.'

Generative AI and search

The power of generative search should not be underestimated in the world of marketing. This AI-powered process is currently being pioneered by search engines and means they can provide users with overviews of search topics, rather than results that involve clicking on individual links.

'In the next 12 months, the world of digital marketing through the lens of Google is going to completely change,' claims Graham Donoghue. 'When you look at organic search and organic listings, they're going to be pushed further and further down the page and to the point where there may not necessarily be any organic listings on page one.'

As a result, he urges hospitality brands to lean into a lot of the products that the likes of Google offer, such as Performance Max, which uses AI across bidding, budget optimization, audiences, creatives, attribution and more, to make sure their product is visible so a search engine can integrate that product into generative search results, and in particular for hotel and vacation search results.

Currently, brands will bid and buy certain keywords. However, the technology with generative search can be more opaque. Donoghue compares it to a 'black box' into which the search engine places your advertising request and expected return on investment, and then automatically creates a marketing campaign. 'It's taken away a lot of the skill that a lot of the smart marketers and agencies had. Search engines are working through that sort of a model; they don't share that data back with you, so that's quite difficult as well. But you can't ignore them because it's so powerful,' Donoghue says. 'Test and learn, lean into the technology, because it's really smart and it will help you.'

The solution

Forge Holiday Group leverages a wide mix of marketing strategies and technologies, which Donoghue likens to 'a three-dimensional game of chess'. It already has relatively high direct and repeat booking levels. Sykes Holiday Cottages, for example, has a direct booking rate of 75 per cent, with the wider Forge Holiday Group seeing about 58 per cent of its guests rebook. But the CEO's mantra is: 'Drive as much direct booking as you possibly can, incentivize customers, because it's better to pay them to return, than pay someone else.'

To do this, the group looks at recurring revenue from three sources: SEO, its Customer Relationship Management platform and direct bookings (including via its app). These are classified as 'free' or low-cost when compared to traditional marketing campaigns like radio or TV campaigns.

The group slots customers into different cohorts, which will be targeted with different media messages.

'We ultimately follow people, using platforms like Google's Performance Max. Some of the AI technologies we've got allow us to attract people, to keep reminding them and to nudge them,' says Donoghue, adding that programmatic bidding technology also allows the group to buy advertising media across a wide range of platforms.

As an example, he says someone might see a search advert on Google, then within the next minute a video on YouTube, and then a banner on Facebook. They might also get sent an email with a special offer, or a message to remind them they have left something in their basket and would they like to continue.

'There's a lot of sophistication used to remind people we're here, and we'll then offer discounts or nudges to get them just to jump over the line,' he says.

The group does not have a fixed marketing budget, which Donoghue says 'blows some people's minds'. Instead, the company acts on the rationale that as long as there is a return on investment, then it keeps spending. It evaluates the different marketing sources and the different customers who are coming in, and blends the data together to calculate an overall blended cost per acquisition.

The marketing team's job is to pull all those different levers to work out where to spend more.

'What you're looking at is the type of customers you're acquiring, the likelihood of that customer rebooking and the value that customer is bringing, whether that customer is likely to buy ancillary products and spend more money on location, or more likely to spend more on a particular sort of a property,' he adds. 'Lifetime value is really important to us because we're willing to spend more to acquire a customer who is going to be more "sticky" with us, and come back directly.'

Forge Holiday Group also capitalizes on timely messaging and, similar to many brands, targets a guest once they've been on holiday during 'a moment of truth', according to Donoghue: 'If they've had a really good time, how do we get them to rebook early?'

That push over the line can take the form of incentives. 'I'd rather give a customer 10 per cent off their next holiday if they book it within the first 30 days, than pay 50, 60, 70 pounds to some other third party to acquire that customer six months down the line,' he adds.

Conclusion

This UK-focused holiday group operates a highly sophisticated marketing operation. It leverages a range of advertising and marketing channels to increase direct and repeat bookings. It also continually assesses the results, which is a reminder that even for hospitality brands with advanced marketing, there's no room for complacency. A focus on investing in brand awareness and direct marketing also makes economic sense as new challenges come into play, including new data privacy legislation that can make the tracking of customers more difficult, and the emerging trend of guests booking later.

The role of loyalty programmes and technology

Big brand loyalty programmes are booming and it's in the loyalty programmes that many hotel brands are focusing their marketing efforts. Loyalty programmes have emerged as a cornerstone of hotel industry strategy, often even overshadowing individual brand identities.

Major hotel companies like Marriott, Hilton and Wyndham view their loyalty programmes as the crucial link connecting their diverse portfolio of brands and properties as well as connecting with guests. The programmes serve multiple purposes, from retaining guests within the company's ecosystem and encouraging direct bookings to reducing dependence on OTAs. In addition, loyalty members typically demonstrate higher value, with increased frequency of stays, higher spending and a preference for direct bookings. The scope of loyalty programmes has expanded beyond simple point accrual for free stays, and they now encompass partnerships, exclusive experiences and credit card rewards. As of writing, Marriott Bonvoy has 200 million members, with Hilton closely following. It's also not just the OTAs realizing the power of loyalty. Expedia Group now operates its three biggest platforms (Vrbo, Hotels.com and Expedia) under the One Key programme and Booking.com has its Genius programme.

It's clear that loyalty programmes will continue to be a powerful tool for driving customer engagement and repeat business in the highly competitive hospitality sector. It is just as likely to be much more difficult for the smaller brands to compete on the scale and breadth of the bigger hoteliers with their programmes. On the other hand, there is also a cost: for hotel owners, there is a significant cost per booking that comes with loyalty programmes.

'We have lost the individualization, the personalization of when you want to book a room. I mean, we are sacrificing personalization over automation because we manage categories and simplified categories.'

Markus Mueller, Co-founder and Managing Director, GauVendi

Future trends in hospitality marketing and personalization

At its core, personalization is about tailoring the guest experience to individual preferences and needs. It's not a new concept. Good hoteliers have always tried to remember their regular guests' preferences. But what is new is that technology has supercharged their ability to personalize at *scale*.

This technology change has, of course, encompassed AI and machine learning. But how quickly will the industry see fundamental change? During the dot-com boom of the early 2000s, there were exaggerated expectations about the internet's immediate transformative power. These predictions initially fell short due to limitations like insufficient broadband infrastructure. However, over time, the internet has fundamentally changed society, albeit more gradually than initially anticipated. Now, it's so deeply integrated into daily life that it's difficult to imagine a world without it. This will be the same for AI and machine learning. The impact of AI will be slower than we all anticipate, but the outcome, once fully felt, will be just as seismic – especially for the marketing industry.

Will we also see a difference in marketing and personalization between luxury, select service and budget hotel options? Potentially the ultra-high-end, famous hotel brands will continue to thrive with or without more automated personalization. Famous hotels are famous for a reason and travellers will always aspire to stay in them. They tend to have a secure place in the market. By contrast, budget accommodation and select service hotels face a more challenging future. They will need to carefully reconsider their approach to technology, likely having to embrace it more fully to remain competitive and relevant in an evolving market landscape.

KEY TAKEAWAYS

Guests want personalization: In hospitality, 71 per cent of consumers expect personalized experiences and 76 per cent become frustrated when it doesn't happen. Personalization builds customer loyalty, starting from the early search and planning stages, not just during the stay.

Data collection is fundamental: True personalization requires collecting guest data beyond basic demographics. This allows for tailored experiences and customer intimacy, which can drive revenue growth. However, integrating and utilizing this data effectively across various systems remains a challenge due to data silos.

Privacy needs to be accounted for: While consumers value personalized experiences, they are also concerned about privacy. Brands must ensure transparency in data collection and usage to build trust. Responsible use of data can lead to enhanced guest stays and increased business growth.

Shifting marketing approaches: Marketing strategies should evolve from broad approaches to more targeted, individualized marketing (one to one). This involves understanding specific guest needs, preferences and behaviours, similar to account-based marketing in B2B industries.

OTAs have a key role: OTAs like Expedia, Booking.com and Airbnb invest heavily in personalization and data-driven marketing strategies. They help operators with tailored recommendations, dynamic pricing and customer retention, but they also present challenges in controlling guest relationships for direct bookings.

Changing search dynamics: The world of search in hospitality is transforming with AI, voice search and visual content. Personalized search results based on user behaviour and preferences, including generative AI, will expand guests' options.

Omnichannel marketing: Successful marketing strategies now involve omnichannel approaches, ensuring consistent messaging and interaction across various touchpoints like websites, social media, apps and direct mail. This is essential for meeting modern consumer expectations during the extensive travel research process.

Direct booking vs reliance on OTAs: While investing in direct booking strategies is often costly, relying solely on OTAs puts hoteliers at risk.

A mixed distribution strategy is recommended to ensure hoteliers can foster guest loyalty through direct relationships while leveraging OTAs for broader exposure.

Attribute-based selling (ABS): ABS, a growing source of revenue, allows guests to select and pay for specific room features they value, offering customization over traditional room types. This approach can optimize revenue and enhance guest satisfaction, although implementation is complex and requires advanced data systems.

The power of loyalty programmes: Loyalty programmes have become a cornerstone of hotel industry marketing strategies, especially for big brands like Marriott and Hilton. These programmes help retain guests, drive direct bookings and reduce dependency on OTAs. Members typically demonstrate higher frequency of stays and increased spending. Smaller brands face challenges competing with the scale of such programmes, but customized experiences can help build loyalty.

Real-World Example – Forge Holiday Group: Leading with data, marketing and personalization for high direct and repeat bookings, and guest satisfaction scores.

Notes

1 McKinsey (2021) The value of getting personalization right – or wrong – is multiplying, 12 November, www.mckinsey.com/capabilities/growth-marketing-and-sales/our-insights/the-value-of-getting-personalization-right-or-wrong-is-multiplying (archived at https://perma.cc/42KG-7QFW)
2 Skift (2024) Airbnb CEO Brian Chesky at Skift Global Forum 2024: Expanding Airbnb beyond accommodations, www.youtube.com/watch?v=V9W2HP53Kro (archived at https://perma.cc/AQU2-YAXH)

6

Revenue management: Getting the price right

In the not-too-distant past, room rates were mostly static. Hoteliers would have priced with variation, only really allowing for a low season and a high season or the difference between midweek and the weekend. Rates would have been set and published in a fixed brochure, given to partners, and perhaps added to a website. The point is that rates were published and couldn't easily be changed or updated. They were effectively 'set in stone'.

This traditional approach limited revenue growth potential as it failed to capture the nuances of fluctuating market dynamics. In more recent years, pricing has become more flexible and dynamic, with hotels hiring revenue experts and using software tools to set prices. However, it's still not universal for operators, particularly independent hotels and the short-term rental (STR) sector, to use dynamic pricing or follow a revenue management strategy.

But for today's 'tech-enabled' hospitality operators, revenue management has become a cornerstone of financial success and profitability. It is a complex, sophisticated and vital part of the machine that integrates pricing, distribution and operational decision making to optimize the flow of cash. Gone are the days when setting room rates meant simple seasonal adjustments or matching competitor prices. Modern revenue management blends art and science, leveraging data analytics, AI and human expertise to ensure that hospitality businesses maximize their income potential while offering competitive rates that attract and retain guests.

Today, revenue management also integrates advanced forecasting, distribution management and a deep understanding of customer segmentation. This holistic approach ensures every aspect of the guest experience aligns with business objectives, from the initial booking to post-stay engagement. The ability to strategically adjust rates and availability in response to demand enables hotels, resorts and STR operators to achieve higher yields and better occupancy rates.

Moreover, technology has played an indispensable role in transforming revenue management from a reactive process to a proactive strategy. Automated systems and AI tools now support managers by processing vast amounts of data to provide actionable insights, so they can make informed decisions faster than ever. These advancements have equipped managers with the means to anticipate market changes and respond with precision, significantly enhancing a property's financial performance.

So, today's revenue manager is tasked not just with setting prices but with ensuring these prices reflect real-time market conditions, maximizing profitability and sustaining a competitive edge in a crowded hospitality sector.

'Previously, pricing was straightforward, with set rates for high and low seasons and occasional holiday adjustments. Now, software enables daily rate changes, adapting to every demand curve. With instant booking on online travel agencies (OTAs), occupancy shifts quickly, so pricing tools must immediately adjust to reflect these changes and stay competitive.'

Thibault Masson, Head of Product Marketing, PriceLabs

The core principles of revenue management

Revenue management in hospitality is underpinned by fundamental principles that enable operators to optimize their pricing and operational strategies effectively. Understanding and implementing these principles is essential for maintaining a competitive position in the market.

Supply and demand dynamics

The foundation of any pricing strategy in hospitality is a deep understanding of supply and demand. Unlike physical products that can be stockpiled, hotel rooms and vacation rentals are perishable inventory. An unsold room for the night is revenue lost forever. This reality drives the need for dynamic pricing that can respond to fluctuations in demand. Hospitality properties operate in markets where demand can fluctuate dramatically based on various factors such as seasonality, holidays, local events and economic conditions. We've all seen the impact of big events, the so-called 'Taylor Swift effect', on room prices, and we've all felt the difference in our wallets as guests when needing to book during school holidays.

A successful strategy hinges on a hotel operator's or STR property manager's ability to anticipate these changes and adjust pricing accordingly. Putting that simply, it means that during peak periods when demand surpasses available supply, properties can implement higher pricing. Conversely, in low-demand periods, competitive pricing and value-added offers can attract guests and prevent rooms from sitting vacant. Managers use forecasting tools, such as Duetto, BEONx, Beyond and IDeaS, among others, to predict demand trends, allowing them to make data-driven decisions. This predictive capability helps ensure that pricing remains flexible and responsive, aligning with market conditions to optimize both occupancy rates and income.

Segmentation and market positioning

Another core principle is understanding market segmentation. Guests do not represent a homogeneous group but have different needs, spending capacities and booking behaviours. Effective revenue management involves segmenting the market into categories, such as business travellers, leisure tourists, long-term-stay guests and group bookings. Each segment may respond differently to price changes, promotional strategies and service offerings.

For example, business travellers typically prioritize convenience and are less price-sensitive. They will typically stay during weekdays, although with the growth in 'bleisure' travel, they may add weekend nights to a stay. In contrast, leisure travellers often plan in advance and are more sensitive to deals and competitive rates, especially on weekends or during holiday periods. Tailoring pricing and promotional strategies to these segments ensures that properties attract the right guests at the right time, optimizing income across different market conditions.

KEY METRICS IN REVENUE MANAGEMENT

Measuring the success of revenue management strategies involves tracking several key performance indicators (KPIs):

ADR (average daily rate): This metric represents the average revenue earned per occupied room and is a straightforward measure of pricing effectiveness.

GOPPAR (gross operating profit per available room): This metric is increasingly important as it takes the channel/distribution cost into consideration.

RevPAN (revenue per available night): This metric is especially important for STR properties. Unlike traditional hotel metrics, RevPAN takes into account properties that may not be available every night due to owner usage or maintenance. It helps gauge the revenue efficiency based on available nights rather than total potential nights.

RevPAR (revenue per available room): RevPAR combines occupancy and ADR to provide a holistic view of revenue performance. It reflects how well a property is balancing room rates with occupancy to maximize revenue.

By focusing on these metrics, managers can monitor and adjust their strategies in real time, ensuring that pricing, availability and distribution align with the overall revenue goals. When effectively applied, these principles enable hospitality businesses to navigate complex market dynamics, attract the right mix of guests and sustain profitability over time.

'First of all, AI has been used by revenue management companies, like ours, forever. We've had AI as part of our solution from day one. Already with *2001: A Space Odyssey*, the movie from Stanley Kubrick, people talked about talking to a computer and talking to AI.'

Klaus Kohlmayr, Chief Evangelist, IDeaS

Dynamic pricing: moving beyond traditional approaches

Dynamic pricing has really changed the hospitality industry's approach, moving beyond traditional, static pricing models to more adaptive and real-time strategies. This approach allows properties to adjust rates based on a multitude of factors, aligning prices with current market conditions, maximizing revenue and enhancing competitiveness. The practice is also being used across hospitality spaces, such as event spaces, lobbies and parking spaces, rather than just rooms.

Understanding dynamic pricing

Dynamic pricing involves the continuous adjustment of room rates in response to supply and demand fluctuations, competitor pricing, local events and broader economic trends. Unlike the fixed pricing models of the past, dynamic pricing uses technology to make real-time changes to rates, ensuring that properties can capture peak demand and maintain occupancy during slower periods. This flexibility not only optimizes revenue but also aligns with customer expectations for value, ensuring that guests perceive their stay as fairly priced.

For example, a hotel near a convention centre might see rates surge during a major industry conference due to increased demand. Similarly, dynamic pricing tools can help lower rates and attract more budget-conscious travellers during quieter seasons or weekdays without sacrificing profitability.

In order to work, dynamic pricing leverages sophisticated algorithms that analyse historical data, current booking patterns, competitor prices and market conditions to determine optimal rates.

These systems can be programmed to consider a wide range of variables, including:

Competitor pricing: Monitoring competitors' rates ensures that prices remain competitive.

Guest booking behaviour: Advanced systems analyse guest booking windows and patterns to optimize pricing. For example, last-minute travellers may be willing to pay higher prices, whereas early bookers might be incentivized with lower rates.

Local events: Real-time updates factor in local events such as concerts, festivals or sporting events that impact demand.

Occupancy levels: Rates increase as room availability decreases, capitalizing on high demand.

Seasonality and time of year: Adjustments are made to account for peak and off-peak travel periods.

Most hospitality businesses use specialized software platforms to manage dynamic pricing effectively. These tools automate much of the pricing process, offering real-time data insights and customizable pricing rules that align with an operator's specific goals.

> 'I'm actually really excited about artificial intelligence and what it can do for the future. As an industry, we're a little bit behind some of the other industries out there in their adoption and use, but it's really emerging and it's changing quickly.'
>
> **Leah Rankin, Chief Product Officer, SiteMinder**

The Taylor Swift effect

One of the defining features of dynamic pricing is its responsiveness to external events. A city hosting a high-profile concert or sporting event will likely experience a spike in hotel and STR prices due to increased demand. Properties that employ dynamic pricing can adjust their rates in real time to reflect this surge, capitalizing on the temporary increase in interest. Without such a strategy, a property risks either underpricing its rooms and missing potential sales or overpricing and failing to secure bookings.

Across each city and country that she has played in, Taylor Swift's 'The Eras Tour' has emerged as a business phenomenon, with its influence extending far beyond concert venues. Taylor and her tour even coined a new economic term, '*Swiftonomics*', to explain the impact on local businesses and the wave of economic benefits they bring. While 'Swiftonomics' also benefits retail and food and beverage, the bulk of money has flown into hospitality and tourism, with lodging taking the main slice of the pie. This ability to adapt pricing based on local, national or even global events helps operators stay ahead of the competition and maintain profitability in varying market conditions.

Advantages of dynamic pricing

Dynamic pricing offers several clear advantages. It maximizes revenue potential by capturing value during high-demand periods and supports steady income during low-demand periods by attracting more guests. This approach also aligns with consumers' growing expectations for value-based pricing, as guests are increasingly accustomed to fluctuating rates influenced by availability and market conditions.

Moreover, properties that effectively implement dynamic pricing can achieve higher levels of occupancy while maintaining optimal rates, fostering a healthier balance between volume and revenue per room. Moving beyond traditional approaches to embrace dynamic pricing equips hospitality operators with the tools needed to stay competitive and responsive in a fast-paced market. With the right blend of data, technology and strategy, dynamic pricing can significantly boost both income and guest satisfaction, making it an essential component of modern revenue management in hospitality.

TECH LEADER INSIGHT

Consumer intent and the importance of looking inside the mind of your guest – David Kelso, CTO and Co-founder, Beyond

The hospitality sector remains too focused on looking at historical data when it comes to pricing. That's according to David Kelso, co-founder and Chief Technology Officer of revenue management platform Beyond.

He is calling for a better understanding of search patterns and behaviours, and is on a mission to democratize access to such data for STR operators and independent hoteliers. These sectors are highly fragmented, and because of that, getting a clear picture of how to price in the future can be challenging.

More advanced revenue management techniques tend to be limited to larger hotel groups, which have access to significant booking data from their own hotels – not to mention financial resources to employ dedicated revenue management specialists.

'Accessibility to data is absolutely key. Operations in hotels have traditionally been based on historical data and historical booking pacing,' Kelso says, with booking pace a revenue management metric that shows the rate at which reservations are made for a specific date.

'That works fine when you have a big portfolio of 1,000 or 2,000 rooms. But when you've got five rooms, it doesn't really work,' he continues. 'You can't pace out five rooms. You get one booking and say "Oh, we're 20 per cent occupied." It doesn't work.'

Beyond was founded in 2008, and originally called Beyond Pricing. It was set up to give hospitality operators the means to price their properties and rooms more effectively. Over the years the platform has evolved to offer real-time pricing, and now relies more heavily on forward-looking market occupancy rather than historical pacing.

Mastering the power of intent

Beyond collects data in a variety of ways, including partnership deals with various booking sites. It can also install tools on its clients' websites to retrieve data, which when combined with other sources reveals the bigger picture of pricing.

'They can share their data and get aggregated data back, and they can use that aggregated data to help their pricing decisions as well,' says Kelso.

But it's the ability to look even further forward that stands to help operators the most. Fortunately, there are various signals out there. 'You'll often find a customer's intent before they actually go through with the booking. And that intent, in aggregate across multiple sites, across multiple destinations, shows identifiable patterns before a booking is even made,' he says.

Kelso cites the example of a Taylor Swift concert announcement: 'You have all these people rushing to search and book. You have to react quickly because you're never going to react faster than a Swifty.' He also gives the example of how a lot of people might decide to book a particular destination for a vacation because it's been a viral hit on TikTok.

Weather is another case in point: 'The forecast changes. And the rain that was happening isn't happening there anymore. It can be subtle, it doesn't have to change a lot, you actually don't need that much data before you have something usable, especially since there are millions and millions of consumers searching all day, every day.'

An automated approach to revenue management means a hotel or apartment operator can monitor such events, catch changing consumer intent – and react with relevant pricing. 'We want to free people from the minutiae of pushing a price up 10 per cent or down 10 per cent day over day based on some random event, fluctuation or competitor change, and remove the manual work,' he adds.

Embracing dynamic pricing

Pricing this way is a form of dynamic pricing, which is a pricing strategy that involves adjusting the cost of goods or services based on various factors in real time. Kelso knows from Beyond data that has been aggregated over a decade that the majority of STRs are still not dynamically pricing their rooms, despite the consumer shift.

'When Uber first came out with dynamic pricing, or surge pricing, there was a big uproar. The same thing happened when airlines and hotels first did it, and when vacation rentals first did it too,' he says. 'But the reality is that it's becoming more accepted. Now you're even seeing it in food and beverage, which would have been inconceivable even five years ago. Now all of a sudden there's digital menus everywhere; it's becoming massively normalized in a consumer mindset.'

Monitoring search behaviour across multiple sites can also result in lower pricing, if an event does not produce the demand that was initially expected. 'It's not always just about raising prices, it's about finding the ideal price point,' says Kelso.

Looking at consumer intent is a well-established practice in other industries, most notably direct to consumer and e-commerce, but Kelso argues they have a different and somewhat easier problem to solve. 'We're trying to perfectly price each piece of inventory,' he says. 'They have millions of the same inventory. So it's a different challenge, but an interesting one that I was drawn to because it's unique to the STR industry.'

Leveraging generative AI to interpret data

AI touches many areas of hospitality, but one of the biggest areas will be pricing, owing to the large amounts of data that need to be processed. Machine learning has been a mainstay of revenue management software for a long time, but the next iteration, generative AI, will create new efficiencies.

'A lot of the strategies we build out, a lot of the methodologies of recommendations, we've been doing that for quite a while,' says Kelso. 'But generative AI is big. It's what's brought AI back into the spotlight again, because it's cool and you can do things with it that were previously thought kind of impossible.'

One of those things will be helping people interpret data, beyond just accessing it. 'You don't have to think ahead of what your consumer wants to see, it can just move on the fly,' he says. 'There will be a lot more tooling coming over time where people can mash together different data sources, and use AI to generate insights and tease out patterns.'

And in his opinion, he believes this will be an area of focus for many hospitality technology startups, and perhaps less for the major players, who 'have already got their entrenched products' and in many cases move slower than their entrepreneurial counterparts.

Forward-looking data, AI and the shift away from historical data

The hospitality industry has long relied on historical data to inform pricing and revenue management strategies. While past performance remains a valuable reference, it is no longer sufficient in itself as a reference. Over the past decade or so, relying solely on historical data has proven to be increasingly ineffective due to changes in travel behaviour, external disruptions and unpredictable global events.

Historical data can tell operators how a property performed under similar circumstances in previous years, but it does not account for unprecedented changes such as the Covid pandemic or sudden shifts in travel trends or the Taylor Swift effect of large events and movements of travel. These types of events can render past data less relevant and reliable. As a result, managers are now turning to forward-looking market data to complement their strategies.

Forward-looking data focuses on real-time insights into future booking patterns, market demand forecasts and occupancy trends. By leveraging such data, hospitality operators can anticipate shifts in guest behaviour, align their pricing strategies with upcoming demand and prepare for sudden changes that historical data might overlook. This proactive approach enables hotels and STRs to react quickly to market shifts, making it a powerful tool for maximizing sales in uncertain and competitive environments.

'What we see coming online right now with artificial intelligence assistance for the hospitality industry, that's a huge wave.'

Ulrich Pillau, Co-founder and CEO, Apaleo

AI and machine learning in revenue management

AI and machine learning (ML) are essential to modern revenue management, offering capabilities that go far beyond manual analysis. AI algorithms can analyse massive data sets faster and more accurately than any human ever could, identifying patterns that inform pricing and operational decisions. Machine learning tools are particularly effective at refining their models over time, learning from past data to improve future predictions, and many pricing tools have been using ML for many years already.

Revenue management platforms enhanced with ML can predict booking behaviours with greater precision. For example, these systems can identify demand peaks based not just on past trends but on a range of variables, such as real-time market conditions, competitor pricing and even local events or economic shifts. This predictive power allows managers to set prices that align with actual demand and adjust those prices as necessary without significant manual intervention.

The integration of ML also helps with pricing optimization. AI-powered systems can recommend targeted pricing strategies that cater to different market segments by assessing factors such as guest segmentation and booking window trends. These tools don't just stop at predicting prices; they can also provide insights into distribution channel performance, helping operators optimize their presence on various platforms, including OTAs and direct booking channels.

Limits of AI in decision making

Despite the advanced capabilities of AI, it is not without its limitations. One of the main challenges lies in AI's reliance on data patterns, which can make it less effective when handling subjective decisions that require human judgement – for now, anyway. For instance, while an AI tool can analyse thousands of data points to recommend a price, it might not account for non-quantifiable factors such as the property's brand value, customer loyalty considerations or nuanced market conditions that a human would recognize.

'A revenue manager has a risk tolerance. They have a framework for judging how to push for more or hedge and de-risk by reducing rates and things like that. Generative AI just doesn't yet have comprehensive access to data that can inform it to be reliable. So revenue managers will always be double-checking the decisions AI might recommend. I think where it's going is how we can use AI to perform like an analyst. Then the revenue manager can approve or disapprove, which over time will reinforce the AI's ability to think more like the revenue manager it is supporting.'

Oliver Stern, Account Executive, Wheelhouse

Risk tolerance is another area where AI still falls short. Revenue managers often need to make strategic decisions that involve a degree of calculated risk, balancing aggressive pricing strategies with the potential impact on customer perception and brand reputation. While AI can provide data-backed recommendations, it cannot always gauge these subjective elements, meaning human oversight is essential for final decision making.

Moreover, AI models depend on the quality of data input. If the data used to train these models is outdated or biased, the predictions can be misleading. This underscores the importance of continuous data validation and model updating to ensure accuracy and relevance.

The future of AI in pricing

AI is expected to move from its current analytical and predictive roles to more prescriptive ones as technology evolves. In the next five years, AI could evolve to not only forecast pricing changes but also suggest comprehensive strategies that include marketing, distribution and guest engagement initiatives. Advanced AI systems might integrate seamlessly with broader Property Management Systems (PMSs), facilitating real-time adjustments across multiple operational areas.

These AI advancements could lead to the creation of hyper-personalized guest experiences through dynamic pricing. By leveraging guest data such as booking history, preferences and loyalty programme participation, AI-driven tools can create customized offers that align with individual guest profiles. This would not only enhance sales through targeted pricing but also improve guest satisfaction by aligning prices and offers with guest expectations.

Further, as AI tools become more sophisticated, their use in strategic scenario planning is likely to expand. Revenue managers could use AI to run simulations, evaluating potential outcomes based on different pricing models and market conditions. This type of prescriptive analysis would empower decision makers to test multiple strategies before implementing them, reducing risk and enhancing strategic foresight.

The move towards forward-looking data and AI in pricing is shaping the future of the hospitality industry. While these tools provide invaluable predictive power and operational efficiency, human expertise remains essential for interpreting data, assessing subjective risks, and guiding overall strategy. The next frontier will see AI becoming even more integrated into decision-making processes, offering prescriptive solutions that allow revenue managers to stay ahead in an increasingly competitive and tech-driven marketplace.

REAL-WORLD EXAMPLE

Resident Hotels are breaking down silos to boost revenue

Founded in 2006, Resident Hotels is a collection of city centre hotels with four properties in London (Covent Garden, Kensington, Soho and Victoria), one property in Liverpool and another in Edinburgh. The group aims to provide heartfelt hospitality to guests and facilitate connection with local communities and neighbourhoods by partnering with nearby restaurants, bars and places of interest in order to provide guests with offers and discounts to help them discover and enjoy the local area.

Challenges and opportunities

Hotel companies typically have separate divisions for functions like revenue management, marketing and sales. But for privately owned Resident Hotels, originally each division was working towards its own priorities and metrics and not always aligned with each other. So they identified opportunities to collaboratively work on strategies and KPIs by aligning departments to strategically work towards common objectives.

The siloed approach led to inefficiencies and missed opportunities, according to Alessandra Leoni, Head of Commercial, who has been with the group for 13 years. As one of the earlier employees and when she was just looking after one hotel, she recalls, 'As a General Manager I benefited from a unique opportunity to align all workstreams within my role and responsibilities, as we were a much smaller group with limited resources. Thus I was the revenue, sales and marketing manager for the property I managed, and so I could only debate strategies with myself and senior leadership.'

She later took on a role at the group's headquarters as its first revenue manager. Here, she often found herself discussing strategy with other workstreams, such as sales and revenue. For instance, each department has unique strengths and skill sets to drive, at times, strategies that may not necessarily align, or to drive revenue at all costs to achieve occupancy and ADR. On the other hand, the sales team may focus on the delivery of corporate segments which historically deliver lower ADRs, while marketing might focus on brand and delivery of direct channels away from distribution channels such as third-party agents.

On other occasions, sales teams would secure volume-driven corporate contracts, but they did not always align with revenue management strategies.

Harnessing tech for the next workforce

Tourism was hit hard by the pandemic. Hotels, restaurants and bars were the first to be impacted and took a long time to recover as people slowly began to be reaccustomed to socializing in public.

During this period, many skilled professionals left hospitality jobs to retrain, in search of more stable employment. This is still being felt today as hotels struggle to recruit and retain people.

Alessandra Leoni began her career as a reception manager and is worried that because there are fewer people joining the hotel industry today, the number of professionals working their way up the ranks will be reduced.

'The industry is suffering from a lot of recruitment issues. Hospitality experts have left the industry for alternative careers. People who had 20 years' experience are migrating to another sector. The new generation is leaner and leaner,' she warns.

With fewer people in entry-level roles like waitressing, or food and beverage, fewer future 'stars' will progress into other roles across operations, sales, revenue or marketing. But technology can help with new skills and talent, she argues.

'The new generations have employment expectations and technology is now part of daily life. It is embedded into younger generations. They don't live without their phones and apps, and everything is at their fingertips. There is an expectation that when they are employed in a role, they'll have access to technology, to automated data entry and admin tasks. Putting people in front of data entry, you're just not going to retain them. So technology is going to have to be part of what we do.'

The solution

In 2021, Resident Hotels integrated these multiple departments into a unified commercial team, the idea being that collaboration would ensure that all departments align with common goals, such as driving overall revenue, improving the channel and distribution mix, and so improving its financial position.

Technology played a key role. The PMS, as can be expected, lies at the core of operations. But of note is how Leoni ensured each commercial team member was trained on how to use it. 'We ensured everyone across the teams is able to use all the unique functionalities that each technology employed within the company can offer,' she notes.

Different team members can then appreciate their peers' perspectives by accessing the technology available through the business. As an example, collaboration extends to producing the newsletter and discussing its content. As part of those conversations, the team looks at the data to share what's needed from a revenue perspective in terms of lead time, booking windows, and who's booking international versus domestic.

'There is a lot of validation across all departments, a lot of discussion to build that marketing campaign and for revenue to create a sales offer to be distributed across different channels,' Leoni says.

She also leverages the latest technology to give Resident Hotels the edge regarding marketing to a changing audience, with changing needs and expectations.

'Guests and bookers from top of the funnel to conversion, from a marketing perspective, are transitioning to desire content such as video through social media, TikTok, it's all of it,' she says. 'We are working towards creating content to inspire travel to our locations. It is important to embrace technology that enables hotels to promote their brand, reputation and flexibility towards resilience and continuous change.'

The unification ably demonstrates how technology can be used to allow people to focus on what's most important to them too. In this case, an ultra-centralized department means team members across the portfolio of six hotels can focus on delivering exceptional stays.

'From an operational perspective, the teams are not focused on administration, so when guests arrive, they are able to connect and deliver heartfelt hospitality,' Leoni says.

It's equally important to the commercial team. 'We need to use technology to make sure time is freed up from an HQ perspective, to drive strategy, make tactical and reactive decisions, to look at the data and adapt as needed,' she adds.

Overall, the on-site guest focus translates into happier guests. Reviews are an important component for Resident Hotels, operating in highly competitive city centres. Through freeing up team members' time to focus on guest needs, the hotel group is rewarded with top-tier scores on TripAdvisor and other channels.

'Reputation is paramount; reviews allow immediate visibility into the consumer and into the guest,' Leoni says, adding, 'The reputation we benefit from as a brand facilitates the brand visibility and awareness, and advocates for the brand and the values of the company and the teams.'

While the idea of merging revenue, marketing and sales into one came organically to Leoni, having previously been General Manager and overseeing so many different components, the process wasn't easy.

Days were spent sticking Post-it notes on walls, with plenty of conversations and ideas. 'And at the end, we said: this is what we're going to do, these are the actions, this will be the strategy, and everybody's objectives are aligned,' she says. 'We have to grow the sales mix. We have to drive users and conversion to the website. We have to do so while achieving the highest possible revenue through occupancy and average daily rates, and operate in a changing economy.'

With incorporated shared targets, colleagues now bring their own special skills to the table. As Leoni sums up: 'Collaboration is a powerful aspiration which many aim for, but at Resident Hotels, it is at the core of what we do and how we operate.'

From home to hotel

Embracing technology is going to be paramount to the continued success of the hospitality industry, and hotels that embrace it will be more flexible and resilient to change. 'Guest needs and expectations have changed and are continuing to change,' says Alessandra Leoni. 'There is an expectation: "I can stream Netflix here in my house", so why would a guest not be able to stream in the hotel bedroom? I don't necessarily care about the TV package provided and standardized for all guests. I want my home to travel with me in the form of my device.'

As a result, she believes personalization and hyper-personalization are a guest need. 'Personalized content delivery is a must,' she adds.

Conclusion

Resident Hotels' decision to set up a central commercial department that oversees a portfolio of six hotels under the Resident Hotels brand and a further four under the Sleeperz brand was a visionary move by the leadership. Yet it encapsulates how the right technology, when used strategically, can elevate the hospitality experience and increase the bottom line. The TripAdvisor scores speak for themselves, and the group punches above its weight.

As Resident Hotels continues to drive its ambition to grow its portfolio technology, collaboration and strong guest reputation will continue to play a pivotal role in its strategies and communities.

Revenue management across multiple markets and asset types

Scaling revenue management across multiple markets and asset types (aparthotels, villa rentals, hotels, flexible rentals) creates a unique set of challenges for hospitality operators. Managing properties in diverse locations requires a nuanced understanding of each market's demand patterns, competitor behaviour and guest expectations. The complexities of operating in multiple markets stem from the fact that each region can have vastly different economic conditions, seasonality and events that affect demand. Successful operators must develop strategies that can be tailored to local markets while maintaining a cohesive approach across a portfolio.

Successful revenue management implementation across multiple locations involves balancing localized strategies with the hospitality operator's overarching business goals. Each property or region operated in will very likely have distinct demand drivers. For example, a beach resort's peak season may be the summer months, while an urban hotel near a business district could experience consistent demand during weekdays or around convention dates. This variability means that a one-size-fits-all approach to pricing management will fall short.

Hospitality operators and their revenue experts need to leverage localized data to make informed pricing decisions that reflect the specific dynamics of each market. This data may include local events, holidays, economic shifts and competitors' strategies. The ability to segment properties based on these criteria allows operators to tailor pricing strategies that maximize revenue potential in each location. Additionally, technology and advanced software that supports multi-market operations provide vital tools to automate and streamline these complex processes.

The role of data in multi-market operations

Data is indispensable for successful revenue management across different markets. Large operators harness comprehensive market data to benchmark performance, identify emerging trends and adjust pricing in real time. Key performance metrics – such as RevPAR, ADR and market share RGI (Revenue Generating Index) – are tracked to ensure each property meets its targets. By comparing these metrics across locations, operators can pinpoint areas of underperformance and deploy corrective measures swiftly.

Market data also enables operators to set competitive prices that reflect each region's specific demand and supply conditions. For example, data on local booking windows, lead times and cancellation rates can inform more granular pricing strategies. Real-time market intelligence tools also provide operators with insights into competitor rates, allowing them to maintain a competitive edge.

Managing a large portfolio requires efficient portfolio analytics tools that can provide high-level insights and enable detailed analysis when needed. Portfolio analytics software allows revenue managers to monitor and compare property performance at a glance. This holistic view enables them to identify trends, forecast future demand and make data-driven decisions.

Bulk rate adjustments are essential for scaling revenue management effectively. Large operators need the ability to make strategic changes across multiple properties simultaneously. For instance, during high-demand periods triggered by regional events or economic shifts, managers may need to implement bulk price increases or promotions to capitalize on the demand surge. Advanced Revenue Management Systems (RMSs) facilitate these bulk changes while maintaining the flexibility to customize rates for individual properties as necessary.

Overall, the capability to manage multiple markets and properties hinges on a combination of granular market insights, advanced data analytics and scalable tools that support real-time decision making. This approach ensures that operators not only meet goals for individual hotels or units but also optimize revenue across their entire portfolio.

The impact of regulations on pricing

For STR operators, regulations can have a significant impact on pricing strategies. As we've seen in places such as New York, Scotland and Barcelona, the rapid growth of the STR market has prompted many cities and even countries to enact rules to manage the perceived effect of STR on housing availability, community character and tourism. These regulations can limit the number of nights a property can be rented, impose licensing requirements or restrict STRs in certain neighbourhoods. As a result, pricing strategies must adapt to comply with these local rules.

The nature of local regulations can directly influence supply and demand in specific markets. For instance, cities with stringent STR regulations, such as New York City and Amsterdam, limit the availability of rental properties. These constraints on supply can push up rates during periods of high demand, creating opportunities for operators who can legally operate within the market. On the other hand, cities with relaxed regulations may face oversupply, requiring managers to implement competitive pricing to attract guests.

Revenue managers in the STR space must remain informed about regulatory changes and adapt their strategies accordingly. For example, some operators might adjust the availability of their properties to focus on high-demand periods when regulations permit fewer rental days, thus maximizing income within the allowed operational window.

To navigate regulatory challenges, revenue managers often deploy adaptive strategies that balance compliance with profitability. One common approach is optimizing occupancy and rates during unrestricted periods. For instance, in markets where rental days are limited, operators might set higher rates during peak periods when demand is highest, ensuring that profits remain strong.

Flexibility is key in responding to regulatory changes. Revenue managers need systems that allow them to quickly adjust availability, update pricing and manage booking windows in response to new regulations. Advanced software solutions can assist by providing real-time notifications and analysis of how regulatory shifts impact market conditions, enabling quick strategic pivots.

Additionally, operators may explore diversified strategies, such as long-term stays that are not subject to the same regulations as STRs. By incorporating a mix of short-term and long-term bookings, properties can maintain occupancy levels and generate consistent revenue.

Balancing automation with the human element

The role of the revenue manager in the hospitality world has been undergoing significant transformation due to the advancement of RMS technology, business intelligence and pricing tools. Automation, data analytics and AI-driven tools have changed how revenue management functions, allowing processes to become more efficient and data-rich than ever before. However, while these technologies provide powerful capabilities, human expertise still remains a critical component for interpreting data, making strategic decisions and maintaining a competitive edge.

Revenue managers and strategists are no longer just price-setters; they are analysts who bridge the gap between data insights and business objectives. Modern RMSs can generate myriad reports and offer predictive models, but it is the revenue manager who contextualizes this information and aligns it with the broader goals of the property or chain. They bring the ability to understand nuanced market shifts, guest sentiment and the intangible aspects of hospitality that technology may overlook. The capacity to interpret anomalies in data, anticipate guest needs and make informed, creative decisions is where human expertise becomes invaluable.

Revenue managers are now also responsible for integrating technology into the business workflow, ensuring that these tools enhance rather than replace strategic decision making. This requires them to be proficient in data analysis and technology management, making them more versatile and essential than ever.

When to rely on automation vs human expertise

The decision on when to rely on automation versus human input is key to effective revenue management. Automated systems work brilliantly to handle repetitive and data-intensive tasks. Tools can analyse market trends, monitor competitor pricing and adjust rates dynamically to align with real-time demand. This allows properties to respond swiftly to changes in market conditions without the need for constant human oversight. Automated pricing tools can also handle high volumes of data efficiently, reducing the risk of human error and freeing up managers to focus on higher-level strategies.

However, human intervention is crucial in unpredictable markets or when the data presents mixed signals. For instance, during unexpected events such as political unrest, economic downturns or sudden changes in consumer behaviour, automated systems may struggle to provide an accurate response. These situations will require human intuition and strategic thinking to navigate, interpret and assess risk and to consider qualitative factors, such as customer loyalty impacts or brand reputation.

Moreover, when launching new promotions, entering a new market or adjusting long-term strategies, human oversight is essential to align these moves with the brand's image and business goals. These strategic interventions ensure that automation supports the business effectively without leading it astray during nuanced situations.

Training and adoption challenges

Like almost all tech adoption across hospitality operations, bringing a team along so that they buy into the changes that they are implementing and providing suitable training are key to success. Revenue managers need to be well versed in using these tools to their fullest potential, which requires an ongoing commitment to training and professional development. While many tools come with user-friendly interfaces, understanding their deeper functionalities and knowing how to interpret the generated data effectively is key.

Training programmes should focus not only on the technical aspects of using these platforms but also on enhancing analytical and strategic thinking skills. The goal is to empower revenue specialists to harness automation as a complement to their expertise rather than a replacement. Without adequate training, there is a risk of underutilizing powerful features or misinterpreting data outputs, leading to suboptimal decisions.

KEY TAKEAWAYS

The shift away from tradition: There is a shift from traditional static pricing to modern dynamic pricing strategies with technology and advanced data analytics transforming revenue management into a proactive, data-driven process.

Revenue management has core principles: Effective management relies on understanding supply and demand dynamics, strategic segmentation and leveraging key metrics like ADR, RevPAR, GOPPAR and RevPAN to optimize pricing strategies and maximize profitability.

Dynamic pricing and adaptability: The adoption of dynamic pricing tools enables hospitality operators to adjust rates in real time based on factors like competitor pricing, local events and demand fluctuations, ensuring properties remain competitive and maximizing sales.

AI and predictive tools: AI and machine learning play a significant role in analysing complex data sets, predicting market trends, and supporting strategic decision making. These technologies improve pricing accuracy and help operators respond swiftly to changes.

Balancing software with human expertise: While automated systems handle routine tasks, human oversight is essential for interpreting complex data, making strategic decisions and navigating unpredictable market conditions to maintain a competitive edge.

The importance of forward-looking data: Relying solely on historical data is no longer sufficient; forward-looking data provides real-time insights into market trends, helping operators anticipate shifts and align their pricing strategies proactively.

Revenue management across multiple markets: Managing income in different markets requires a localized approach supported by advanced analytics and scalable tools, allowing operators to tailor pricing strategies to regional demand patterns while maintaining a cohesive portfolio strategy.

Challenges and regulation compliance: Revenue managers must stay adaptable and compliant with local regulations, especially in STR markets where rules can directly affect pricing strategies. Successful operators use flexible systems to adjust availability and pricing as needed.

Real-World Example – Resident Hotels: Increasing revenue and guest satisfaction by breaking down departmental silos and forming a unified, tech-enabled commercial team aligned around shared objectives.

7

Sustainability, IoT and hospitality

Sustainability in hospitality is a meaty, important topic that is often misunderstood and can sometimes even be somewhat divisive. Geographic regions can have different takes on the importance of climate change, and guests can really differ in how much sustainable and green initiatives mean to them and how much of an impact the 'greenness' of a hotel or short-term rental (STR) might have, not just on their choice of accommodation but also on their wallets.

In addition, for today's employee market, there is a definite growing trend towards younger generations wanting to work with companies that are not only able to communicate an attractive purpose but are also able to demonstrate commitment to the environment and social impact.

There is a fair amount of debate about how much the lodging industry is really doing in terms of the green economy and environmental and social initiatives that aren't just 'greenwashing'. Being B-Corp Certified is still so rare in hospitality; only a few hotel companies globally meet those highest standards regarding environmental, social and governance (ESG).

That all being said, sustainability, becoming more environmentally friendly as well as more socially responsible, is a growing thread across all of lodging. Many of the operators and tech leaders that I spoke to for this book mentioned its importance to them personally as well as professionally.

In its essence, sustainability in hospitality encompasses a holistic approach that prioritizes minimizing the environmental footprint while enhancing social and economic well-being. Environmentally, which is typically the current main thrust of initiatives that benefit from technology, it involves reducing energy consumption, managing waste, conserving water and promoting eco-friendly practices throughout hotel operations. That could be anything from changing towels less frequently to saving energy on automated lighting and temperature control.

Socially, sustainability focuses on supporting local communities, ensuring fair labour practices and offering inclusive, healthy environments for both staff and guests. Economically, sustainable practices aim to reduce operational costs and create long-term value by maintaining high standards that attract environmentally conscious travellers. There are also increasing regulatory requirements such as the Corporate Sustainability Reporting Directive that will mandate certain ESG requirements and goals.

REAL-WORLD EXAMPLE
Host & Stay's sophisticated approach to total building control

Host & Stay is a UK-based accommodation manager and short-stay lets agency, with about 1,000 properties available. Its in-house property management service focuses on maintenance, housekeeping and compliance. In 2022, parent company, The SDDE Smith Group Limited, acquired property technology firm resicentral, which further enhanced Host & Stay's management offering.

Challenges and opportunities

Host & Stay helps property owners manage and rent out their homes. This combination of offerings clearly shows the daily challenges its owner customers face. One of these is the cost of running a home, with the recent rise in energy prices being particularly felt.

'Our concern 18 months ago was the rise in utility costs,' says Dale Smith, CEO and founder of Host & Stay. 'We thought the rise was going to be prolonged and prolonged. We were worried about owners leaving because it was becoming less financially viable to short let because of rising utility costs. So, we needed a solution to solve that. Otherwise, we were concerned we'd have a higher attrition rate on the portfolio.'

The party's over

One of the biggest fears for a vacation rental owner is an illegal party or a gathering getting out of control. It's one area Airbnb has been clamping down on too; in August 2020 it implemented a ban on parties, which it then codified in 2022.

As well as temperature controls, Host & Stay's property technology system resicentral can monitor noise levels. A prolonged spike in decibels could mean a party is underway, so Host & Stay is able to set up notifications to monitor such spikes. As well as reducing energy bills, this is a case of adopting technology as a security device, and a means to ensure peace of mind for owners.

The solution

Host & Stay offers resiAIR, a product created by sister company resicentral as part of its Signature management package, which comes at a premium 15 per cent over its Classic package. But Smith believes the benefits of seamlessly integrating it into a property outweigh the extra cost for owners. 'Control to us is key,' he says. 'It gives the owner sight of the property. We've got everything in there from a sensor point of view.'

In fact the technology features 12 different sensors inside a home that monitor various aspects, including lighting, noise and sound, as well as temperature, humidity and air quality. It can also digitally control light switches as well as the heating.

So how does it work? As an example, before a guest arrives, the entrance hallway light can be automatically switched on so they don't arrive in darkness, while inside the mood lighting and an ambient temperature can be activated. When the guest isn't present, the temperature can be maintained at 15 degrees. The system also provides information on how long it takes for the property to reach the ambient temperature – meaning an empty home isn't unnecessarily being heated.

As another example, a guest could check in at 4pm. They enter the property, switch all of the lights on and raise the thermostat temperature to 24 degrees. Two hours later they go out for dinner but leave the temperature high and all the lights on.

'If we see that over a 30-minute period there's been no movement, no light switches have been touched and we've got a low CO_2 reading, then we know nobody's in the property,' says Smith. 'So we could choose to switch all of the lights off automatically and reduce the temperature from the 24 degrees that they set, and turn it back down to 18 degrees. The owner doesn't need to get involved in that, we don't need to get involved in that. The property is maintaining itself based on the rules that we set.'

He adds that Host & Stay has seen gas and electricity savings in some properties reach as much as 40 per cent.

What's important to note are the prescribed rules and automation, because Smith says he has seen examples of owners and guests fighting over the temperature, turning it up and down. While they can see what's happening, that doesn't mean they can control everything and override systems. 'With our management scheme, we don't give owners control, however, because it's us that's managing the property. The owners can see what's going on, but it's our team that would respond to any alerts,' Smith says.

A keyless entry system enables guests to receive unique door codes prior to arrival, with different codes provided to housekeepers, so Host & Stay can monitor who's going in and out of the property. In larger properties the technology can detect which bedrooms have not been used, with data passed to the housekeeping team to instruct them there's no need to clean those rooms, which reduces the overall cleaning time and cost. Further ahead, Host & Stay is exploring the use of robot vacuum cleaners.

Tapping Into new markets with sustainable travel certification

Focusing on technology that monitors energy use generates a halo effect for Host & Stay. Not only are costs saved, and guests benefit from a better experience, but it can also help properties gain a stamp of approval. For example, properties that adopt resicentral may benefit from Sustonica certification.

Sustonica is a sustainability badge and recognition, and aims to help guests easily find eco-conscious properties. While there are differing types of certifications, Sustonica focuses on STRs. The initiative helps attract the segment of customers that opt for more sustainable properties, based on the idea that simple badges make it easier for potential customers to discover properties that consider their carbon footprint.

'We see that as one of the key things going forward, we know more and more guests are ESG-conscious and green travel conscious,' says Dale Smith.

The certification falls under Host & Stay's ManageGreen initiative, which aims to 'bring sustainability to the forefront of holiday let management'. The ManageGreen offering also includes partnerships and eco-conscious travel guides.

The technology and dashboard app for hosts is an effective solution, but it wasn't necessarily an easy journey for Host & Stay to set it up as a service. The resicentral system was originally a 'fully cabled solution' and designed for the purpose-built student accommodation and build-to-rent sectors, Smith recalls. So, his company spent 12 months developing a 'retrofit solution' so resicentral could be installed in any property at any point.

Host & Stay directly employs more than 300 housekeepers and has a maintenance team of over 20 people. As a result, Host & Stay can successfully position full end-to-end management as a USP for homeowners.

'We're a big believer in having those skill sets in-house, and deploying that in-house, because it gives us control. We can control the quality end to end; I would rather be in control of it than managing multiple third parties to try to deliver that service,' Smith adds. 'That's core to us, that's where our heart is, that full management piece, because we don't believe that's being done properly across the sector at the moment.'

Conclusion

Successfully executed, the concept of tech-enabled hospitality encompasses more than digital distribution and marketing strategies, or smart ways to message guests; it applies to buildings too. The acquisition of resicentral and the development of the retrofit resiAIR solution has not only proved instrumental in helping Host & Stay reduce energy consumption in the property, driving down utility bills for its customers; it has also opened the door to other benefits.

This UK property management agency's approach is a masterclass in showing how hospitality operators can leverage technology to provide a great guest and owner experience, and unlock cost efficiencies. According to Smith, the numbers speak for themself, as he says 60 per cent of new owners opt for its Signature management scheme, which includes resiAIR, compared to its Classic package.

IoT and smart energy management

A simple explanation of the Internet of Things (IoT) is that it is a network of interconnected devices embedded with sensors and software that collect, exchange and act on data. In hospitality, IoT is now playing a growing role in enhancing efficiency, automating processes and adding value to the guest experience. Smart thermostats, energy-monitoring sensors and predictive maintenance systems are just a few examples of how IoT is used to streamline operations, enhance guest experiences and reduce resource usage.

Connecting sustainability and IoT has allowed the industry to highlight how technology can significantly support environmental goals in the hospitality sector. By integrating IoT solutions, tech-enabled hospitality operators across hotels and STR properties can now optimize energy consumption through real-time data and automated adjustments, reduce waste through predictive inventory and waste management systems, and conserve water by detecting leaks and monitoring usage. This technology helps operators run more eco-friendly and cost-effective businesses, and allows them to align with sustainability objectives and meet the growing demand for responsible tourism and 'green stays'.

It is, of course, no surprise to anyone that the hospitality industry is a significant energy consumer due to the continuous demand for heating, cooling, lighting and various operational needs. Think of all those pools, towels, sheets, corridors to clean, rooms to be kept at the right temperature and lighting that is kept on 24 hours a day. In helping hospitality businesses manage energy more efficiently, reducing costs and environmental impact, IoT technology has emerged as a key mechanism.

By interconnecting sensors and smart controls that adjust lighting, heating, ventilation and air conditioning (HVAC) based on real-time occupancy data and guest preferences, IoT systems can monitor and subsequently reduce energy use and energy waste. For example, a smart thermostat can detect when a guest leaves the room and will automatically adjust the temperature to a more energy-saving setting. Similarly, automated lighting systems can switch off lights when rooms are unoccupied and gradually dim them in common areas during off-peak hours, contributing to energy savings without compromising guest comfort.

These smart systems are designed to learn and adapt over time, analysing usage patterns and making more efficient energy adjustments. They also integrate seamlessly with hotel management software, allowing operators to monitor and control energy settings remotely, optimizing energy use even further.

IoT sensors also play a crucial role by monitoring and tracking energy consumption across different parts of a property. Sensors can provide actionable insights through dashboards that display energy usage metrics, enabling managers to identify areas of excessive energy use or inefficiency. With these insights, operators can implement targeted energy-saving measures, such as adjusting HVAC settings during peak usage times or identifying energy-intensive appliances that may need upgrading.

It is not just about turning off the lights or lowering the temperature; it is also about improving air quality. When multiple people occupy a room, such as in a meeting room or in a hotel lobby, the CO_2 levels naturally increase. IoT sensors measure these levels and adjust the fresh air supply accordingly, increasing ventilation when necessary to maintain air quality. Conversely, if a room is unoccupied, the system reduces the fresh air flow to save energy. Traditional hotel systems continuously pump heating, cooling and fresh air into rooms, but this smart approach minimizes energy waste by adjusting based on real-time occupancy.

Real-time monitoring also helps in setting energy benchmarks and goals. By having a clear understanding of how much energy is being consumed at any given time, properties can make data-driven decisions to meet sustainability targets. This data can be used for reports and certifications, showcasing the hotel's commitment to sustainable practices and appealing to eco-conscious travellers. For example, a hotel operator that is looking to become B-Corp Certified will be able to prove its downward trend of targets through real-time monitoring.

Waste management and resource optimization

Effective waste management can also have a significant impact on hospitality operators looking to do a better job on sustainability targets and also to reduce operational costs. IoT technology provides innovative solutions for optimizing waste management and resource usage, helping properties manage everything from food waste to water conservation.

For example, smart bins equipped with sensors can detect when they are nearing capacity and automatically alert the waste management team to schedule collection at the most efficient times. This approach reduces unnecessary pickups and the associated costs, ensuring that waste is managed only when needed. The technology also helps properties reduce their carbon footprint by streamlining disposal logistics and minimizing truck emissions.

Moreover, these systems can categorize types of waste, providing insights into which areas of the hotel generate the most waste. With this data and the help of AI tools, hotel managers can implement targeted waste reduction strategies, such as adjusting kitchen practices or providing guests with clearer recycling guidelines.

'We've built an online guest portal with all the information about the reservation and the property. We digitize every home to keep energy bills as low as possible and guarantee security through electronic locks.'

Jean-Paul Godfroy, CEO, HUSWELL

Reducing food waste

On the food and beverage side, food waste is a significant issue in hotel kitchens and restaurants, where over-ordering or inefficient food use can lead to excess waste. IoT-enabled inventory and food tracking systems address this by using real-time data to predict usage patterns and inventory needs. These systems can alert staff when food items are nearing their expiration date, suggesting recipes that prioritize those ingredients to minimize waste.

Additionally, IoT-based inventory management tools analyse past consumption trends alongside current reservation data to forecast future needs accurately. This predictive capability helps reduce overstocking and ensures that food items are used efficiently.

Water conservation initiatives

Water is another critical resource that can be managed more sustainably. IoT systems can track usage patterns throughout a property and detect leaks automatically. For example, smart water meters identify unusual spikes in usage, signalling a potential leak that maintenance staff can address promptly. This prevents water wastage and reduces the risk of water damage.

Hotels can also use IoT systems to encourage water-saving habits among guests. For instance, some properties could use an app to inform guests of their water usage and provide tips on reducing it during their stay. This approach can instil a sense of shared responsibility, and it aligns with the preferences of eco-conscious travellers.

By integrating these IoT solutions, hospitality operators can create a more sustainable business model that conserves resources, cuts down operational expenses and aligns with global environmental efforts.

'We are already living up to that idea that the hotel can provide a kind of social structure for an area in the city and really connect not only the internationals but also the locals together.'

Hans Meyer, Co-founder, Zoku

Technology-focused sustainability initiatives that hospitality providers can adopt

AI-powered predictive maintenance: IoT devices monitor the health of appliances and systems, predicting failures before they occur, thereby reducing resource wastage and extending equipment lifespans.

Automated water monitoring and leak detection: IoT water meters track usage and identify leaks early, preventing wastage and lowering water bills.

Carbon footprint tracking for guests: IoT-enabled systems track and display a guest's energy and resource usage during their stay, helping them understand their environmental impact and encouraging sustainable behaviours.

CO_2 and ventilation monitoring: Sensors monitor CO_2 levels in rooms and common areas, adjusting fresh air circulation to maintain air quality while minimizing energy used for ventilation when spaces are unoccupied.

Digital key systems: Mobile keycards eliminate the need for plastic cards, reducing material use and associated waste.

Dynamic energy usage optimization: AI-powered algorithms analyse energy usage patterns and adjust energy consumption during peak and off-peak hours for maximum efficiency.

Eco-mode in smart devices: Smart appliances in guest rooms, such as energy-efficient TVs or air purifiers, automatically switch to eco-mode when rooms are unoccupied.

Guest-controlled smart room features: Mobile apps or voice-activated assistants let guests adjust room settings (temperature, lighting, blinds) to their preferences, reducing unnecessary energy use.

Renewable energy integration with IoT: Smart grids manage renewable energy sources like solar panels, optimizing the balance between on-site energy generation, storage and usage.

Smart energy management systems: IoT-enabled systems use sensors to monitor and control energy consumption, automatically adjusting heating, cooling and lighting based on real-time occupancy.

> 'It's like Maslow's Hierarchy of Needs. You need to focus on the baseline stuff before you can talk about the surprise and delights.'
>
> **Kent Hatcher, Director of Product, Mint House**

Automated maintenance, predictive analytics and supply chain

Essentially, IoT solutions enable properties to function more effectively with fewer resources. However, one of the most significant ways IoT contributes to operational efficiency is through automated maintenance and predictive analytics. By monitoring the performance of critical systems such as HVAC, elevators and kitchen appliances, IoT sensors can track key metrics like temperature fluctuations, energy usage and system vibrations to detect anomalies that could signal an impending failure.

When potential issues are identified, the system alerts maintenance staff, enabling them to address problems proactively before they escalate into costly repairs or service disruptions. For example, if an

HVAC system shows irregular energy consumption patterns, the IoT system might indicate a clogged filter or failing component that needs attention. This predictive approach minimizes equipment downtime, extends the lifespan of assets and enhances guest comfort by avoiding unplanned outages. It may also mean that rooms will be 'out of action' less often, which of course contributes directly to revenue.

IoT systems, alongside AI analytics, can enhance inventory and supply chain management through real-time tracking of supplies such as toiletries, cleaning products and kitchen ingredients, helping to ensure timely restocking while avoiding overstocking, which can lead to waste. IoT-enabled inventory systems will track usage patterns and automatically place orders when supplies reach predefined thresholds. For example, a smart inventory system might detect that a hotel is running low on eco-friendly soap and automatically send a purchase request to the supplier. This ensures that essential items are always available without overburdening storage or creating excess waste.

TECH LEADER INSIGHT

Building trust through technology – Jessica Matthias, Global Sustainability Director, Sabre

With 10 years working at global travel technology company Sabre, Jessica Matthias has had a front-row seat witnessing a number of hospitality trends over the past decade. One of the most dominant is the mounting pressure on the travel industry to transition to becoming more sustainable.

While the aviation sector has come under the spotlight in recent years, with calls to reduce carbon emissions, the attention is now turning to accommodation. At the same time as the hospitality sector is still recovering from the pandemic, Matthias finds herself focusing on educating the industry on how best to implement more environmentally friendly practices.

Her advocacy efforts span, naturally, technological solutions. Sabre has a global perspective of industry challenges, courtesy of the millions of people who interact with its technology, in one form or another, on a daily basis. The US company's technology footprint spans everything from mobile apps and airport check-in kiosks to OTA websites and airline reservation systems.

On top of software, Matthias's role increasingly involves collaborations and campaigning.

Visualizing the bigger picture

One of the biggest challenges she perceives is that many hospitality brands are first and foremost focusing on generating income, in some cases in order to survive. Hotels tend to operate on tight profit margins, a problem exacerbated by the pandemic, which hit both revenue and staffing levels. Currently, she says, hotels are looking for short-term gains rather than long-term cost benefits.

'One of the main barriers to adoption at the moment is the idea of the upfront cost and integration challenge,' she says. 'For a lot of hotels... dedicating budget towards investing in sustainability technology does offer a return on investment in the long term, but it does involve quite a bit of a cost investment and time investment upfront.'

Matthias argues that integrating any new technology can be time-consuming and complex, but there is a further issue with sustainability-related technology in terms of proving the ROI. 'It's not so straightforward to say, if you implement this, you're going to see this much improvement in your sustainability performance or in your profit,' she says. 'It's hard to quantify that and justify that upfront cost and integration investment.'

Technology integration impacts

There's a significant education aspect to Matthias's role, especially around smaller properties or hotel chains that may be unaware of the vast range of solutions available that can make a difference. 'At Sabre, our challenge is to help overcome some of those barriers in terms of raising awareness and developing cost-effective solutions for a range of different types of hotels, and developing partnerships,' she says.

Sabre is well known as a Global Distribution System (GDS), which means it connects travel bookers and suppliers, such as airlines, accommodation providers and other travel-related services. The company continuously receives feedback from hotels that they want to see their offerings represented in a more lively and colourful way, Matthias says, rather than just a listing. She notes that Sabre does this already, bringing rooms and more to life through so-called rich content that includes photos, descriptions and more, but is increasingly exploring how to enhance showcasing a property's sustainability features.

'We're showing things like whether a property has an electric vehicle charging point. And guests want to know what type of charging point it is, whether it's for a Tesla or another type of car. There are all these different intricacies of offerings that hotels are creating on the sustainability front that they want to see represented in the GDS,' Matthais says.

Meanwhile, Sabre's Hospitality division provides solutions such as Nuvola, for hotel task management and guest engagement, and SynXis Retailing, for selling ancillaries. Both of these solutions can boost a hotel's sustainability efforts.

Nuvola, for example, can automate operations such as housekeeping, configure room cleaning and linen change frequency, and monitor energy and water usage, which helps hotels minimize emissions.

Features such as smart room controls have sustainability benefits too. The temperature of a room can be set automatically, and sensors detect when the guest is going in and out, and so automatically shut off the heating until they return, when the room returns to the desired temperature. The same principle applies to air conditioning or lighting.

'Obviously the hotel will be saving on energy usage after implementing a system like that,' Matthias argues. 'But also for the guest, it is easier to control than a lot of those other systems you get in the room, where it can be clunky, with so many different settings you just don't know how to use.'

There are great tech solutions to enable hotels to monitor energy efficiency, water and waste reduction. The net result is a hotel can see results in terms of a reduction in carbon footprint, and then translate that into cost savings as well. 'Nuvola can also remind the hotelier to conduct preventive maintenance, extending longevity and reliability of elevators, mini fridges, and more,' she adds.

Her overall message is that technology can enhance the sustainability performance of a hotel while also improving the guest experience.

A softer approach

More subtle but equally important options take into consideration what takes place outside a hotel. Matthias recalls how Sabre acquired a gifting platform called Techsembly in 2023. It brings marketplace and gift card retailing capabilities to its SynXis Retailing platform. The software is used by luxury hotel brand Capella Hotels and Resorts across its properties in Singapore, Bangkok and the Maldives, allowing it to offer an itinerary of workshops and activities to experience culture, community and tradition.

Hotels are therefore easily able to curate sustainable experiences and initiatives, and promote these to guests.

'We have some customers who specifically use it for pushing out their local ocean conservation-based experiences. They can be centred around local wildlife conservation, or responsible whale watching. And then some of the proceeds of that go to those local charities,' says Matthias.

In the public eye

Leaders in any field need to be visible, and Matthias has embraced her role as Global Sustainability Director over the past year, leaning on her public relations experience to champion the cause at events and conferences.

Then there are partnerships, including a notable one with Travalyst, the not-for-profit organization founded by Prince Harry, The Duke of Sussex. Sabre joined the coalition, which is developing a clear, consistent and credible sustainability information framework for travel sellers, in February 2024. Other Travalyst partners include Amadeus, Booking.com, Expedia Group, Google, Skyscanner, Travelport, Trip.com Group, Tripadvisor, Visa and Mastercard.

The goal is that with so many global players, Travalyst can accelerate and scale its mission to create sustainability standards, including providing consistent flight emission estimates across booking platforms.

'When I book a hotel, it's just still not obvious whether it is a really genuinely sustainable property, because there are so many different types of certifications available at the moment for hotels. You don't know which one is a credible certification, and which is something somebody made up that doesn't have any validation behind it,' she says.

Matthias was also recently appointed to the Global Business Travel Association Foundation's Sustainability Leadership Council. The foundation is the charitable arm of the association and it aims to 'drive positive change for People and Planet'. As well as championing climate action in business travel, the foundation looks at ways to empower women in their careers, and to help develop the next generation of business travel professionals.

'There's still a lot of work to be done by technology companies like Sabre, and the industry in general, to promote the most sustainable hotels and build that trust among consumers for what is actually a sustainable property,' she concludes.

Challenges and considerations
when implementing IoT for sustainability

Implementing IoT for sustainability in hospitality presents significant opportunities, but it also comes with challenges. From financial considerations to infrastructure compatibility and workforce adoption, understanding these obstacles is crucial for a successful transition.

One of the primary challenges of IoT implementation is the significant initial investment that can sometimes be required, at least for large and ambitious initiatives. The costs for full implementation include purchasing IoT devices, installing sensors, upgrading infrastructure and integrating systems into existing operations. For example, intelligent energy management systems and IoT-enabled waste solutions may require specialized hardware and software, and expert consultants to set them up. These upfront expenses can be daunting, especially for smaller operators with limited budgets and when there may not be an articulated return on investment (ROI).

However, IoT solutions can offer a compelling ROI over time. Energy savings, reduced operational costs and improved resource management can offset the initial outlay. Communicating potential ROI figures can help stakeholders justify the initial costs and build confidence in IoT adoption.

Data security and privacy

IoT devices collect vast amounts of data, including sensitive guest information, making data security and privacy a top priority. Hotels must ensure that the data collected through IoT sensors and smart devices is encrypted, securely stored and compliant with regulations such as Europe's General Data Protection Regulation or the California Consumer Privacy Act. Breaches risk financial penalties, damage to the operator's reputation and erosion of guest trust.

To address these concerns, operators should implement robust cybersecurity protocols, including firewalls, regular audits and staff training on data handling. Partnering with reputable IoT vendors that prioritize security features in their products is another critical step in safeguarding guest data.

Integration with legacy systems

Many hotels operate with legacy systems incompatible with modern IoT technologies, creating integration challenges. For example, older HVAC systems may not support the connectivity required for smart energy management, necessitating costly upgrades or replacements, or the hotel management software doesn't easily and affordably integrate with IoT software. Operators can adopt phased implementation strategies to overcome this, starting with areas that provide the highest ROI. Partnering with vendors offering modular IoT solutions that integrate with legacy systems ensures a smoother transition.

Training, adoption, and bringing the team with you

Even the most advanced IoT systems can fail to deliver value if staff are not adequately trained to use them. Resistance to change and a need for more understanding about how IoT works can hinder adoption across the organization. To address this, hotels must invest in training programmes to familiarize staff with new technologies and their benefits. Hands-on workshops, easy-to-use interfaces and continuous support from IoT vendors can help employees feel more confident using these systems. Encouraging feedback and involving staff in the implementation process also encourages buy-in and ensures that IoT systems are effectively integrated into daily operations.

In conclusion, while implementing IoT for sustainability involves challenges related to cost, data security, infrastructure compatibility and staff adoption, careful planning and strategic investment can help hotels overcome these obstacles and unlock the full potential of IoT-driven sustainability.

KEY TAKEAWAYS

Towards a holistic approach to sustainability: Sustainability in hospitality is multifaceted, encompassing environmental, social and economic dimensions. It involves reducing energy consumption, managing waste, conserving water and fostering inclusive and socially responsible practices that appeal to eco-conscious guests and employees.

IoT as a sustainability enabler: IoT technology supports sustainability by optimizing energy use, monitoring waste levels, conserving water and improving operational efficiency. These interconnected systems enable properties to run more eco-friendly and cost-effective operations.

Waste and water management innovations: IoT-based solutions like smart bins and water monitoring systems optimize resource usage, reduce waste and prevent water leaks.

Enhanced guest experience through technology: IoT-powered smart rooms, guest apps and CO_2 monitoring systems personalize guest experiences while promoting eco-conscious choices. These technologies align with the growing demand for sustainable travel.

Challenges in IoT implementation: Key challenges include high upfront costs, integrating IoT with legacy systems and ensuring data security. Addressing these issues with phased implementation, strong cybersecurity measures and staff training is critical to successful adoption.

Return on investment (ROI) potential: Despite initial expenses, IoT can offer long-term ROI through energy savings, reduced operational costs and increased guest satisfaction. Effective communication of these benefits can encourage stakeholder buy-in.

Real-World Example – Host & Stay: Not satisfied with what was available in the market and concerned about rising energy costs, this operator bought in to a proprietary technology solution to manage energy better, with great results.

8

Hospitality's backbone:
Operations, security
and guest access

Across hospitality operations, security, housekeeping and access control form the backbone of a successful guest experience. These elements are interwoven into every aspect of a property's daily functioning, ensuring not only guest satisfaction but also operational efficiency and profitability. Together, they represent the critical pillars that support seamless service delivery, staff productivity and the overall safety and comfort of guests.

When we think about operations, we are really looking at the complex coordination of activities and processes, from managing bookings and front desk interactions to ensuring the smooth functioning of behind-the-scenes processes such as housekeeping and maintenance. A well-orchestrated operational framework minimizes errors, reduces downtime and enhances the overall guest experience. Tech and specifically Software as a Service (SaaS) solutions are increasingly playing an important role in smooth operations for hotel and short-term rental (STR) operators.

Security and safety within hospitality are vital in building trust with guests. Modern solutions extend far beyond traditional locks and cameras, incorporating advanced systems like biometric access controls and Internet of Things (IoT)-powered monitoring. Physical security solutions and cyber security also play a crucial role in safeguarding sensitive guest data and financial transactions.

Housekeeping, often viewed as a routine function, directly impacts guest perceptions and reviews. Cleanliness and preparedness are the absolute basics of any lodging offering, from the most basic budget accommodation to the most luxurious of hotels. Without housekeeping and maintenance, no hotel or STR brand would stay in business for very long. Efficiency in housekeeping ensures timely turnover of rooms, cleanliness standards and resource optimization. Advances in automation, IoT and operations-focused software have revolutionized this area, enabling data-driven decision making and sustainable practices.

Over the last few years, and especially in the aftermath of the global pandemic, access control has undergone a digital transformation, shifting from physical keys to digital keys. We are still seeing huge opportunity for access and guest welcomes to be even more digitally guest-centric. These innovations not only streamline the check-in and check-out processes but also enhance security and provide guests with greater convenience and control over their environment.

In addition, AI-driven predictive maintenance and IoT-enabled devices are helping operators optimize costs, reduce manual workload and still deliver personalized experiences.

'I can see a future where there's no check-in process at all – guests just walk in and feel at home.'

Hans Meyer, Co-founder, Zoku

IoT and its impact on security

Security is a fundamental element of hospitality operations, encompassing guest safety, data protection and asset management. Traditional security systems, while foundational, are being increasingly supplemented or replaced by smart, IoT-enabled solutions that deliver enhanced efficiency, responsiveness and peace of mind for both operators and guests.

For decades, hospitality security relied on manual checks, basic key systems and analogue surveillance cameras. While effective in their time, these systems often fell short in offering flexibility, scalability and proactive monitoring. The advent of IoT-enabled solutions has brought about real-time monitoring, automated responses and seamless integration with other operational systems.

IoT-powered systems can also employ interconnected devices to monitor, detect and respond to security threats. For instance, sensors embedded in hotel rooms can detect unauthorized entry or environmental anomalies, such as smoke or excessive humidity, and trigger alerts. This proactive approach minimizes risks and enhances safety by addressing issues before they escalate. Noise and occupancy monitoring is another growing area where software and IoT devices are increasingly used.

Access control systems and their use in hotels and other lodgings have seen remarkable growth. There's been a move away from traditional metal keys to keycards and now to digital solutions. Digital keycards, mobile app access and even biometric systems (although it's still very, very early days) are becoming a potential new standard for ensuring guest and property safety.

Biometric systems: 'Tech-enabled' hospitality providers are increasingly using biometrics for seamless and contactless services, enhancing convenience and security. Key applications include facial recognition for check-ins, keyless room entry and secure payment systems. These innovations will reduce the need for physical cards or keys. For instance, biometric systems can grant guests access to amenities like gyms and pools based on facial scans, providing a frictionless experience. Furthermore, hotels can personalize services by using biometric data to recall guest preferences, such as room temperature or dining habits. Security is also bolstered, as biometric identification minimizes fraud and unauthorized access.

Digital keycards: Widely adopted, these allow guests to access their rooms securely while reducing the risk of unauthorized duplication. Keycards can also be configured to grant access to specific areas, such as gyms or conference rooms, enhancing operational control, while at the same time making things better for the guest.

Mobile app access: Mobile-based access eliminates the need for physical keys altogether. Guests can unlock their rooms or other designated areas using their smartphones. Keys can be added to Android or Apple wallets and integration with guest profiles allows apps to adapt to personalized settings, such as preferred room temperatures or lighting upon entry.

Data, privacy and the path to autonomous hospitality –
Nils Mattisson, Co-founder and CEO, Minut

Swedish company Minut makes property sensors for monitoring noise, smoke, energy and occupancy. But for Nils Mattisson, its co-founder and CEO, there's much more at stake than simply manufacturing devices that can detect when people are smoking a cigarette or throwing a raucous party.

That's because the notion of putting monitoring technology in a hotel room or vacation rental raises a host of other questions, from reducing reliance on on-site staff and driving the shift towards 'autonomous hospitality' to associated privacy and socio-economic issues.

Emerging hospitality technology continues to have a fundamental impact on the way buildings are run. Many brands are moving towards features like digital check-in and keyless entry, but leveraging numerous benefits from sophisticated monitoring too.

Minut has 'evolved from discovering adverse events' such as cigarette smoke, noise, over-occupancy or people bringing in pets when they're not supposed to, says Mattisson. Today, as well as checking for nuisances, sensors enable operators to maximize the efficiency of a building. For example, they can determine if guests have shown up or left, whether it's time to send in cleaners or if it's possible to offer an early check-in.

Foundation of autonomous hospitality

In general, Mattisson breaks hospitality technology down into two areas. The first (and perhaps the most common) is as a means to free up an employee's time so they perform fewer monotonous tasks, such as administration, and instead spend more time on interacting with guests.

The second is autonomous hospitality, where a building is able to function with as few people on-site as possible – or none at all. The main reason is to lower operating costs. 'We don't like to say that, but I mean that's what's happening,' says Mattisson.

The former Apple engineer notes that Minut works across both scenarios. 'With autonomous hospitality, we probably see faster growth. You see a lot of hotels that aren't really viable anymore. Labour costs are higher than they used to be,' he says, citing one customer who successfully operates a building with 300 rooms with just one member of staff.

Tied into this cost-saving narrative is the pursuit of securing more direct bookings, as that then reduces the number of commissions paid to the OTA. To promote their brand directly and better compete, Mattisson says they need five-star reviews and a stellar reputation.

'How do we put technology in the service of making sure the guest is having the best possible stay when you can't have a person checking them in?' he asks. 'We have customers where maybe five years ago they would take all of their bookings to Airbnb, Booking.com or Expedia, now they are getting half of them direct, so they started brand building to get repeat business.'

In a traditional hotel setup, a guest can ask a concierge for a new pillow, tell them their neighbour is noisy or ask for help with the thermostat. 'Even a small miss can easily get to that four star or worse. So, you have to come up with a system with no people, where you are still guaranteeing that the guest is going to have a good night's sleep,' he adds.

Another Minut customer has several buildings across London that do not have on-site staff, but there is a 'central back office' from where they can dispatch someone if needed.

'That's not something they want to do. And that's only something that they would do in a rare circumstance,' Mattisson says. 'But then you can get to less than one person on average in a building. I would say that the best solution is to either have one person there 24/7, or you really have to make everything tip-top with technology.'

In this case, the operator needs a 'known margin of error – especially with access. You can't lock people out.'

Monitoring and reducing energy usage is another appealing area. Growing numbers of tourists are opting for more sustainable stays, and lower carbon emissions result in lower operator costs.

'I'm a big believer in aligning incentives, between what's good for the planet and what's good for the operator,' Mattisson continues. 'Anything where you can save a little bit of money can make a big difference on the bottom line, so we've started doing more work with the likes of Nest and Ecobee to make sure apartments are run more efficiently from a heating and cooling point of view.'

Ethical questions

In parallel to all this data collection, privacy is paramount.

'There is a whole grey area where there is more data that we can get, but there are ethical questions that we as an industry have to figure out where the right balance is,' Mattisson says.

For example, Minut is working on a people-counting system. The CEO is exploring whether it is an invasion of privacy to know how many people are in a hotel room.

'You can obviously imagine scenarios where that is sensitive. But likewise, that data can help the operator run their business in a better way,' he observes.

'We want to make sure we don't go too far on the data collection side and get a backlash. And we want to make sure the balance is such that everyone feels like they're a winner. With these increased capabilities, there is more of a grey area. It's mostly an ethical question more than a tech question.'

Privacy issues also vary depending on the type of accommodation or the purpose of the guest stay. Long-term tenants may have a higher expectation of privacy than a short-stay guest, for example. Another scenario could involve a business traveller booking a hotel room for one, but sensors reveal several people in the room. That too could be sensitive.

Social aspects

Meanwhile, operational technology plays a wider societal role. In the residential sector, and particularly across social housing and student living, or buildings where more vulnerable people live, Mattisson thinks the advantages go beyond smoke detectors; it could help save lives.

For example, he says noise is one of the main drivers of mental health issues among students. 'They never get a break if they have a bad neighbour,' he says. 'I think we can contribute positively there.'

It's a similar situation in social housing. In buildings that provide shelter for vulnerable people, the fact that an antisocial neighbour is watching movies at 3 am could push people over the edge. 'There's plenty of technology that can help, there just needs to be a feeling of responsibility,' he adds.

But overall, the entrepreneur is excited about the STR sector, which allows tourists to mix with locals. And it's in these situations where he feels Minut's technology lends itself best.

'You absolutely need monitoring to make sure neighbours are not disturbed. Because what's going to happen is there will be a party, even if it's every other weekend, and the family living next door will be badly affected. They'll go to the local council and politicians, and then when you get this backlash, in terms of regulation, it's all wiped out.'

He claims Minut's technology can reduce complaints by 85 per cent.

Fits and starts

As for innovation in the space over the next five years, Mattisson predicts the focus will be spent learning about emerging tools and about how people respond to them.

He thinks the recent generative AI 'breakthrough' and adoption of Large Language Models over the past couple of years changed the game, but it's unlikely a similar seismic development will appear anytime soon.

'Progress happens in fits and starts,' he says. 'Large Language Models are very good and they are going to continue to get better. I don't know if it's going to change the circumstances in which we build technology. There is a time before and after they arrived on the scene. Over the next few years, you're going to see things play out based on the things that have happened over the last two years.'

Part of that will involve consolidation, Mattisson adds, which is already happening at pace.

'AI is really setting the stage for the next few years,' he continues. 'I don't think we need another big breakthrough in order to achieve interesting products and growth. Even if there was no development whatsoever in terms of new breakthroughs over the next three years, we still have a lot of work to do with just what's become available recently.'

The tech future of housekeeping and maintenance

As we all know, housekeeping and maintenance are the unsung heroes of hospitality operations, operating behind the scenes to make sure that everything runs smoothly and the guests get the best experience possible. If a room isn't clean, if elements of the property just don't work or it's slow to service a room, you've lost any guest loyalty you might hope for and you're pretty much guaranteed a poor star rating or review.

The operational area of housekeeping and maintenance, once the domain of spreadsheets, paper and pencils, is benefiting hugely from technology, particularly in data-driven solutions and automation. By embracing innovative platforms, IoT integrations and sustainability initiatives, hotels and STR operators can achieve unprecedented efficiency, cost savings and guest satisfaction.

'The technology allows us to create a frictionless experience where the guests can access their apartment for their stay in the city without ever seeing or talking to a Mint House employee if they don't want to.'

Kent Hatcher, Director of Product, Mint House

Housekeeping management platforms and automating tasks

Housekeeping management platforms have evolved into indispensable tools for modern hospitality operations. These platforms use data from the Property Management System (PMS) to automate task assignments based on real-time guest activity, such as check-ins, check-outs and special requests. By integrating directly with the PMS, housekeeping platforms ensure that tasks are prioritized logically and efficiently. This saves on time and resources as well as minimizing human error when it comes to planning workloads. Some PMSs also have this functionality built in.

When a guest requests early check-in or when a guest checks out early, the platform can automatically notify housekeeping to prioritize cleaning that specific room. Conversely, late check-outs are flagged to delay cleaning tasks, optimizing staff schedules and reducing idle time. This dynamic scheduling approach eliminates guesswork and maximizes labour efficiency.

With IoT systems in place, hotels can monitor and manage room readiness. Sensors embedded in rooms can detect occupancy, air quality and light usage, providing real-time updates to housekeeping teams. Motion sensors, for example, can identify when a room is vacant, signalling that it's OK to go and fix something that has been requested. This eliminates unnecessary interruptions for guests and allows for more precise task management.

IoT-enabled systems also enhance predictive maintenance by monitoring room conditions. For instance, sensors can alert staff to issues like leaks, heating, ventilation and air conditioning (HVAC) inefficiencies or low stock of consumables, enabling proactive responses. By integrating these systems with housekeeping platforms, operators can address problems before they impact guests.

> 'There are two things that you want to know about the check-out. Number one: I want to get my cleaner in there as quickly as I can. Number two: I want to be able to offer it for an early check-in for the next guest, either as a delighter or as a revenue-enhancing feature that I'm going to charge for.'
>
> **Nolan Mondrow, CEO, Remote Lock**

Sustainability, conservation and efficiency

Sustainability is a growing priority in housekeeping operations and IoT solutions are central to achieving environmental goals. Smart water meters, for example, track usage during cleaning and detect anomalies like leaks. Similarly, IoT-enabled devices optimize energy consumption by adjusting lighting and HVAC settings based on room occupancy.

Towel and linen reuse programmes, often communicated via guest-facing apps, can also reduce resource usage. Many hotels now offer incentives for guests who opt out of daily cleaning. These programmes, coupled with IoT monitoring, allow operators to cut water and energy consumption as well as people's time while maintaining high cleanliness standards.

REAL-WORLD EXAMPLE

Simple tech innovations help Íslandshótel break housekeeping rules

Family-owned Íslandshótel was founded in 1992 when Hotel Reykjavík opened in the capital with just 30 rooms. Today it's the largest hotel chain in Iceland, with 18 properties, representing 2,000 rooms and ranging from three to four stars. The chain is also the first in the country to achieve full Green Key certification across 17 of its properties. Green Key is a standard of excellence for environmental responsibility and sustainable operations within tourism and is recognized in more than 60 countries.

Challenges and opportunities

When you think of technological innovation in the context of hospitality, cleaning rooms and maintenance might not always be front of mind. But in Iceland, Íslandshótel has adopted a new tech platform and change in mindset that has produced dramatic results for the chain.

Staff overheads are often one of the biggest costs for hotels today, with front desk, housekeeping and maintenance labour costs adding up. In the highly competitive hospitality industry, brands continually search for ways to lower payroll costs, and new technology often steps in to address pain points.

In Íslandshótel's case, the group wanted to address inefficiencies in how it prioritized cleaning rooms, responded to guests checking in early and communicated maintenance issues.

'We always had some problems with communication between housekeeping and the front office,' recalls Hjörtur Valgeirsson, Chief Operating Officer, Íslandshótel. 'The issue sometimes is understanding how long it takes, and how much effort it takes, for a housekeeper to clean a room. This is something that the front desk just doesn't always understand.'

He reels off one example: a seemingly simple request to split a bed into two. As well as the significant time it takes to do this (it may look like a simple job, but in reality it isn't so simple), it can also disrupt the housekeeper's operations. Meanwhile, Valgeirsson adds that a receptionist could be faced with a guest checking in early and requesting a room to be ready. 'There's potential for conflicting priorities, which is always happening across hotels. In the past, prior to using the platform, we would have people running around a lot up to the floors to check things. So, it's a lot of time wasting,' he says.

As well as reducing operational costs, hotels strive to operate in a more environmentally sustainable manner – which itself often leads to cost savings but equally reassures guests who are increasingly searching for greener vacations.

How Lego inspires usability

New technology can sometimes be met with trepidation, as staff may question how much extra training will be needed. That wasn't the case for Íslandshótel's integration of housekeeping and task management app Sweeply.

Hjörtur Valgeirsson calls out Sweeply's big, bright buttons. 'I think they call it a Lego format,' he says. 'There are really clear, colourful buttons and you can understand it easily. It's simple to use when you're working on something else under pressure. Using their phone, the housekeeper just clicks when they start the room and clicks again when the room is finished.'

The solution

In May 2023, Íslandshótel decided to use Sweeply, a software company based in Reykjavik, to run its housekeeping and maintenance management. The hotel group also jumped on this occasion to trial an unorthodox approach to its hotel operations.

For Valgeirsson, Sweeply's housekeeping and task management dashboards provided a solution that meant they did not have to juggle between different platforms, including messaging app Slack.

Sweeply integrates with Íslandshótel's PMS, and staff, including receptionists, are able to clearly identify which rooms are available. 'The rooms get allocated, and they go into a procedure when they need to be cleaned, so it solves this communication issue,' Valgeirsson says.

The tech also speeds up maintenance requests, as the platform allows staff users to take a photo of something that is broken, and tag the right person, with the request entered as a dedicated maintenance task list. 'It's all in the same system,' he notes. 'The housekeepers, who are always in the rooms, have the system open so they can quickly take a picture of an issue and report it. It's practical and seamless.'

Íslandshótel also took advantage of the tech transformation to trial a new way of operating. They decided to ask guests to opt in for daily housekeeping, in a bid to further drive down costs, be more sustainable and as a response to what the hotel felt were changing customer needs. The approach was in part due to Covid altering the behaviour of guests. 'We saw a change since Covid where people valued more privacy, and in some cases, privacy was valued above service. There are guests who just want to be left alone,' Valgeirsson says.

Discussions followed around how the hotel group could implement optional housekeeping as a new service offering, with the offering being, we will leave you alone! 'When we are checking in the guest, this needs to be in the welcome speech, presented to the guest in a way they understand that it is their choice if they want us to come into the room and clean,' says Valgeirsson. 'If not, we will leave you alone.'

The rollout of this shift began in one of Íslandshótel's properties and has since been implemented in all but one of the chain. Before implementing, Valgeirsson was initially concerned guest satisfaction would dip when the optional housekeeping model began, and there were some teething issues related to communicating the offering.

'You would have guests who come in, and they would expect the cleaning, but they were not informed of the "opt-in" system. So, we needed to be very careful in how we designed the pre-arrival information, how we communicated, all over the hotel's public spaces and in the rooms themselves,' he says.

Eventually, guest satisfaction improved, and today more than 65 per cent of Íslandshótel's guests choose to forgo daily cleaning, while 35 per cent 'opt in'.

Tapping into culture

Íslandshótel's decision to make housekeeping optional is unusual for a hotel, but it isn't too dissimilar from a common daily activity in our lives: shopping at the local supermarket. According to Hjörtur Valgeirsson, we've all been accustomed to scanning and bagging our purchases ourselves for several years now.

Cutting the hotel cleaning service is not something you would have thought of doing a few years ago, nor even just asking if this was a possibility that a guest would entertain. 'But it's changing so fast,' says Valgeirsson. 'People want to be able to adjust the service the way they want to. People have more opinions about what they want, and some people want privacy.'

He also likens the transformation to service in the airline sector. 'It's interesting how this will develop in the hotel industry. I mean, we see with airlines you have to pay for everything. It may not work for full-service hotels, but it's interesting to explore for hotel service in the future,' he adds.

As automation and a do-it-yourself ethos become more prevalent in our daily lives, Íslandshótel's adoption of Sweeply is an example of how technology can also transform mindsets.

Conclusion

Íslandshótel's implementation showcases how technology can drive operational and guest satisfaction improvements and highlights how hospitality software innovation can extend beyond pricing algorithms, marketing strategies or channel distribution.

As Valgeirsson says: 'The benefit is in meeting the guest requirements. We have less workload for the staff, we are saving on labour costs, we are saving on raw materials and it saves time on communication because it's more seamless. As a bonus, it's more environmentally friendly. We are also a part of Green Key, which means we are always looking to be more environmentally friendly and conscious. And this fits into that.'

Perhaps more importantly, it reveals how important it is to take risks, because, as this pioneering hotel group found out, rewards are there for the taking.

Gamification of training tools

Innovative training tools, powered by AI and gamification, can be used to improve staff engagement in housekeeping and we are starting to see a jump in usage. Gamification platforms turn routine tasks into rewarding challenges, where employees earn points or rewards for completing tasks efficiently and maintaining quality standards. Leaderboards and recognition programmes can lead to healthy competition, boosting morale and productivity.

AI-driven tools also offer tailored training programmes that adapt to individual staff needs. For instance, new hires can access step-by-step tutorials, while experienced employees engage in advanced problem-solving simulations. These tools also improve job satisfaction, reducing turnover in a traditionally high-churn sector. The hospitality sector – which traditionally struggles to hold on to talent – is looking at different ways to keep staff motivated.

By integrating data-driven platforms, IoT technologies and innovative training tools, the future of housekeeping is one of enhanced efficiency, sustainability and employee satisfaction. These advancements not only streamline operations but also align with the evolving expectations of eco-conscious travellers and modern hospitality standards. The result is a win-win scenario where guests enjoy a seamless experience and operators benefit from lower costs and empowered teams.

'We have an Employee Net Promoter Score (eNPS) because we think if people are not happy, we can't be a good hospitality company.'

Begum Agca Okutgen, Head of Partner Network, Blueground

KEY TAKEAWAYS

Modern security measures: Physical security has evolved from traditional systems to advanced digital solutions like biometric access, IoT-enabled monitoring and noise and occupancy detection. These innovations enhance guest trust and property security.

Digital transformation of guest access: The shift from physical keys to digital solutions such as keycards, mobile apps and biometric systems is changing guest access and how operators welcome guests.

Efficiency in housekeeping: Automation and data-driven tools have transformed housekeeping, ensuring timely turnover and optimized resource use. This directly impacts guest satisfaction and operational efficiency.

Ethical and privacy considerations: As the use of monitoring technologies grows, there is an increasing need to address privacy and ethical concerns. Transparent practices and responsible data usage are essential to maintaining guest trust.

Towards autonomous hospitality: The concept of autonomous hospitality, powered by minimal on-site staffing and advanced technology, is gaining traction. This model, while cost-effective, emphasizes the importance of maintaining service quality through robust technological infrastructures.

Real-World Example — Íslandshótel: Iceland's largest hotel chain has used technology to offer guests an 'opt-in' model for housekeeping. The initiative has been hugely successful, with 65 per cent of guests forgoing cleaning, saving the chain time, energy and resources.

9

Revolutionizing guest communication

Communication has become the cornerstone of every successful guest experience. As travellers become increasingly accustomed to digital interaction in their daily lives, their expectations for seamless, immediate and personalized communication with hotels or short-term rental (STR) operators have grown exponentially.

The hospitality industry, historically slow to adapt to technological shifts, is now at the forefront of a revolution in guest communication. Adopting new tools has also prompted many hotels and STR property managers to rethink how they engage with guests throughout the entire journey – from the moment they consider booking to long after they check out.

'Technology should be removing those points of friction, removing inconveniences, ultimately making guests have a much better experience. It's about ensuring that the technology we use enhances the guest experience by making their stay seamless, intuitive and tailored to their individual preferences.'

David Peller, former Global Managing Director, Amazon Web Services Travel and Hospitality

The evolution of guest communication technology

Guest communication technology for hotels has evolved significantly over the past decade. Gone are the days when a phone call to the front desk or a face-to-face interaction with a concierge was the primary method of communication. Today, a suite of digital tools has emerged, transforming how hotels interact with their guests.

The rise of digital messaging platforms has been one of the most significant developments in hotel guest communication. Platforms like WhatsApp, SMS, iMessage, WeChat and Facebook Messenger have become preferred channels for many guests, providing a quick and convenient way to reach out to hotel staff. These platforms enable real-time, two-way communication, allowing hotels to respond instantly to guest enquiries, concerns and requests.

This shift to digital messaging adds convenience and aligns with the broader trend of mobile-first communication. As more guests use smartphones as their main means of communication, hotels have had to adapt by integrating messaging platforms into their operations. These platforms offer numerous advantages, including handling multiple conversations simultaneously, tracking communication history and providing a seamless experience across different stages of the guest journey.

Generative AI has transformed guest communication even further. Hotels and STR operators are increasingly using chatbots, powered by generative AI, to manage routine enquiries and provide 24/7 support. These AI-driven tools answer frequently asked questions, assist with bookings and even handle more complex tasks like recommending local attractions, negotiating discounts or managing check-ins and check-outs.

The key advantage of AI chatbots is their ability to deliver personalized responses based on guest preferences and past behaviour. By analysing data such as previous stays, booking patterns and guest feedback, AI can tailor interactions to meet the specific needs of each guest. This level of personalization leads to a more engaging and relevant experience. For example, guests might use a hotel's app to customize their stay by selecting pillow types, setting room temperatures or choosing dining preferences – all before they even arrive at the property.

The proliferation of mobile apps and in-room devices has further revolutionized guest communication. Many hotels now offer mobile concierge apps that allow guests to access services, make requests and communicate with hotel staff directly from their smartphones. In-room devices, such as tablets or smart TVs, also serve as communication hubs, enabling guests to order room service, book spa appointments or request housekeeping services.

REAL-WORLD EXAMPLE
How Bob W is digitizing the customer journey

Finland's Bob W was founded in 2018 and is a tech-led hospitality provider that offers a hybrid between hotels and conventional private rentals – otherwise known as the 'Best of Both Worlds'. Bob W opened its first property in the Punavuori district of Helsinki in 2019.

With a focus on sustainability, the brand operates across 10 European countries, and calls its employees 'Bobstars'. It is expanding rapidly, having announced a joint venture with Osborne+Co Investment Management in July 2024, with plans to turn a further 25 buildings into between 1,500 and 2,000 units with an estimated gross development value of £400 million.[1]

Bob W's main proposition is to use technology to give every guest a high-quality, 'live like a local', contactless experience, at scale. Part of that plan means digitizing the guest journey, which, according to Chief Operating Officer Jeremy Slater, emerged from a need to offer a better alternative to the classic front desk experience.

'That's our whole product ethos: to make it easier than a hotel without any of the overheads of having an additional headcount at the front desk,' says Slater. 'There are a few use cases where the front desk is part of the experience itself. Whether that's the Plaza in New York or Four Seasons Hotel Madrid... for a five-star luxury resort-style hotel, it's part of the experience – and you want it.'

He thinks this desire for such a traditional experience now applies to just a 'very small slither' of people and believes overall that the front desk experience slows guests down, acting as a barrier between them and their apartment or room. 'And that barrier often has a queue, or you have to wait for mad things like for them to print stuff out. Why are they printing stuff? Why are they giving you key cards that don't work two hours later?' he adds.

Leveraging guest communication to secure repeat bookings

Bob W's laser focus on the digital journey isn't just to make life easier for guests; it's also a strategy to increase the hospitality group's chances of converting the guest to a repeat booker, or convert them from an online travel agency (OTA) booking to a direct booking.

That might be in six months, or six years, and Jeremy Slater believes that, due to the strength of the brand and consistent messaging with a defined tone of voice, the guest will return to its own website to book again, rather than through another channel.

Challenges and opportunities

How can a relatively new hospitality brand harness technology to improve the experience, boost guest satisfaction and retention, and drive awareness? These are the main questions this European challenger brand is addressing.

The solution

Bob W uses a third-party 'core' Property Management System (PMS) across its apartments and then builds its own products on top of that. That includes a Customer Relationship Management (CRM) platform called Houston, which receives details from the core PMS. Houston can tell by a guest's email address if they have stayed before, for how many nights and how much money they spent.

Behind the technology is its 'guest success team', with half the staff based in an office in Estonia and the rest in digital nomad hotspots such as Lisbon, parts of Spain and the Canary Islands.

This strategy enables Bob W to digitize the guest journey from start to finish but with a human touch, making the experience as seamless as possible. For example, if a guest last stayed at Bob W Hyde Park and needed help with their suitcases as there was no elevator, the guest would be called to ask if they required assistance again.

The company leans on WhatsApp as its preferred communication tool. Before the stay, a guest will receive a WhatsApp message. If they don't have WhatsApp, they use SMS. 'About 97 per cent of our communications come through WhatsApp, which is how we want it to be,' notes Slater.

However, in a bid to better connect with guests, the company leverages its brand. 'Bob W is speaking to them,' says Slater. 'Bob W is the avatar of the perfect host and the channels he uses to communicate with the guests reflect that.' WhatsApp is used as it's how a friend of a friend would message, Slater continues, 'and that's how we want Bob to be seen'. WhatsApp as a platform is also easier for the team to manage or 'triage' questions compared to incoming phone calls.

Beware the spammers

The fine art of guest communications is a balancing act. Too little leaves guests feeling lost; too much and they feel like they're being spammed. That's according to Jeremy Slater. For example, the apartment operator uses WhatsApp as a means of communication, but it needs to engage with guests the right amount so they know it's there to help, like a virtual concierge. It tries not to overstep the mark.

'We've seen that work, and we've seen how that can also really fail,' says Slater. 'I've done that at previous businesses where we've thrown the kitchen sink, everything, all the proactive comms, and the guests are like, "Whoa, stop. Calm down!" And then they just stop reading and responding because they just think it's spam. It's a fine line.'

Conclusion

There probably aren't that many hospitality companies that have opted for a name as their brand, but in a competitive environment where marketing is key to standing out, it certainly makes it more personal. Branding is one thing, but then applying that throughout the guest experience is key. Controlling much of its technology in-house, Bob W is able to achieve a high degree of consistency.

The company's proposition is that Bob W, effectively an avatar, is the perfect host. It wants guests to understand that Bob is hosting them. As Slater says: 'It's not just the company name.'

Personalizing through data

The power of personalization in guest communication lies in the ability to harness and analyse vast amounts of data, transforming it into actionable insights. In the hospitality industry, data is the lifeblood of effective communication, enabling hotels to move beyond one-size-fits-all approaches and towards tailored, individualized interactions with each and every guest.

Hotel and STR operators have access to a wealth of data, collected from various touchpoints throughout the guest journey. This includes website views, booking history, preferences noted during previous stays, feedback provided through surveys or online reviews, and even real-time data collected during the current stay. By integrating this data into their communication systems, hotels can develop a comprehensive profile of each guest, capturing their unique preferences, behaviours and expectations.

The ability to tailor communication is one of the most powerful aspects of modern guest communication technology. Hotels can now collect and analyse vast amounts of data on guest preferences, behaviours and feedback. This data-driven approach allows hotels to tailor their communication strategies to each individual guest, offering personalized recommendations, special offers and tailored experiences.

For example, a hotel might send a custom-made welcome message to a returning guest, referencing their previous stays and offering an upgrade or a complementary service. By leveraging data in this way, hotels can create deeper connections with their guests, enhancing the overall guest experience and boosting loyalty. This level of personalization enhances their overall experience by anticipating and meeting their needs before they even have to ask, making guests feel valued.

Benefits of advanced guest communication technology

The adoption of advanced communication technologies offers hotels myriad benefits, from improved guest satisfaction to increased operational efficiency. One of the most immediate benefits is the significant improvement in guest satisfaction. By providing multiple communication channels and ensuring that these channels are responsive, hotels can meet guest needs more effectively. And, as hospitality operators are effectively held to ransom by the customer review, being able to respond at warp speed is vital.

Real-time communication means that issues can be resolved quickly, requests can be fulfilled promptly and guests can feel more connected to the hotel throughout their stay. Moreover, the ability to personalize communication based on guest data adds a layer of care and attention that can turn a good stay into a great one. When guests feel that their individual preferences and needs are being recognized and met, their overall satisfaction with the hotel increases, leading to higher ratings, positive reviews and repeat business. We will explore this more in Chapter 11 on enhancing the guest experience.

Beyond enhancing guest satisfaction, advanced communication tools also improve operational efficiency. By automating routine tasks and streamlining communication, hotels can free up staff to focus on more critical, high-touch aspects of guest service. For instance, AI chatbots can handle a significant volume of inquiries, reducing the burden on front desk staff and allowing them to dedicate more time to the type of complex requests that might elevate a guest experience.

Additionally, integrating communication platforms with other hotel systems, such as PMSs or CRM tools, ensures that all guest interactions are logged and accessible in one place. This centralization of information minimizes errors, reduces miscommunication and allows for more coordinated and efficient service delivery. It is also in this vein that unified inboxes, which is when all messages for all the various platforms (email, WhatsApp and booking platforms) are accessible in one place, are so important.

'The future of technology in our industry is going to be centred around guest communication tools. Platforms like Enso and Breezeway will lead the way, focusing on enhancing the guest experience from the moment they arrive at the destination through seamless interactions and personalized services.'

Terry Whyte, The Vacation Rental Software Guy

Increasing revenue-generating opportunities

Guest communication platforms are also powerful revenue drivers. By using these platforms to promote upsells, add-ons and special offers, hotels can enhance the guest experience while simultaneously increasing their revenue. For example, during the booking process, a chatbot might suggest upgrading to a suite or adding a spa package based on the guest's past behaviour or preferences.

Similarly, bespoke messaging during the stay can prompt guests to take advantage of on-site services, such as dining in the hotel restaurant or booking an excursion. By strategically using communication tools to highlight these opportunities at the right moments, hotels can boost their ancillary revenue without appearing pushy or intrusive.

Whether it's a late-night room service request or an urgent maintenance issue, guests can rest assured that their needs will be addressed promptly. Sometimes they are also happy to pay extra for this.

While the benefits of advanced guest communication technologies are clear, implementing these tools is not without its challenges. Hotels must navigate a complex landscape of technology options, integration issues and the need to maintain a human touch in an increasingly digital world.

TECH LEADER INSIGHT

Understanding the guest's lifetime value with better data management –
Willem Rabsztyn, CEO and Co-founder, Bookboost

Guest communication is a fast-evolving domain within hospitality technology. How people communicate with each other is in constant flux, with the shift from email to messaging apps and other social platforms accelerating.

Understandably, hospitality brands make every effort to be where their customers are, to speak with the right tone of voice and to deliver relevant messages based on the individual's profile. Those brands that can build a picture of their customers tend to reap the rewards of offering a better guest experience, which in turn leads to revenue opportunities.

Visualizing the customer through effective data management isn't easy, however. And historically the focus has been on communication before the guest's stay to secure bookings. Today, there's an emphasis on extending the conversation, during and long after the guest has checked out, in order to maximize the guest's lifetime value. But data is becoming more 'scattered', according to Willem Rabsztyn, CEO and co-founder of Bookboost, which is on a mission to consolidate and optimize guest data from all sources and solve personalization and communication at scale.

He argues that the CRM platform has never been so important, as the number of digital interactions a hotel can have with a guest exponentially increases. For example, he suggests that if a guest has stayed three or four times with a hotel group, there could be 30 to 50 customer profiles generated, from the OTA, PMS and hotel website through to point-of-sale systems, newsletters and channel manager.

'Every tool in the customer journey might send a different email with different branding,' Rabsztyn says. 'Maybe the PMS sends a booking confirmation, the OTA sends a booking confirmation, the check-in tool sends a pre-stay message and so do some other tools in the customer journey, all with different layouts, different languages and not taking into account what the guest's needs are.'

Mapping the guest's digital journey

While a PMS deals with the operational side of a hotel, the CRM will focus on all things customer-related. As well as communication, it can also touch upon loyalty, marketing automation, upselling, cross-selling providers and reputation management, often connecting into other third parties.

There are many benefits to better data management. Hotels might want to have a different narrative towards first-timers vs returners, lower spenders vs high spenders or business guests vs families.

'Bringing customer data together to map out the whole customer journey, we can recognize the individual guest. For example, they're coming for the third time with a friend to this hotel for business purposes,' Rabsztyn says. 'Based on what we have seen, they usually book a certain type of room, or usually have dinner at the hotel restaurant. So based on that, we can personalize that communication and create revenue opportunities.'

The CRM could also promote a dinner table booking for a leisure couple, or recommend reserving a workspace area for a corporate guest.

From Bookboost's perspective, it brings 'scattered' customer data together into a single place and is then able to distribute that again to various customer-focused solutions. Taking things further, Rabsztyn says filters can also apply to location too. If the hotel guest lives locally, the hotel can then engage with them to promote offers to friends. 'In this way, you can really personalize your sub-segments, the sub-populations, in your guest population,' he says.

Identifying 'moments of truth'

Rabsztyn also says there are different points within a customer journey that he identifies as so-called 'moments of truth.' For example, besides the check-in, another moment could be when the guest walks into the room for the first time. 'What is their first experience?' he says. 'Is everything according to what they expected? Maybe housekeeping has forgotten about something? So this is one moment to check in proactively with the guest at scale,' advises Rabsztyn

Moments of truth can also include when a guest shares a negative sentiment in a feedback form – a comprehensive CRM would then engage with the guest. If a guest leaves with a positive sentiment, the CRM can put extra focus on getting that review onto other platforms, such as Google Maps, TripAdvisor or the OTA.

Further ahead, say 50 days after the booking, a smart CRM will also identify that a loyal guest has not yet made a future booking. 'So we keep engaging with the guests, offer them something because we see that this guest is booking every time in October, and automatically invite the guest to book again,' Rabsztyn says.

'In the past, everything has been reservation focused. Today the hospitality movement is set to become more customer focused. So where hotels in the past talked about RevPAR (revenue per available room), we talk about Customer Lifetime Value (CLTV). How to maximize CLTV based on buying behaviour, based on the past customer data, and looking at the bigger picture of what certain types of guests do in that hotel.'

And with many hotels now diversifying their spaces and increasingly tapping into communities, so too will their demand for more cohesive data on their guests increase.

'I've seen examples where a hotel also cleans the rooms or offers a service to do housekeeping in the neighbourhoods. So hotels become more integrated community systems, especially in cities,' Rabsztyn adds.

Choosing the right guest communication technology

The sheer number of guest communication tools available today can be overwhelming. Hotels and STR managers must carefully evaluate their needs, resources and guest demographics when looking to choose the technologies that deliver the most value.

However, the key is to ensure that whatever technology is selected aligns with the hotel's overall guest experience strategy. Technology should enhance the guest experience, not detract from it. This means considering not just the tool's functionality but also its ease of use, integration capabilities and support options.

Here are some things to consider.

Integration and data management

Effective guest communication relies on seamlessly integrating various systems, from PMS and CRM platforms to messaging apps and AI tools. Ensuring that these systems work together harmoniously can be a significant challenge, particularly for hotels with legacy systems or limited IT resources.

Data management is another critical consideration. As hotels collect more data on their guests, they must have systems in place to manage and protect this information. This includes ensuring compliance with data protection regulations, such as the General Data Protection Regulation (GDPR) in Europe, and implementing security measures to prevent data breaches.

Maintaining the human touch

As hotels increasingly rely on technology to manage guest communication, they risk losing the personal, human touch that is so central to what is traditionally thought of as hospitality. While AI and automation can handle routine tasks and inquiries, it's essential that hotels that still want to offer 'human hospitality' strike the right balance between technology and human interaction.

For hotels still looking to maintain the balance between tech and human input, one way is to use technology to empower staff rather than replace them. For instance, AI can handle initial inquiries, but human staff should be ready to step in for more complex interactions. Similarly, personalization tools can also be used to enhance human interactions, not replace them. By leveraging technology in this way, hotels can ensure that their communication remains warm, personal and genuinely hospitable. This, of course, may not be the case for hotels that appeal to guests who either actively don't want 'human hospitality' or are happy with an automated experience.

Training and staff adoption

Successfully implementing advanced communication technologies involves using the right people to bring about change. Hotels should also invest in training staff to use these tools effectively, from the technical aspects to a broader education on the role of technology in modern hospitality.

Adoption can also be challenging, particularly if staff are resistant to change or the technology is perceived as too complex or time-consuming. Hotels should approach technology adoption with a clear plan, including pilot programmes, phased rollouts and ongoing support to ensure staff are comfortable and confident using the tools.

> 'In the luxury sector, it's not reasonable for us to expect our guests to do anything at all. They should be telling us how they want to communicate and how they want to work with us.'
>
> **Andy Evers, Group Director of IT, Rocco Forte Hotels**

The future of guest communication

As the hospitality industry continues to evolve, so too will the technologies and strategies used to message guests. Several trends will likely shape the future of guest communication.

AI and machine learning

Machine learning algorithms will be playing a key role in predicting guest needs, personalizing interactions and optimizing communication strategies. AI-driven tools will become more sophisticated, capable of understanding and responding to a broader range of guest inquiries and preferences.

In the future, AI may also play a more significant role in managing the entire guest journey, from pre-booking to post-stay. For example, AI could be used to analyse guest feedback and automatically suggest improvements to hotel operations or communication strategies. This level of automation and intelligence will enable hotels to continuously refine and enhance the guest experience.

Integration of the Internet of Things (IoT)

IoT devices like smart thermostats, lighting systems and keyless entry can be integrated with communication platforms.

For instance, a guest might receive a welcome message on their smartphone as they approach their room, with the room's temperature and lighting automatically adjusted to their preferences. These kinds of integrated, personalized experiences will become increasingly common as IoT technology advances and guests' expectations become more sophisticated.

Voice-activated communication

Voice assistants like Amazon's Alexa or Google Assistant are already being integrated into some hotel rooms or STR properties, allowing guests to control various aspects of their stay using voice commands.

In the future, this could extend beyond the room, enabling guests to interact with hotel services and staff through voice commands from anywhere on the property. This hands-free approach could enhance convenience and accessibility, particularly for guests with disabilities or those who prefer not to use mobile devices.

Sustainability and ethical considerations

As sustainability becomes an increasingly important issue in the hospitality industry, hotels will need to consider the environmental and ethical implications of their communication strategies. This might include using digital communication tools to reduce paper waste, leveraging AI to optimize energy usage or ensuring that guest data is managed in a way that respects privacy and security.

Hotels that prioritize sustainability in their communication strategies can reduce their environmental footprint and appeal to the growing segment of eco-conscious travellers. As such, sustainability will likely become a key consideration in developing and implementing guest communication technologies.

Embracing the future

The revolution in guest communication technology is reshaping the hospitality industry, offering hotels new ways to connect with guests, improve their experience and streamline their operations. By embracing these technologies and integrating them thoughtfully into their operations, hotels can meet the evolving expectations of today's travellers while staying true to the core values of hospitality – warmth, personalization and exceptional service.

Hotels that are proactive in adopting and adapting to this revolution will be well positioned to lead the industry, delivering stays that are deeply personal and memorable. The challenge is finding the right balance – leveraging technology to enhance, rather than replace, the human touch at hospitality's heart.

KEY TAKEAWAYS

Digital transformation: Guest communication has evolved from traditional methods to digital platforms, emphasizing real-time, mobile-first interactions through messaging apps, AI-driven chatbots and mobile concierge services.

Personalization through data: Modern guest communication is heavily reliant on data to personalize interactions, enhancing the guest experience by anticipating needs and offering tailored services.

AI and automation: AI and automation are central to improving efficiency in guest communication, handling routine inquiries while allowing staff to focus on high-touch and high-value interactions.

Maintaining the human connection: Despite the increasing reliance on technology, maintaining a personal, human touch is, for some customer segments, still crucial. For operators serving this market, technology should empower staff to enhance guest interactions rather than replace them.

Balancing communication: Effective guest communication requires a balance to avoid overwhelming guests with information while ensuring they feel supported. This involves the strategic use of communication tools like WhatsApp to engage guests without spamming them.

Real-World Example – Bob W: Bob W's experience illustrates how a tech-enabled hospitality brand leverages digital communication to provide a seamless, personalized guest experience while driving brand loyalty and repeat bookings.

Note

1   Bob W (2024) Bob W partners with Osborne+Co to build a £400 million portfolio of high-quality serviced apartments, https://bobw.co/articles/bobw-partners-with-osborneco-120m-fund-serviced-apartments?lng=de (archived at https://perma.cc/CB9T-LTK3)

10

Financial technologies and hospitality

The growing impact of financial technology (fintech) on hospitality has been fascinating to begin to understand and to watch unfold. As an industry, lodging is exiting the dark ages and entering a world offering more flexibility, choice and benefit for both the operator and the consumer. Gone are the days of payment machines and long nights of reconciling payments and credit inconsistencies. As with all areas of modern life, fintech innovation has dramatically impacted the consumer user experience and instilled feelings of trust and financial security.

The hospitality industry thrives on delivering seamless, memorable experiences, and fintech has become indispensable as a facilitator. At their core, fintech systems and services have been created to facilitate smooth, secure and efficient financial transactions that are undeniably vital at every touchpoint of the guest experience; it's only a matter of time before they become universal for hotels and short-term rentals (STRs).

Within hospitality, financial technologies encompass a wide range of tools and systems designed to simplify payment processes, reduce errors and improve operational efficiency. They enable businesses to cater to a digitally savvy, convenience-driven customer who expects the same level of ease and security in their transactions as they do when buying from any e-commerce retailer. Whether through digital wallets, contactless payments or advanced fraud detection, fintech bridges the gap between guest expectations and operational realities.

Payment technologies are strategic enablers. Hoteliers and STR operators can improve cash flow management, enhance reconciliation processes and integrate seamlessly with other essential platforms like the Property Management System (PMS) to provide a holistic operational framework. By automating mundane tasks and reducing the reliance on manual interventions, these solutions free up staff to focus on creating personal, value-added stays for guests.

A short history of payment solutions in hospitality

The transformation of payment solutions in hospitality reflects the sector's broader evolution from manual processes to cutting-edge technologies. Traditionally, payment methods relied heavily on cash, cheques and rudimentary credit card systems. However, these legacy systems were cumbersome and prone to errors, delays and inefficiencies. Manual credit card checks often led to discrepancies in billing, while night audits consumed valuable staff hours that could have been redirected towards guest services.

The introduction of electronic payments marked a turning point. Credit and debit cards became mainstream, offering guests greater convenience. However, early systems still required significant manual intervention, from reconciling transactions to managing chargebacks. Though incremental improvements were made, these processes still left room for errors and bottlenecks.

The digital revolution further transformed the landscape, introducing online booking platforms and mobile payment solutions. Suddenly, guests could pay from anywhere in the world, using a variety of currencies and methods. Accelerated even more during the pandemic, mobile wallets like Apple Pay and Google Pay gained traction, offering convenience and security. At the same time, automation began to play a more significant role in reducing the burden of manual reconciliation and fraud management.

Today, while still far from having universal adoption, payment technologies can be deeply integrated into hospitality operations. The rise of contactless payments, powered by near-field communication

(NFC) technology, has reshaped guest interactions, particularly during the pandemic. Instant refunds and buy now, pay later (BNPL) models have emerged as guest-centric innovations, catering to a demand for flexibility and immediacy.

This change highlights a dual focus: enhancing the guest experience and improving operational efficiency. By addressing traditional pain points and leveraging technological advancements, modern payment solutions ensure that transactions also contribute to the broader goals of guest satisfaction and profitability.

'Those who innovate first are starting to see the rewards.'

Spencer Hanlon, Chief Operating Officer, Nium

Core components of fintech in hospitality

As with all technology solutions that address various pain points, fintech in hospitality is constantly developing. Here are some current use cases.

Automation of routine tasks: Manual tasks like night audits and transaction reconciliation are time-consuming and prone to human error. Payment technologies automate these processes, ensuring that accounts are balanced, no-show fees are processed and refunds are issued without manual intervention. This not only saves hours of labour but also reduces stress for finance teams.

BNPL models: This flexible payment solution has gained limited traction in the hospitality industry. However, this may change as it becomes more common elsewhere and hoteliers grow to trust it. BNPL systems, such as Klarna and Clearpay, allow guests to book accommodation or services and pay in instalments without incurring interest. This model appeals to budget-conscious travellers and potentially opens up new revenue streams for operators.

Cryptocurrencies: Though still in its infancy in hospitality, cryptocurrency payments are gaining attention. Cryptocurrencies eliminate the need for intermediaries, such as banks, significantly reducing transaction fees. This reduction in costs can lead to more competitive pricing for hotel services, an advantage that both businesses and customers can appreciate, with Bitcoin and similar digital currencies offering secure, decentralized payment options. While adoption remains limited due to volatility, processing speed and regulatory challenges, forward-thinking operators are exploring their potential as a differentiator in niche markets.

Digital wallets: The rise of digital wallets, such as Apple Pay and Google Pay, has transformed the payment landscape everywhere, not just hospitality. These tools offer convenience and security that appeal to tech-savvy travellers and those used to the convenience of touching a screen. By eliminating the need for physical cards, digital wallets enhance the speed of transactions and contribute to a frictionless guest experience. Adopting digital wallets also builds trust for hoteliers, demonstrating a commitment to modern, secure payment methods.

Dynamic currency conversion: This allows international guests to pay in their own currency, offering transparency and convenience. For hotels, it generates additional revenue through transaction fees and exchange rate markups, making it both a guest-friendly feature and a strategic financial asset for operators.

Integration with PMS: The ability to integrate payment solutions with PMS platforms is a game-changer for hospitality operators. A synchronized system ensures that every transaction, from booking deposits to room service charges, is recorded in real time. This centralization reduces discrepancies, streamlines reporting and provides a holistic view of financial performance.

Payment gateways: Payment gateways are the backbone of digital transactions, connecting guest payments to hotel accounts. These systems enable real-time processing, ensuring that funds are transferred securely and promptly. By integrating with PMS platforms, gateways are seamless, reducing errors and speeding up transactions.

Streamlining operations: Fintech tools allow for the centralization of financial data, enabling faster decision making. For example, real-time dashboards can provide insights into payment trends, guest preferences and operational bottlenecks. This visibility empowers management to make better decisions that align with business goals.

Ultimately, payment technologies have the power to redefine operations. Eliminating inefficiencies and empowering teams enable hospitality businesses to focus on their core mission: delivering exceptional stays.

'There's an untapped white space of technology adoption that still will happen over the next few years. As technology gets cheaper, it's easier to adopt. The learning curves will decrease. The barriers are coming down.'

Klaus Kohlmayr, Chief Evangelist, IDeaS

TECH LEADER INSIGHT

Putting payments at the centre of hospitality – James Lemon, Global Industry Lead – Hospitality, Travel and Leisure, Stripe

A smoother customer experience, new ancillary revenue streams, more efficient operations, faster innovation. As far as wish lists go, these four items would rank highly for any type of accommodation operator.

And they are all achievable by adopting a strategic approach to payment technology, according to James Lemon, Global Industry Lead – Hospitality, Travel and Leisure at Stripe, the fast-growing financial services and software company.

'Payments are strategic,' he declares. 'It literally is the money that your business takes. It's probably the most important part of a business... and it's the most important part of a technology stack as well.'

Payment technology is just as important as a PMS, or guest messaging platform, and deserves its place as another core element of a property's digital infrastructure. It also needs to seamlessly integrate with the myriad systems the business needs to operate successfully.

Back to the money – Lemon claims payment technology can unlock growth for hotels when market uncertainties prevail.

'It is a fascinating time for hospitality. Everyone is incredibly bullish on the long-term for the industry. People have an inherent need to travel. They want to explore the world. They continue to set aside chunks of their household incomes and their company budgets to do so,' he says. 'But it's also an industry that was relatively exposed during Covid and now is seeing potentially a second softening of demand.'

He thinks payment technology can help hospitality companies innovate and provide more opportunities to gain revenue.

Frictionless booking

Lemon has extensive travel industry experience with multiple vantage points, having worked for both hotels and the technology firms that serve them, including Travelport, IHG and Hostmaker. He also co-founded Otolo, an online community for hospitality employees to receive mentoring and develop their careers.

He argues that one of the biggest advantages from installing sophisticated payment software is that it eliminates friction, which is crucial for hotels aiming to drive direct sales on their website booking engines.

'For any company, from the smallest individual host to the largest hotel chain, it's now possible to have access to the same kind of checkout experience as the online travel agencies have been doing for years,' he says.

It's important because the last decade has seen a rise in the number of ways customers want to pay. Accepting a credit card or debit card would probably have been the default method 10 years ago, but around the world, they're no longer the main way people want to pay.

'You're seeing a big rise in digital wallets,' Lemon says, adding that new payment mechanisms have grown because of the popularity of Apple Pay and Google Pay, as well as third-party payment platforms like Alipay and GrabPay.

As a result, he argues, every website should be able to accept these payment methods to eliminate friction. Notwithstanding local currencies, these new payment types are increasingly geographically varied. Local payment methods can be preferred for a variety of reasons, depending on government legislation, or cultural, political and economic reasons.

'There are going to be hundreds more of these coming over the next few years. It's not going to get any easier,' he adds. 'And if you're a hotel chain trying to capture demand in all these countries, you're sitting there going: well, how on earth do I offer this kind of localized checkout experience to all customers?'

Therefore, effective payment technology can provide one integration that allows different payment methods to be used, providing a different checkout experience depending on the location.

Why is it so important to get the payment checkout right? Because it complements a hotel's marketing activities. 'They are spending on the marketing funnel – right from the highest acquisition on your Google and meta searches, you're optimizing all of your content, your video, your descriptions, your languages, yet something like 70 per cent of people still abandon the booking at the checkout page,' Lemon says. 'So, if you can expand that funnel by a few basis points, you have a huge impact on your direct bookings and a huge impact on your bottom line.'

Ancillaries and new business models

He also identifies other benefits that place payments in the spotlight: namely, ancillary revenue, greater trust and improved business intelligence insights.

'Travel companies and hospitality businesses are coming to realize they're not always able to rely on the same revenue streams they had before. It may not be enough to just fill your beds, but it's important to look at other revenue sources,' he says.

Effective payment technology remembers the user, so brands can more readily enter other areas of trip spending. From Stripe's perspective, because it comprises a series of products that also include physical payment terminals and its Connect platform, which allows users to embed payments into their products, it is able to offer a range of customer behaviour insights.

For example, in the STR sector, he sees hosts renting kayaks and bikes, helping with grocery shops or organizing the transfer from the airport. Behind the scenes, hosts take a commission for selling the ancillaries.

'Once you save their payment type, they can use it again and again. You can create what I would call new purchase moments,' Lemon says. 'You could go to the guy who rents bikes down the street, or your local taxi firm, and onboard them to your marketplace. Suddenly, a host can now step into other parts of the travel spend that otherwise would have been complicated to set up.'

He argues that previously a host would spend a lot of time discussing payment terms and end up forgetting to focus on the partnership and how to grow it. 'That stuff's all taken care of, everyone's got their own dashboards, it's incredibly transparent, it's all automated. So at the end of the quarter, you can sit down and go, actually, how's this gone? What do we work on next? You're not sitting there going, I think you still owe me money, or this customer didn't turn up,' he adds.

A greater level of trust also comes with advanced payment technology. The hotel guest may be staying in a location they don't know, so advance payments can remove any concerns they might have around knowing where to shop, or having to stop at a cash machine before arriving at the apartment. 'Now suddenly it's like a trusted checkout,' Lemon says.

And he adds that, because international payment providers like Stripe allow users to embed payments into their products, they can provide a range of customer behaviour insights.

'You can actually turn that data into something not just the finance team uses, but actually something the marketing team can use. What are that family's spending habits? How much do they spend in the resort? How much do they spend with us each year? You could feed that into your marketing engine so that your payment data could become the new kind of marketing data,' he says.

'There's an increased technology lens and an interconnectivity we need to provide for our customers, more than ever before,' Lemon concludes. 'I'm bullish on both the ongoing need for passionate professional hospitality leaders, but also the need that we should all have a bit more of a grasp around hospitality tech and what it can do, and why it's good for our teams and our guests.'

Catering to a globalized market

The hospitality industry is fundamentally global, catering to guests from diverse cultural and economic backgrounds. As a result, multi-currency support and localized payment methods have become essential for meeting the expectations of global audiences.

Adapting to source markets

To best cater to international guests, 'tech-enabled' lodging providers are increasingly looking to tailor their payment solutions to align with the preferences of key source markets. For example, WeChat Pay and Alipay dominate the payment landscape for Chinese travellers, making them critical for hotels targeting this demographic. By offering region-specific payment options, operators demonstrate an understanding of their guests' unique needs, helping to promote trust and encouraging bookings.

In addition to alternative payment methods, operators increasingly understand the need to consider cultural nuances. For instance, Japanese travellers may expect detailed receipts, while European guests tend to prefer instant refunds. Recognizing and adapting to these expectations can boost guest satisfaction and loyalty.

> 'We are only really scratching the surface in terms of the penetration of these new modern payment tools in the travel segment. The travel segment is still largely dominated by some very large players and they have for the last 80 years maybe dictated how things work.'
>
> **Spencer Hanlon, Chief Operating Officer, Nium**

Multi-currency payments and global payment providers

A seamless multi-currency payment system reduces the friction associated with international transactions. When guests can pay in their local currency, they avoid the inconvenience of exchange rate conversions and associated fees. This transparency not only improves the booking experience but also builds trust in the hotel's financial processes. For hoteliers, multi-currency support reduces disputes and chargebacks by ensuring accurate billing in the guest's preferred currency. Advanced payment platforms automatically calculate exchange rates and provide real-time conversions, ensuring smooth transactions for both parties.

Hotels with diverse guest demographics benefit significantly from partnering with globally recognized payment providers. Platforms like PayPal, Adyen and Stripe offer extensive coverage and integrate easily with PMSs. These providers support multi-currency transactions, enabling hoteliers to cater to guests from virtually any market without requiring additional infrastructure. Alternative payment methods also appeal to younger, tech-driven travellers who prioritize convenience and security. Digital wallets and mobile-first solutions resonate with this demographic, emphasizing the importance of choosing a payment provider capable of supporting innovative technologies.

'We actually have one hotel on our platform that offers bitcoin payments. I feel like it is a good idea and in the future there will be more of these sorts of transactions. But the reality is it's in the very early stages.'

Antonia Bernhardt, Head of Sales and Business Development, Like Magic

The democratization of fintech tools for hospitality

In the past, sophisticated financial technologies were the domain of major hotel chains with vast resources. However, the democratization of fintech, as with much else of tech development in hospitality, has enabled even the smallest operators to access advanced tools that allow them to operate on a more level playing field. Independent hoteliers or STR operators can now implement systems that offer the same level of convenience, security and customization as those used by global chains.

Payment platforms have revolutionized financial management for small businesses by offering micro-account capabilities. For instance, an independent property manager can onboard local service providers – such as taxi companies, tour operators and catering services – onto a single payment platform. These micro-accounts allow operators to seamlessly split payments, ensuring each service provider is compensated while the hotel collects a platform fee. This approach also creates new revenue streams.

The rise of democratized fintech empowers small businesses to elevate their operations, enhance guest experiences and compete effectively in a highly dynamic market.

The role of AI in payments

The ability of AI to analyse vast amounts of data and predict trends has made it an indispensable tool for hoteliers seeking to optimize their financial processes.

Integrating AI into hospitality payment systems has changed how properties handle transactions and manage financial operations. AI-powered fraud detection identifies suspicious activities in real time by analysing patterns and anomalies. This proactive approach allows operators to investigate potential fraud before it escalates into chargebacks or significant losses, with systems automatically flagging unusual patterns, such as sudden spikes in high-value transactions from a single location.

This same analytical power extends to personalization, where payment data provides crucial insights into guest preferences, allowing properties to tailor their offerings, such as presenting business travellers with express check-out services or offering leisure guests instalment plans for luxury upgrades.

REAL-WORLD EXAMPLE
Rocco Forte Hotels balances digital efficiency with personalized service

Rocco Forte Hotels comprises a collection of luxury hotels, resorts and private residences in leading destinations across the globe. Sir Rocco Forte, son of the late hotelier and businessman Lord Charles Forte, established Rocco Forte Hotels with his sister Olga Polizzi in 1996.

Challenges and opportunities

At the higher end of the hospitality spectrum, guests in luxury hotels have different expectations compared to mainstream hotel stays. These can cover aspects such as how and when they pay for their stay, the requirement for an individualized service and attitudes towards technology.

For example, most budget hotel bookings incentivize guests to pay for their stay up front. The five-star guest, however, prefers to pay when checking out.

Luxury guests are also typically less inclined to download additional apps or engage in more complex digital interactions, like setting up accounts or entering multiple steps for a simple service such as ordering a drink through an app.

The challenge for Rocco Forte Hotels is how to balance preferences such as these, while leveraging the efficiencies new technologies can bring. With a portfolio of almost 20 properties, the group will look to use technology to enhance services through a more seamless, personalized journey, but it needs to avoid adding complexity to the guest experience.

The solution

To address these challenges, Rocco Forte Hotels focuses on 'meeting guests where they are', according to Andy Evers, Group Director of IT.

That mostly entails making sure it uses popular platforms like WhatsApp for communication – and soon payments.

'In the luxury sector, our guests should be telling us how they want to communicate and how they want to work with us,' the Director says. 'Something I'm keen on avoiding is introducing things that add resistance.'

WhatsApp is commonly used because a hotel can initiate communication, and once the guest responds, the hotel can continue to use that channel. That's not to say apps are not used in the luxury market, but Evers believes a hotel group with 200 luxury hotels would probably see more success getting guests to 'buy in' to the app.

If the guest has not paid in advance for their holiday, the hotel is able to capture a pre-authorization payment on the guest's card and a 'token' will follow the guest throughout their stay. For example, it will integrate into the point-of-sale (PoS) systems and the PMS so purchases can be charged at the end of the stay. This can lead to a more seamless experience and one that removes the need to interrupt the guest with a card machine for every transaction.

The hotel group is also always reviewing its payment platforms to suit the clientele.

For example, WhatsApp payments are growing in popularity, with the benefit that the app can be used to send a payment link, with the guest then authorizing it using Face ID. For example, a guest could be in town and in need of a taxi. They contact the hotel concierge through WhatsApp and receive a link: the guest can pay for it then and there or charge it to their room.

With an international clientele, the company is also exploring a range of other international payment platforms that guests are used to in their own country. 'We'll do whatever it is that the guest wants in support of the fact that they tell us what luxury means for them,' Evers notes. 'Again, we'll meet guests where they are.'

Another benefit of digital payments and integrated platforms is that the flow of data helps build a picture of the guest's activities and Rocco Forte Hotels can help department heads plan their resourcing.

For example, bar staff need to know the hotel's occupancy in order to determine how many staff they will need and at what times.

'If you're not getting data to people who can activate that data from an operational perspective, then you have to ask why you're getting it at all. If we know that you've got a reservation at the restaurant for 7 pm, that's great. The restaurant needs to know that, but also housekeeping because they will then know that you're likely not to be in the room at that time.'

Therefore, there's a need to 'push' that data around to inform workload across every operational department. The data flow between food and beverage ecosystems, restaurant management systems, PoS systems and front-of-house and maintenance management systems is critical.

On the guest side, should guests change their mind about doing something, the hotel needs to react quickly. 'The key point is communication – quick, correct and accurate communication between teams and departments,' Evers says.

The right tools for the job

At Rocco Forte Hotels, the mindset of 'meeting customers where they are' and being wary of forcing them to download new apps applies to employees too. Andy Evers believes that his department is one of many that will contribute to selecting the most appropriate software and systems relating to guest service projects. The hotel company will also always take consultation from business leaders whose role it actually is to handle guest experience.

'Looking at this from a technology professional's point of view, I don't run a hotel, I've never served a drink, I've never checked a guest in,' he says. Based on their experience and expertise, he believes the IT department's responsibility is to equip other departments with the right tools and, most importantly, enable that critical data flow.

'My duty then becomes how do I get these systems to talk to each other in a meaningful way, so that when a guest checks in at the front desk, the staff there can help them know there's an opportunity for them to make a reservation at the restaurant, to enjoy drinks at the bar. They can help them make it happen so that the whole guest experience is one journey,' Evers adds.

Conclusion

Rocco Forte Hotels' approach to technology and digital payments is in tune with its demographic: the guest has to come first, and none more so than the five-star guest.

The hotelier doesn't want to insist on new apps because so-called app fatigue is already fairly common. But by integrating familiar technologies and thoughtfully integrating existing systems with each other, the group is minimizing friction for both guests and staff.

The challenges with payment technology

While fintech solutions offer clear benefits, implementing them requires operators to navigate significant challenges, particularly costs and integration. The adoption of advanced payment technologies often demands substantial upfront investment, and integrating these systems with existing platforms like a PMS can be time-consuming.

The challenge extends beyond technical considerations to meeting evolving guest expectations. Modern travellers expect seamless payment experiences across multiple platforms and touchpoints, requiring hoteliers to maintain user-friendly, responsive systems capable of supporting a diverse range of payment methods. Successfully addressing these challenges requires a strategic approach that balances operational needs, security requirements and guest preferences, enabling operators to harness fintech solutions' full potential while protecting their operations and reputation.

'We don't want a human being to interact with payments anymore. It's error-prone.'

Antonia Bernhardt, Head of Sales and Business Development, Like Magic

KEY TAKEAWAYS

Fintech as a strategic enabler: Financial technologies are no longer mere transactional tools but strategic enablers that enhance operational efficiency, improve guest satisfaction and unlock new revenue streams.

The shift from legacy systems: The evolution from manual payment processes to automated, tech-enabled solutions has streamlined operations, reduced human errors and provided faster, more secure transactions for both guests and operators.

Core components of hospitality fintech: Payment gateways, digital wallets, BNPL models and AI-driven fraud prevention systems are critical tools.

Globalization demands multi-currency support: Multi-currency payment options and localized methods like WeChat Pay and Alipay are essential for accommodating international travellers and building trust in a globalized market.

Democratization of fintech tools: Platforms like Stripe have empowered small operators to adopt advanced financial solutions, creating a level playing field and boosting innovation across the industry.

The role of AI: AI enhances security, enables predictive analytics and delivers personalized guest experiences through data-driven insights into spending behaviours and preferences.

Emerging trends in payment technology: Contactless payments and sustainable practices like digital receipts are shaping the future of hospitality payments.

Navigating implementation challenges: Despite its benefits, adopting fintech solutions requires overcoming challenges such as high upfront costs, integration complexities and maintaining data security.

Real-World Example – Rocco Forte Hotels: Rocco Forte Hotels demonstrates how luxury operators can integrate fintech solutions to enhance a guest's stay. Leveraging digital payments throughout the stay means the group minimizes guest friction, so staff across its properties can focus on providing a five-star experience.

11

Guest experience:
The bedrock of hospitality

In the world of hospitality, guest experience is the very essence of the industry. Every interaction, from the first click on a booking website to the final 'thank you' email, contributes to the overall guest experience. In a time where travellers have countless options at their fingertips, delivering exceptional, unique experiences is essential for a brand to set itself apart, build solid customer relationships and grow the bottom line.

But what exactly constitutes a great guest experience? We probably understand more about what it isn't rather than what it is. We know that it is, in part, a delicate blend of comfort, convenience, personalization and those intangible moments that leave a lasting impression. It's the warm smile at check-in, the perfectly fluffed pillow, the restaurant recommendation that leads to an unforgettable meal, and the seamless technology that makes everything just a bit easier.

It is generally seen as a given that customer-centric companies are more profitable than those not focused on the customer. In the hospitality industry, where the customer is quite literally at the centre of everything, this takes on even greater significance.

However, long gone are the days when a clean room and a comfortable bed were enough to satisfy travellers. Today's guests are savvier, more connected and have higher expectations than ever before. They seek stories and memories.

Technology has played a significant role in shaping these evolving expectations. Guests now expect the same level of digital convenience they enjoy in other aspects of their lives. They want to book with only a few taps on their phone, check in without queuing at a front desk (or not check in at all) and control their room environment with voice commands.

Personalization is another key driver of changing guest expectations and travellers expect hotels to know and cater to their preferences. Whether it's remembering their favourite type of pillow or recommending activities based on their interests, personalization can transform a standard stay into a tailored experience.

> 'It's less about just the room, it's about the experience.'
>
> **Leah Rankin, Chief Product Officer, SiteMinder**

The link between guest experience and profitability

Elevating guest stays can directly impact a property's bottom line. Satisfied guests are more likely to return, recommend the property to others and leave positive reviews. Social media also significantly influences booking decisions today.

The financial impact of guest experience is substantial. In the context of hospitality, this could mean the difference between a one-time stay and a loyal guest who returns year after year, perhaps even becoming a brand ambassador.

Moreover, positive guest experiences boost ancillary revenue. Satisfied guests are more likely to use additional services, from the hotel restaurant to the spa. They're also more likely to be understanding if something goes wrong, giving the property a chance to rectify the situation rather than immediately posting a negative review.

Where does technology fit with experience?

Technology is revolutionizing the way hotels interact with and serve their guests. From AI to the IoT, tech solutions empower properties to deliver more personalized, efficient and memorable visits.

Many of the 'tech-enabled' hospitality providers covered in this book are leading the charge here, and their approach exemplifies how technology can create frictionless experiences. But it's not just about replacing human interaction with technology because many successful operators use technology to enhance, rather than all-out replace, the human touch. AI-powered chatbots, for instance, handle routine inquiries, freeing up staff to provide more personalized attention where it matters most. Mobile check-ins and digital keys mean no waiting in line for the front desk. Virtual concierge services enhance the traditional front desk.

'We refer to our on-site team as the host role. And I think that sometimes gets misconstrued. People think a host means someone who is standing there and greeting people. All a host really means is that our technology is running the task-oriented portion of the hotel on autopilot in the background, but the host on-site can get you a cocktail. They can show you to your room, they can talk to you, they can tell you where in the city to go.'

Ryan Killen, Co-founder and CEO, The Annex

Creating a seamless booking process

We all know that a vacation begins long before check-in. A hotel or rental apartment's ability to influence how a guest feels about a brand and their subsequent stay starts with the booking process. Here, a smooth, intuitive experience sets the tone for the entire stay and can be the deciding factor in whether a potential guest chooses your property or that of a competitor. It also sets expectations and helps to build trust and good feelings between a customer and an operator. A poor booking experience will either turn a potential guest off or set the stage for potential conflict right from the start.

Having a mobile-optimized website set up for bookings is crucial. With more and more travellers using phones to research and book accommodation, a clunky mobile interaction equates to lost bookings. The power of self-service shouldn't be underestimated, with most customers preferring to self-serve to source information. This means providing comprehensive information about rooms, amenities and local attractions on your website, as well as offering easy-to-use booking tools.

Effective communication is the backbone of great guest experiences. In our hyper-connected world, guests expect to be able to reach out to properties through their preferred channels, whether that's SMS, WhatsApp, iMessage, WeChat, Facebook Messenger, or a proprietary app. Multi-channel messaging platforms allow hotels to meet guests where they are, providing timely responses and proactive communication. This could mean sending a pre-arrival message with check-in details, responding to a mid-stay request for extra towels, or following up post-stay for feedback.

'You need to invest in technology. What a guest sees in their daily lives when they go to the supermarket or when they go on their phone and connect to apps that give them a very personalized experience, they will expect the same in a hotel. And if you, as an operator, are not able to provide that experience, then you're going to be lagging.'

Wouter Geerts, Director of Research and Intelligence, Mews

The importance of mobile

Hotel-specific mobile apps have become powerful tools to enrich guest experiences. These apps can serve as a one-stop shop for guests, offering features like mobile check-in, room selection, service requests and local recommendations.

The Hilton Honors app is a prime example of how mobile technology can transform the stay. It allows guests to use their phones as room keys, select specific rooms and even control in-room features like lighting and temperature.

Moreover, hotel apps can be valuable marketing tools, allowing properties to send personalized offers and updates directly. They can also provide valuable data on guest preferences and behaviour, informing future improvements.

When it comes to the stay experience, there's a saying: 'Whoever owns the door, owns the stay.' This means if you take care of access to a property or room, you can control other aspects of the in-room stay through smart technology. It also means that if you manage the actual room/unit/property and that's your domain, then you are the one responsible for the experience. The online travel agencies (OTAs) don't have this yet; they just have control over bringing the booking, although they are working hard to get more of the traveller journey on their platforms, such as check-in, check-out and payments.

But first, providing a seamless experience when it comes to check-in and room access should be the priority for hospitality operators. With the wealth of technology available – the ability to retrofit locks, build virtual check-ins and verify documents through apps – no guest should ever have to wait in a long line or be locked out of their room again. However, as guests, we know that as an industry, we are not there yet. Friction is still rampant when it comes to checking in.

For the actual room or property, digital room keys accessed via smartphones are rapidly becoming the norm in many hotels, although we know key cards are still popular. These mobile keys offer numerous benefits for both guests and properties. For guests, they eliminate the need to keep track of a physical key card and reduce the frustration of demagnetized cards. They also allow for a smoother arrival, with guests able to bypass the front desk and go directly to their rooms.

For hotels, mobile keys can also reduce front desk traffic, allowing staff to focus on more complex guest needs. They also offer enhanced security, as digital keys can be instantly deactivated if a phone is lost or stolen.

TECH LEADER INSIGHT

Deploying technology that puts guests front and centre – Steve Davis, CEO, Operto

In the complex business of running a hospitality company, nothing is more valuable than a satisfied customer. Yet, according to Steve Davis, CEO of Operto, a property operations platform for vacation rentals, hotels and serviced apartments, not enough technology providers are focusing on the guest experience.

The benefits go beyond creating a loyal guest or word-of-mouth marketing, he argues, because perfecting the art of the guest experience can, in fact, enhance a property's operational efficiencies.

In the same way Uber improved the booking journey (and paved the way for an easy way to tip drivers), so too should hotels leverage technology to provide better experiences.

As an example, Davis imagines a display on a phone that shows staff appearing as 'buzzing bees' as they go about their work. 'For example, you can see 28 Uber cars on your screen... in the same way you're tracking towels at the hotel,' he says.

Another scenario? The guest could receive an alert on their phone, thanks to smart locks, that tells them the cleaners have just arrived in their room. That prompts the question: would you like to request anything? The guest could reply they need extra towels, or extra soap, or the mini-bar topped up. The housekeeping staff can even take a photo of towels and the soap – and it gives the opportunity to thank them and perhaps leave a tip.

In the same vein, an app could allow staff to be rewarded for stellar service. Another means to enhance the experience is by incentivizing staff, particularly because the hospitality sector is renowned as one of the least financially rewarding industries to work in. In some cases, in certain parts of the world, employees cannot survive without tips.

'If the employee is providing great service, and can be tracked, they could end up actually doubling their salary because they're doing all these high-impact things for guests,' Davis says.

Another tie-in with a hotel's operations here is that this lowers the level of staff turnover, and all because there was a technology solution in place that provides guests with an easy way to tip the person doing the task, he notes.

'If you take that guest-centric approach to everything, the knock-on effect will always hit the front desk, and hit the back office, because of that commitment to the guest,' he says.

'The downstream effect of building great technology for the guest is that it lightens the load on the operator. At the end of the day, what are operators gunning for? They are gunning for five-star reviews, repeat bookings and word of mouth to friends and family. Maybe they go on social media and they rave about a stay, and all those happen because of a happy guest – not because you've got the most incredible messaging system that can auto-reply to someone's request.'

Davis also thinks a great guest experience is one where you offer 'optionality' around checking in. A business guest might want to check in online before they arrive, or if they are with their family and have lots of different needs, they might prefer to talk to someone in person at the front desk.

It's notable that Operto's first foray into technology was digital access and keyless entry.

'As the technology continues to improve, and things become cheaper and faster, you get that technology adoption curve. You naturally see Property Management Systems (PMSs) and individual independent technology providers starting to merge.' With this in mind, Davis notes that Operto remains 'PMS agnostic', so can operate with other systems, acting as an overlay to a property's existing system.

While he may think many hospitality technology companies are putting too much emphasis on building software for employees, such as general managers or housekeeping, the mindset is now starting to shift.

'More and more companies are starting to figure that one out. If you've got the most amazing back-of-house scheduling and a ticketing kind of service, that doesn't touch the guest. It might enable some of this, but it's not putting the guests at the front and centre of the conversation,' he concludes.

The virtual concierge

For a certain level of hotel service, the concierge sitting in the centre of the lobby has been a mainstay of service and decorum, providing that sense of being truly looked after. But, today, AI-powered virtual concierges, sometimes also called digital concierges, are beginning to change the way hotels provide information and services.

These digital assistants can handle guest inquiries 24/7, from providing information about hotel amenities to making restaurant reservations or booking local tours. But what these services really represent is a democratization of a luxury service. It's now no longer just the privilege of the four- to five-star traveller who receives such assistance to add experience to their stay – it's open, potentially, through mobile, for all types of hotel or lodging to provide the value-add service. This also goes for the short-term rental operator who typically, due to the logistics of operations and placement of properties, has not been able to offer a traditional concierge service. Another way of looking at it is that this evolution doesn't mean the end of human concierges, particularly in luxury properties. Instead, it allows human staff to focus on providing more personalized, high-value services while routine inquiries are handled efficiently by AI.

'I think the role of concierge will evolve over time. It could be more a combination of receptionist and concierge, who will be an ambassador, doing everything you need at a hotel level.'

Ulrich Pillau, Co-founder and CEO, Apaleo

In-room experiences

The in-room/in-property experience is a critical component of overall guest satisfaction, and technology is enabling hotels to take this to new heights. Smart room controls let guests adjust lighting, temperature and even window shades with the touch of a button or a voice command. Voice-activated assistants like Alexa Smart Properties for Hospitality can provide information, play music or even order room service, all hands-free.

Personalized content recommendations, whether for in-room entertainment or local tours and activities, can make guests feel truly understood and catered to. Brand-owned apps are also being created as an alternative to the in-room tablet.

The key here is to use technology to enhance comfort and convenience without making the room feel cold or impersonal. The best in-room tech seamlessly integrates into the environment, providing functionality without overwhelming the guest. It's also about keeping that sense of hospitality and service at the forefront.

Are the robots coming?

While it might sound like science fiction, robots are finding their place in the hospitality industry. Since opening in 2015, Japan's Henn na Hotel, the world's first robot-staffed hotel, offered a glimpse into a future where robots could assist in hospitality. However, the impact on the industry has been limited, although they are now being effectively used in different scenarios, from robot butlers delivering items to guest rooms to AI-powered cleaning robots. It's important to strike a balance. While robots can handle certain tasks efficiently, the hospitality industry is fundamentally about human connections. The goal can be either to use robots and automation to enhance rather than replace human interactions or, in the case of cleaning robots and even room service robots, to replace staff.

> 'At the end of the day in the hospitality business, you need to make amazing experiences for people who are coming to create memories, and that's what we are here for.'
>
> **Shahar Goldboim, Co-founder and CEO, Boom**

Data analytics

In the age of big data, leveraging guest information for personalization is crucial. By analysing data from various touchpoints – bookings, on-property behaviour, feedback surveys and more – hotels can gain valuable insights into guest preferences and behaviour.

Furnished apartments and vacation rental provider Mint House's approach (see the following Real-World Example) exemplifies the potential of data analytics in enhancing guest stays. This data-driven approach allows hotels to anticipate guest needs and continuously improve their offerings. It can inform everything from room assignments to marketing strategies, helping properties deliver more targeted, relevant experiences to each guest.

Virtual and augmented reality

Virtual and augmented reality (VR and AR) technologies are opening up exciting new possibilities in the hospitality industry. These immersive technologies can enhance guest stays in numerous ways, from pre-stay to on-property experiences. A couple of years ago, at a large hotel technology conference, there was a holographic 'machine' that was making big waves on the trade show floor. The holographic machine demonstrated how a team member, perhaps a concierge, could be 'deployed" to any location. This potentially means that a concierge, front desk or call centre could have a real human person in location but 'beam' them down in real time across multiple locations, thousands of miles apart. It gives distributed and centralized teams a new twist.

VR has also grown, with virtual property tours that allow potential guests to explore a hotel or rental before booking, increasing confidence in their choice and potentially boosting conversion rates. Once on property, AR can be used to create interactive local guides, bringing destinations to life in new and engaging ways.

REAL-WORLD EXAMPLE

How Mint House uses tech to guide guests through the unfamiliar

Founded in 2017, Mint House offers apartment-style accommodation with the amenities of a premium hotel. It focuses on providing hospitality with 'smart technology' features including keyless entry and a 24/7 digital concierge. Mint House currently has 13 properties across 10 cities in the United States, with growth plans in the works.

Challenges and opportunities

While Airbnb is known for offering stays in unusual places, including a yellow submarine or a home 'suspended' by a hot air balloon, Mint House does the same – although in less extreme circumstances.

Its guests don't need to access a floating house by crane, but Mint House does still need to help familiarize guests with relatively new and different experiences: a hotel-branded experience within apartment buildings.

Many of the properties it uses vary from one another, and may not be branded on the outside as a hotel would. For example, Mint House offers apartments located in multifamily buildings, which means the building could have many different uses, from residences to offices.

As a result, it focuses on mapping out the steps where it sees technology having the most dramatic impact, making entry into the property easy. Or, as Kent Hatcher, Director of Product, Mint House, puts it, bridging the digital and the physical.

'We're operating in an atypical or non-traditional model where we don't have control over the full building,' he said. 'Oftentimes, we don't have staff there 24/7, depending on the model that we're operating in a particular building.'

Getting feedback mid-stay

Mint House is pioneering an innovative approach to guest feedback and issue resolution using artificial technology. It is implementing a mid-stay survey that combines numerical ratings with free-form text responses. While guests often give high overall scores, they may mention specific issues in their comments. To address this, Mint House is experimenting with Large Language Models (LLMs) to analyse the free-form text. This AI-powered system aims to identify actionable insights, such as recurring problems with specific room amenities or immediate guest needs.

The goal is twofold: to spot trends that could lead to proactive improvements (like replacing a frequently mentioned faulty coffee maker) and to trigger real-time responses to guest needs (such as promptly providing fresh towels). Although still in its early stages, this application of AI in guest experience management shows promising potential for enhancing service quality and operational efficiency in the hospitality industry.

The solution

Mint House leverages technology to create a frictionless experience for guests when accessing their apartments. As guests will have expectations of how to arrive and check in to a hotel, Hatcher says technology guides them through a different set of paths: into a building, then into their room, then onto the WiFi.

In keeping with many 'tech-enabled' hospitality companies, it does this by creating the right 'infrastructure' for people to contact Mint House if they need to. 'That's through an 800 number, through QR codes posted strategically around the building, through chat functions, all those types of proactive ways that we can show we're there because it's an atypical experience for them,' Hatcher says.

'Regardless of the time of day, you can get in touch with a Mint House support person. And they are able to resolve 99 per cent of the things over the phone, whether it's check-out, check-in issues, building access issues, technology issues, all those sorts of things,' he adds.

Operating a 'zero-fail' approach

Mint House uses a range of different technology systems and processes, including its own app, to make the guest experience as seamless as possible – with the check-in perhaps the most important.

Kent Hatcher likens it to a Jenga tower with 'these pieces of the puzzle at different stages that help us create this experience'.

There's potentially more room for error due to the complexity, but Hatcher says Mint House is constantly re-evaluating those steps on the customer journey.

'The thing with those steps is they're a zero-fail type of thing. It could work 99 out of 100 times, but that hundredth person, if it doesn't work... and they haven't stayed at a place like this, it's going to jolt them,' he says.

'And so that's why we're constantly re-evaluating those steps on the customer journey, looking at all the permutations of how we can fail at one of those steps, whether it's a technology failure, it's a human error on our side, or it's a human error on the user side. And how do we take them from being off of the happy path and help them get back onto the happy path, which is getting into their room,' he adds.

Meanwhile, Mint House constantly assesses emerging technology providers, and stays up to date with the providers it currently uses, which will often launch new products as part of their own release cycles.

Technology also enables Mint House to cope with extra layers of complexity, from complying with municipality rules and ID capture to handling specific rules related to the specific property and landlords' rules regarding who they allow into their buildings, such as background or credit checks.

'Where the technology comes in is allowing us to enable those types of experiences and get guests into buildings and hotels that are completely unique, and stays that they've never had before,' says Hatcher. 'It's like Maslow's Hierarchy of Needs. You need to focus on the baseline stuff before you can talk about the "surprise and delights". And so, in our context, it's about getting our guests to the property, inside the property and then in their room and logged into WiFi as seamlessly as possible.'

In terms of its approach to investment and development, Hatcher says it's an 80/20 split of buy versus build, as its technology stack is primarily built on other software providers. 'We're not going to build the best access control system. We're not going to build the best guest verification system. So, we go out and partner with companies like Operto and Autohost to help handle those steps along the journey, which are zero-fail opportunities,' he says. 'And then we plug in specific technology along the way to help fill those gaps that the companies just haven't developed yet.'

One example of this is a 'proactive notification system' for guests when they first arrive, so they automatically receive a message welcoming them, and information about the building, and they are asked if they need any help. 'That's not a fault of any of our partners, it's just not something that they have actively developed, or they are in the process of developing,' Hatcher says. 'And these are things that I can quickly build and launch, so we're not fully reliant on the Software as a Service platforms we're using.'

Conclusion

Mint House signposts the guest journey as much as possible, reassuring guests at every step. As well as this sophisticated, thoughtful approach to how it uses technology, its 'tech-enabled' hospitality mantra has other benefits. For example, the model is attractive for building owners and operators looking for a low-risk way to diversify their offering, rather than fully commit to a single hotel or apartment brand.

Staff training

While technology plays an increasingly important role in enhancing guest experiences, well-trained staff remain the heart and soul of hospitality. Technology can be seen as a way to reduce staff costs or as a tool to empower staff, not replace them. As Ryan Killeen, co-founder and CEO of The Annex, a tech-focused boutique hotel based in Toronto, Canada, says, 'No one knows their own property better than the team on the ground.' This highlights the irreplaceable value of well-trained, empowered staff who can provide personalized service and handle complex situations that technology alone cannot. Training programmes should focus not just on technical skills but also on emotional intelligence, problem solving and how to effectively use the property's technological tools to enhance guest experiences. Staff should be empowered to make decisions and go above and beyond to ensure guest satisfaction.

Issues management

In hospitality, it's not a question of *if* issues will arise, but more a question of *when*. The key to maintaining guest satisfaction often lies in proactive issue detection and swift, effective resolution. It's also about effectively communicating before, during and after issues are raised. Technology can play a crucial role in this process. AI-powered systems can analyse patterns in guest behaviour and feedback to identify potential issues before they escalate. For instance, if multiple guests comment on slow WiFi speeds, the system can flag this for immediate attention.

When issues do arise, having streamlined processes for resolution is crucial. This might involve using a centralized system to track and manage guest complaints, ensuring nothing falls through the cracks. The goal should be not just to resolve issues, but to turn potentially negative experiences into positive ones through exceptional service recovery.

Housekeeping and maintenance

Efficient housekeeping and maintenance processes are foundational to guest satisfaction. After all, a clean, well-maintained room is a basic expectation for any traveller no matter what the level of service of the property. Software is transforming these behind-the-scenes operations. IoT sensors can help optimize cleaning schedules, alerting staff when a room is vacant and ready for cleaning. They can also monitor the status of various amenities and equipment, flagging items that need attention before they become a problem for guests.

Mobile apps for housekeeping staff can increase efficiency, allowing for real-time updates on room status and special requests.

Accessibility and inclusiveness

Technology can play a significant role in making properties more inclusive and accessible to guests with disabilities. This might involve providing detailed accessibility information on the hotel website, allowing guests with specific needs to make informed decisions. In-room assistive technologies like voice-activated controls can enhance the experience for guests with mobility or visual impairments. Accessibility also means creating an environment where all guests feel welcome and valued, regardless of their background, age or needs. This might involve offering multi-language support through AI translation services or providing options for guests with dietary restrictions.

Balancing high-tech and high-touch

As we've explored the many ways technology can enhance guest experiences, it's crucial to remember the importance of the human element in hospitality, where that is still a desire from guests. Technology can reduce staff costs, or it can enhance, not replace, human interactions. Jeremy Slater, Chief Operating Officer of short-stay apartment specialist Bob W, articulates this balance well: 'We're tech-enabled, as the title of this book suggests, and we should really home in on that as just being a normal part of running a business in the 21st century. It's about being tech-enabled but human-focused.'

The most successful properties will be those that leverage technology to handle routine tasks and provide convenience, freeing up their staff to focus on creating meaningful, personal connections with guests. After all, it's these human touches – the warm welcome, the thoughtful gesture, the genuine care – that often leave the most lasting impressions.

Enhancing guest experience in the modern hospitality landscape requires a strategic blend of cutting-edge technology and timeless hospitality principles. By embracing innovation while keeping the focus on human connections, properties can create stays that exceed the expectations of today's travellers. In doing so, they can drive guest satisfaction, loyalty and, ultimately, business success in an increasingly competitive industry.

'The front desk experience isn't adding anything to the guest journey, it's just slowing them down. It's basically putting up a barrier between the guest and their bedroom. And that barrier often has a queue or you have to wait for things like them to print stuff out.'

Jeremy Slater, Chief Operating Officer, Bob W

KEY TAKEAWAYS

Guest experience is critical: Exceptional guest experiences are at the core of hospitality. Personalization, convenience and memorable moments can set a brand apart in a highly competitive industry. It should begin from the search phase through to post-stay.

Technology can enhance human interaction: The best properties use technology like AI, mobile check-ins and virtual concierges to streamline operations and allow staff to focus on more personal guest interactions.

Personalization is key: Guests increasingly expect tailored experiences that cater to their preferences, from personalized recommendations to room preferences.

Seamless access is essential: Mobile keys, virtual check-ins and digital concierge services are increasingly important in providing convenience and frictionless experiences.

The link between guest experience and profitability: Satisfied guests are more likely to return, spend on additional services and provide positive reviews, directly impacting a property's revenue.

AI and automation: AI-powered systems can handle routine inquiries, optimize guest feedback responses and assist in housekeeping and maintenance, improving efficiency and guest satisfaction.

In-room tech for a better experience: Smart room controls, voice-activated assistants and personalized content are increasingly being used to make in-room experiences more comfortable and engaging.

Balancing high-tech and high-touch: Successful hospitality operators find the right balance between using technology to handle tasks and preserving the human touch, which is critical for creating lasting, meaningful experiences.

Real-World Example — Mint House: Mint House exemplifies how tech-enabled hospitality can create seamless guest experiences, from keyless entry to 24/7 digital concierge services. Its focus on bridging the digital and physical aspects of hospitality helps guests navigate non-traditional accommodation effortlessly while also ensuring operational efficiency.

12

Artificial intelligence: The robots are coming

While AI seems to dominate almost every conversation about the future of technology, its practical impact on hospitality isn't always clearly understood. For hoteliers and property managers, AI represents immense opportunity but also potential confusion and even overinflation, at least in the short term.

Many, or even most of us, have had to learn from scratch what AI actually is, and then we've needed to get to grips with what AI can do for business and what it still can't. As is often said, technological innovation is moving fast, but we also mustn't forget that many tech innovations of yesteryear, such as the electric lightbulb, the telephone and personal computers, were just as seismic in their time. The saying that we tend to overestimate tech transformation in the short term, but underestimate it in the long term, seems as apt today as it has ever been.

For operators, many are already using machine learning and generative AI (AI that uses models to produce text, images, videos or other forms of data) for a variety of task-based applications. It's been part of revenue management for some time, and many are using tools such as ChatGPT, Claude or Gemini for research and copywriting but are not yet using AI for more business intelligence or strategic tasks. For many, it is still a confusing topic, so understanding AI's role in hospitality and how operators can separate genuine innovation from marketing hype can be difficult.

At its very basic level, AI in hospitality refers to automation through software that can perform tasks typically requiring human intelligence or at least human time resources. These systems can analyse data, recognize patterns, make decisions and even engage in conversations. But unlike the future vision of robots running hotels, today's AI works largely behind the scenes, enhancing rather than replacing human hospitality, although that is rapidly changing with the advent of AI sales agents and customer service personas.

The transformation of hospitality through AI is happening incrementally, focusing on specific pain points and opportunities rather than totally revolutionizing the sector. At least for now. Revenue Management Systems use machine learning to analyse market data and suggest optimal pricing. Guest communication platforms employ natural language processing to handle routine inquiries. Computer vision helps monitor property security and maintenance needs. Each application addresses a particular challenge while contributing to overall operational efficiency.

It's good to also understand that AI has evolved significantly from its early conceptual stages to today's transformative applications. Traditional AI focused on rule-based systems, but machine learning brought a shift by enabling algorithms to learn from data. More recently, generative AI has garnered widespread attention. However, the next frontier is agentic AI, which introduces autonomous decision-making systems that can plan, learn and adapt independently. While generative AI is reshaping current business processes, agentic AI promises to disrupt the future with even more sophisticated, self-governing capabilities, marking a new era in AI innovation.

Modern hospitality businesses face increasing pressure to deliver personalized experiences while maintaining operational efficiency. Competitive markets, higher guest demands, the general move towards digital experiences and relationships, squeezed margins and higher operational costs are putting pressure on operators. AI can either be viewed as a welcome tool to help remove obstacles, reduce labour around mundane tasks and create better business decisions or it can be taken by teams as just another distraction, a tool to 'learn'.

Yet the industry's adoption of AI remains measured and practical. Rather than pursuing AI for its own sake, successful operators are beginning to focus on specific business problems where AI can deliver tangible benefits. They recognize that AI can enhance guest experiences and streamline operations while still offering guests *hospitality* in the way they want to receive it.

'We're integrating artificial intelligence where we think we can do a better job for our guests or for our teams, without decreasing the quality of what we are doing.'

Ryan Killeen, Co-founder and CEO, The Annex

Democratizing hospitality through AI

Perhaps one of AI's most significant impacts on hospitality is its democratizing effect. Advanced technology that was once the exclusive domain of major hotel chains has become accessible to operators of all sizes. Hospitality technology availability, in general, is levelling the playing field and transforming how smaller properties compete in an increasingly digital marketplace. AI now sharpens that levelling of the playing field because it allows for the deeper understanding that only distilling complex data analysis can bring, but without the need for specialist skills.

This democratization that AI brings manifests in several ways:

- Simplified user interfaces that make advanced tools accessible to non-technical users
- Natural language summaries that translate complex data into any language
- Automated decision-making tools that don't require extensive training
- Affordable pricing models that make enterprise-grade technology accessible to smaller operators

The impact extends beyond just making tools more accessible. By democratizing access to sophisticated technology, AI is enabling smaller operators to make data-driven decisions that were once the preserve of large chains. This significantly levels the competitive playing field while raising the overall standard of hospitality services.

Enhancing guest experience through AI

Arguably, the true potential of AI in hospitality lies not in replacing human interaction but in enhancing it. Today's guests expect personalized, efficient service at every touchpoint of their journey, and AI helps deliver this by processing vast amounts of guest data to create more meaningful, personalized experiences. It also deals with mundane, repetitive tasks while freeing staff to focus on high-value interactions. Which operator doesn't want that!

AI's ability to analyse guest preferences and behaviour patterns, thereby enabling a level of personalization that would not be possible to achieve manually – that is the magic sauce. By bringing customer data together to map out the whole customer journey, we can recognize the individual guest. For instance, we are able to see that they might be visiting a hotel for the third time for business purposes, and based on what we've observed about their preferences, we can personalize their experience accordingly.

This might include customized room settings based on previous stays, targeted activity recommendations, dining suggestions aligned with dietary preferences, tailored marketing communications and proactive service interventions. The key is using AI to handle routine tasks while enabling staff to focus on meaningful 'in-person' guest interactions.

Smarter communication through AI

The art of guest communications is always a finely tuned balancing act. Too little communication can leave guests feeling lost and not cared for. But doing too much can feel like they're being spammed.

AI-powered communication tools have transformed how properties interact with guests. However, the key is to find the right balance between using tools and providing human interaction so that guests aren't left feeling either under- or over-served. And getting the frequency right.

The ways in which operators are currently using AI tools to improve communication include handling routine inquiries 24/7, providing instant responses in multiple languages and routing complex queries to appropriate staff. AI tools can also help to maintain a consistent brand voice and provide the ability to learn from each interaction.

'I don't think anyone could have predicted the immediate impact that generative AI, with companies like OpenAI and DeepSeek, would have on our daily lives and operations. So much has changed in a year. So to predict what's to come in the next five years is nearly impossible.'

Wouter Geerts, Director of Research and Intelligence, Mews

Being predictive and proactive

Another of AI's most powerful applications is its ability to anticipate guest needs before they arise. For example, early identification of potential issues can have a significant impact on guest satisfaction and subsequent review scores. Proactive maintenance scheduling can ensure that niggly issues are dealt with before they become a larger and more complex problem needing significant room/unit/home downtime to fix, or much more labour and time or money. AI can also predict and allow for better resource allocation and service delivery needs.

'We're testing taking all that freeform text from guest feedback, running it through a Large Language Model. We hope to identify trends like "Room 302 is always talking about this coffee maker" and trigger proactive maintenance.'

Kent Hatcher, Director of Product, Mint House

AI's natural language-processing capabilities are also changing how brands and operators handle guest feedback. Left solely to AI, review feedback and response can feel very robotic still, but using AI to flag issues, prioritize and sort reviews while bringing in some human element to add final touches can work incredibly well to save time, build relationships with guests and potentially turn the complainers into raving fans. AI tools can also be used to monitor online reviews in real time, track sentiment trends and measure the impact of service and product improvements. There is really so much, with more to come, to help hospitality businesses increase both their service offerings and also business processes.

TECH LEADER INSIGHT
The domino effect of artificial intelligence – Shahar Goldboim, Co-founder and CEO, Boom

From budget motel chains to luxury hotel groups, AI is set to make its biggest impact over the coming years. And, according to Shahar Goldboim, co-founder and CEO of Boom, companies that fail to adopt it won't just be left behind, they'll be replaced by the companies that do.

Boom is a short-term rental property management platform with a mission to 'empower property managers to streamline their operations, increase revenue and reduce operational costs'. It claims to be the world's first AI-powered Property Management System, or AiPMS.

Through its booking engine, channel manager, operational tools, review analysis, reputation handling systems and more, it wants to help its property manager customers automate routine tasks, optimize pricing and deliver exceptional service at scale.

Its latest product development is less around the physical, operational side, but more to do with selling to guests by using chatbots, which is one of the fastest-growing areas in technology. Boom's 'AI sales agent' is able to provide support through text, voice or video, and unlike real humans will be working 24 hours a day.

'First of all, AI can speak in any language, and it can understand the habits of the person speaking that language,' Goldboim claims. 'Someone from China will have a different way of communicating than an American. For example, how they view discounts and what kind of approach they want. So you have the ability to talk with each person in their own language, with their own habits and even culture. On top of that, your answering time will be much quicker.'

Goldboim also thinks a virtual salesperson will be able to connect the dots better and maximize every opportunity to upsell. 'Somebody who was supposed to come in May, but didn't end up booking with you. But during the inquiry process they told you via chat they were going to be visiting their parents for an anniversary, or Christmas, next year,' Goldboim says. 'So two months before this date, you send them a message: hey, are you coming to visit this location again?'

This is an example of information being used for guest personalization – the holy grail of the tourism industry – and the sales agent may then be able to negotiate a best price, while answering in less than 15 seconds. As well as adapting to multiple languages and negotiation styles, the AI sales agent could also offer airport transfers or an early check-in or late check-out.

'You only need one sales agent. You wouldn't need 5 or 15, you don't need to scale the amount of sales agents,' he adds.

While the debate continues around how much 'emotional intelligence' chatbots will have, it's clear that, as the technology advances, the ability to mimic real people will only grow. But the key point for Goldboim is that AI saves time.

Philosophy and perceptions

The emerging theme around AI is that it can improve the hospitality experience by freeing up time for employees to spend with guests, or on actions that enhance their stay.

Goldboim goes a step further and thinks that if AI has the ability to reduce costs, by freeing up more time, a property manager should then reinvest those savings.

'It's not just about cutting costs, it's about deploying that investment into something that directly impacts the guest experience, which then leads to more repeat bookings,' he says.

He cites a company with a payroll of $100,000 as an example. Using AI, it can be lowered to $40,000, producing a 'gap' of $60,000, which can then be redeployed and dedicated to the guest experience.

He believes the principle can apply to any type of hospitality brand. 'You have Motel 6 that's selling a room for $80, and they are the cheapest when you are driving around, or you have Four Seasons,' Goldboim says. 'So every company should use it to make their brand better. It will be up to them how they view AI, but at the end of the day, they will need less customer support, fewer salespeople, or they will tackle much more than they used to. So they can scale operations in a better way with the same amount of people.'

Elsewhere, the founder is applying AI technology to areas like revenue management to accelerate A/B testing around pricing algorithms. Content is another strand, as Goldboim says AI can be integrated into how the first property image is displayed on a website. Online travel agencies (OTAs) have long tested how website visitors react to certain images, whether they are clicked on or later boost the conversion rate.

Goldboim wants to offer that capability across the hospitality sector. 'Is the listing good enough that people will book it?' he says. 'Then I can look at all of that and extend my reach with Google. I can do more social media. How do you connect all of the systems to give an output? This is how I view the system: everything is an ecosystem and it's a domino effect.'

Rise of the robots

Many people will have seen short videos of robots doing somersaults in the air, and equally catastrophic ones of them performing everyday tasks badly. But that could soon change with developments like the Tesla Bot gaining pace. The company describes them as 'general purpose, bi-pedal, autonomous humanoid robots capable of performing unsafe, repetitive or boring tasks'.

Goldboim talks about Boom's innovations as additions to its 'AI workforce', but he believes robots such as these will be another crucial element in the future.

'When you look at Boston Robotics, you understand that a robot can do any action that a human can, and more. When you add AI to it, you understand that the robot will be able to do any action that a human does for plumbing, cleaning pools, landscaping, 24/7.'

From a cost-efficiency perspective, he admits a property manager buying a robot would represent a huge initial investment, but in the long term it could become a revenue-generating ancillary. Guests could be given the option of whether they wanted a robot in their rental to clean the dishes, or wash clothes, or act as housekeeper.

'We take two weeks off a year to enjoy our time, or we take a weekend to fulfil ourselves as humans,' says Goldboim. 'So how do we, as an industry, make this experience an amazing experience that recharges people with the energy they need, to create happiness and create memories? To create the dream that we have as humans?' he adds. 'The way to look at it is not that AI is going to replace humans. But companies that won't use AI will be replaced by ones that will.'

Automation and the route to greater operational efficiencies

Operational efficiency is a critical component of success in the hospitality industry, where seamless service and optimized processes directly impact guest satisfaction and profitability. The implementation of AI has introduced the ability to greatly increase operational automation, helping hospitality operators streamline their workflows, reduce costs and improve service.

When it comes to the much talked about 'death of the front desk', many 'tech-enabled' hospitality operators are already providing mobile applications and self-service kiosks to bypass reception queues and manage their own check-ins and check-outs. The automated approach alleviates the workload on front desk staff, enabling them to focus on personalized guest interactions and complex inquiries that require a human touch. AI integrations only complement and enhance these opportunities.

Room allocation is another area where AI has made significant strides. Advanced AI algorithms can analyse current and projected room availability, guest preferences and booking patterns to optimize room assignments. By considering factors such as guest loyalty status, past stay history and specific preferences (such as higher floors or specific views), AI systems can improve the guest stay.

Housekeeping scheduling has also seen improvements through AI-driven tools that predict room turnover needs based on booking data and guest check-out times. Automated scheduling systems ensure that rooms are cleaned and prepared in a timely manner, reducing idle time for housekeeping staff and ensuring that rooms are available for early check-ins when needed.

'Revenue management companies have used artificial intelligence for the last 35 years. What's new is how you're engaging, interacting and communicating with technology through a voice or generative-type interface where the computer gives you better ability to get things done more efficiently than in the past.'

Klaus Kohlmayr, Chief Evangelist, IDeaS

Using AI to support teams

AI is not just for automating guest-facing tasks because it can also play a pivotal role in supporting staff by providing data-driven insights that aid decision making. For example, AI-powered communication tools can instantly notify staff of guest requests, upcoming VIP arrivals or changes in room assignments, helping teams stay informed and responsive. This immediate flow of information enables staff to prioritize tasks more effectively and maintain high standards.

Moreover, AI can assist in managing staff schedules, taking into account occupancy forecasts, seasonal trends and even individual employee performance metrics. By aligning staffing levels with predicted guest demand, AI ensures that properties are neither over-staffed nor understaffed, so it can optimize labour costs while maintaining service quality.

AI tools are being developed to train and motivate teams through 'gamification' too, with the aim of turning routine tasks and learning into engaging competitive experiences that not only boost staff performance but also make work more engaging. AI-driven 'gamification' software might be used to track individual and team performance metrics or award points for completed tasks and guest satisfaction scores. Staff apps might encourage friendly competition through leaderboards, provide real-time feedback and coaching and identify areas for additional training.

For example, housekeeping teams may compete for the fastest room turnover while maintaining quality standards, or front desk staff could earn points for positive guest reviews. AI analyses performance data to ensure fairness and adjusts difficulty levels automatically. The key is maintaining a balance between fun and professionalism, enhancing and not distracting from the core mission of providing exceptional service.

Using AI to predict maintenance issues

One of the most impactful applications of AI in operational efficiency is predictive maintenance. AI-powered maintenance systems use data from Internet of Things (IoT) sensors and equipment to monitor the condition of critical infrastructure, such as heating, ventilation and air conditioning (HVAC) systems, elevators and kitchen appliances. These sensors collect data on usage patterns, temperature fluctuations and other operational parameters, which AI algorithms analyse to detect anomalies or signs of potential failure.

By identifying early warning signs, AI can alert maintenance teams to potential issues before they escalate into costly breakdowns. For example, if an HVAC system shows signs of strain, an AI system can recommend maintenance before the system fails, preventing discomfort for guests and expensive emergency repairs.

The ability to anticipate maintenance needs can help operators allocate resources more effectively. Maintenance teams can prioritize tasks based on urgency and ensure that preventive maintenance is performed during off-peak hours, minimizing disruptions to guests. This level of operational foresight contributes to a more reliable and consistent service offering, plus reducing any potential for wasted costs.

AI in inventory and resource management

AI's role in inventory and resource management is another area where it enhances operational efficiency. In hospitality, managing resources such as food and beverage supplies, room amenities and housekeeping products can be complex, especially during peak seasons or events. AI-based forecasting tools, if used, can analyse past usage data, current booking trends and external factors like local events or weather patterns to predict future resource needs.

This predictive capability allows operators to order inventory just in time, reducing waste and ensuring that supplies are available when needed. For example, an AI tool might anticipate an increase in demand for pool towels during an upcoming heatwave or higher food and beverage consumption during a music festival. Of course, a human would also think to order more towels for the pool during a heatwave, but the point is that with AI capabilities, they don't have to think about it.

When it comes to supply chain management, AI can streamline and optimize the timing and volume of orders by automatically adjusting order quantities based on real-time sales data and supplier availability. This ensures that operators maintain optimal inventory levels without overstocking, not only saving money but also supporting sustainable practices by reducing over-ordering and associated waste.

It is crystal clear that AI is becoming an integral part of achieving operational efficiency in hospitality. By automating routine tasks, supporting staff with real-time data, enabling predictive maintenance and optimizing resource management, AI helps operators maintain high service standards while controlling costs.

'As AI develops human-like emotional intelligence, it can easily replace customer interactions in call centres and front desks, and it would do a much better job than any human can, simply because it will speak any language, has access to an unlimited amount of data and it will never be moody or biased.'

Floor Bleeker, Hotel Tech Expert

Challenges and ethical considerations of AI

The integration of AI in the hospitality industry brings significant advancements. However, its adoption also presents challenges and ethical considerations. Key issues to explore include data privacy and security, job displacement, algorithmic bias and balancing automation with human interaction.

Data privacy and security

AI systems in hospitality rely on the collection and processing of vast amounts of guest data to deliver personalized experiences and operational insights. This data can include everything from personal preferences and booking histories to sensitive payment information. The collection and storage of such data make AI systems a potential target for cybersecurity threats, raising concerns about how guest information is safeguarded.

To ensure data privacy and security, hospitality operators really must implement robust data protection measures, including encryption, secure access protocols and regular security audits. Building guest trust is paramount. Operators must be transparent about the type of data being collected, how it will be used and the measures in place to protect it. Clear privacy policies and the option for guests to manage their data preferences can engender trust and loyalty, reassuring guests that their information is handled with care and security.

The fear of job displacement and workforce concerns

The use of AI in hospitality has led to concerns about job displacement as AI technologies increasingly automate routine and repetitive tasks such as check-ins, room allocation and customer service interactions. While automation can lead to operational efficiencies, it can also create anxiety among workers about job security. The impact of AI on the workforce is a complex issue that requires a nuanced approach, but as we all know, AI *will* change the workforce and the skill sets that are required.

However, rather than simply displacing jobs, AI has the potential to redefine roles within hospitality. Many of the tasks taken over by AI are repetitive or low-skill, which frees up human staff to focus on more complex and engaging responsibilities that require emotional intelligence and creativity – qualities that AI currently cannot replicate and may never be able to do. For example, while an AI-driven chatbot might handle straightforward guest inquiries, more complex or sensitive issues are still best managed by actual people.

To adapt to these changes, hospitality operators will likely be required to invest in reskilling and training programmes for their employees. These programmes should focus on upskilling staff to work alongside AI tools, enhancing their roles to include data interpretation, strategic decision making and personalized guest interactions. By reimagining job descriptions and emphasizing human–AI collaboration, operators can create a workforce that is both tech-savvy and guest-focused.

REAL-WORLD EXAMPLE

From sales to check-out – Blueground's AI journey

Blueground is one of the largest operators of furnished, flexible rentals for 30+ day stays. The company was co-founded by Alex Chatzieleftheriou in 2013, who after many years as a business traveller had experienced first-hand the pain points of living out of hotels while travelling for work for months at a time. He created Blueground to solve the gap in the market for high-quality, consistent, furnished and flexible rentals for individuals and corporate clients.

In 2023 the company launched the Partner Network, adding pre-vetted, third-party furnished apartment providers and their portfolio of units to the Blueground platform.

Challenges and opportunities

Within the hospitality offering, the mid-term apartment sector is growing fast, fuelled by demand for longer stays in accommodation with larger spaces. Operators such as Blueground look to capitalize on the prevalent demand. AI gives hospitality brands the ability to gain a competitive edge, but equally, can be harnessed to encourage collaboration.

The solution

Blueground's AI journey stretches back several years, and today it is utilized across multiple functions, in particular before the guest arrives.

'We're very big on AI, and we've been one of the earlier adopters,' notes Begum Agca Okutgen, Head of Partner Network at Blueground.

Growing numbers of hospitality companies are leveraging the technology to capture bookings, from enhancing marketing and advertising to dynamic pricing promotions and sales engines. On the latter point, Blueground has developed a sales chatbot.

AI extends to guest interactions

Blueground is tapping into AI to assess various interactions it has with guests, in order to measure their experience and examine if there was a root cause if something went wrong. The technology then channels feedback to the team members.

'It's a very instant feedback mechanism. This guest wasn't happy with this interaction. What went wrong?' says Begum Agca Okutgen.

'And that gets communicated to the agent or whoever interacts with the guest, including their manager. It's more instantaneous than oral feedback,' she adds, because Blueground strives to make every interaction as positive as possible.

'When a guest sees a unit, and they inquire about the unit, we have a sales agent called Jarvis that now tackles up to 90 per cent of the initial inquiries for both Blueground-managed and partner-managed units. Jarvis then routes the inquiry to different sellers, depending on the case type,' Okutgen adds. 'Some enquiries that Jarvis deals with will lead to booking all on its own. And that has been dramatically effective, in terms of our sales team productivity.'

This allows Blueground's sales team to focus on the most valuable deals, which are often more complex as the company's average duration of stay is around 100 days. However, she claims that these long-term bookings are mathematically proven to make more money for the company. In fact, more than 50 per cent of the company's revenue comes from six-month-plus stays.

As productivity increases, so does efficiency. But Okutgen says Blueground's NPS (the market research metric Net Promoter Score) has also been increasing. 'AI is a big part of that,' she says.

AI is also being used for photography, and Blueground can automatically filter images. It first rates the quality of the picture and then classifies it, identifying whether it is an image of a living room, bathroom or bedroom, for example. Then, its system will know in which order to display them to optimize the likelihood of converting a website visitor from a browser into a booker.

These AI-powered optimizations are all critical to its newly launched Partner Network, which was launched to cater to increased demand.

The company applies the same logic to its partner listings, in part to ensure that imagery meets certain standards. 'It will reshuffle this to the first photo, or hide some of these because they don't look nice,' she says. Its technology can also add descriptions, even taking locations and nearby attractions into consideration.

Technology and a data-driven approach are also in place to help its partner members adjust their pricing and adopt strategic discounting to drive longer bookings.

Ultimately, the Partner Network is designed to help Blueground scale further and accelerate expansion into markets where it doesn't have enough supply to meet demand.

'Even in the markets we operate with Blueground units, we're adding a lot of units through our partners and it's our growth business at the moment,' Okutgen says. 'Our point of view is we don't so much believe in competition but we know there is demand and we're just trying to serve that by giving as many options to the guests as possible.'

Conclusion

Many companies adopt AI practices to improve operations, but in Blueground's case, it is also tactically using the technology to scale its Partner Network. By showcasing efficiencies and improvements around listings alongside strategies to secure more profitable long-stay bookings, it boosts its chances to bring on more partners and expand its presence further.

Bias in AI algorithms

Bias in AI algorithms is an ethical challenge that can have significant implications for guest experiences and operational decisions. AI models learn from the data they are trained on, and if this data contains biases – whether explicit or implicit – the AI system may perpetuate or even amplify those biases. In a hospitality context, this could manifest in biased recommendations, unfair treatment of guests or flawed decision-making processes.

For example, an AI system trained on historical data that reflects a preference for certain types of guests could inadvertently prioritize or exclude specific demographics. This can lead to a lack of diversity in service delivery and even discrimination, harming the guest experience and violating principles of fairness and inclusivity.

'If enough people say a certain thing, AI might tell you something's true that's not actually true.'

Jason Fudin, CEO, Placemakr

To address algorithmic bias, operators must ensure that the data used to train AI systems is representative and diverse. Regular audits of AI algorithms are also necessary to identify and mitigate biases. Implementing transparency protocols and explainability features in AI tools can help operators understand how AI reaches its decisions, making it easier to spot and correct biased behaviour. On the other side, those who currently use generative AI know that it can be inaccurate in its answers and even make things up, including sources and facts. So 100 per cent reliance, even for things like content and copy, needs to be checked by the human eye.

AI and sustainability in hospitality

Sustainability is an increasingly important priority for both hospitality operators and their guests. AI has emerged as a powerful tool to support these sustainability efforts by making operations more resource-efficient and eco-friendly. From energy management to waste reduction, AI can help hospitality businesses minimize their environmental impact while maintaining profitability and guest satisfaction.

One of the most significant contributions of AI to sustainability in hospitality is energy management. Energy consumption in hotels and large properties can be substantial, driven by the need for heating, cooling, lighting and other services. AI-powered energy management systems optimize energy use by leveraging data from IoT sensors and real-time occupancy information. These systems can automatically adjust room temperatures, lighting levels and other energy-consuming features based on guest presence and preferences. For example, AI can ensure that unoccupied rooms maintain minimal heating or cooling, which saves energy.

These intelligent systems learn from past energy usage patterns to refine their operation over time, ensuring that properties remain energy-efficient under different occupancy levels and weather conditions. The result is a significant reduction in energy costs and a decrease in carbon emissions, aligning with global efforts to combat climate change. By integrating AI-driven energy management solutions, hospitality operators can demonstrate their commitment to sustainable practices while saving money.

> 'I don't think hospitality is one of these areas that will be fully "AI-fied" or automated. It's about real people and how you make them feel. If you want to make them feel like they're in a soulless box powered by robots, then great, go for it.'
>
> **Jeremy Slater, Chief Operating Officer, Bob W**

Waste reduction

As mentioned previously, AI can play a crucial role in reducing waste within hospitality operations, particularly in food and beverage services. Predictive algorithms powered by AI analyse historical data, current bookings and external factors like local events or seasonality to forecast demand for food and supplies. This allows hoteliers with food and beverage offerings to better plan their inventory, ensuring that they stock just the right amount of ingredients and other perishable items. By aligning supply with actual demand, AI minimizes over-ordering and reduces food waste.

Beyond food waste, AI systems can track the usage of non-perishable items such as toiletries and cleaning supplies, adjusting order quantities to avoid excess. By implementing these predictive tools, properties can manage their resources more efficiently, contributing to a more sustainable operation that aligns with environmental and financial goals.

Supporting sustainable operations and guest experiences

Guests today are increasingly looking for eco-friendly options during their stays, and AI can help meet these expectations. For instance, AI-driven guest apps can prompt visitors to make sustainability-conscious choices, such as opting out of daily towel and linen changes or participating in water-saving programmes. These small actions can significantly reduce water and energy consumption over time.

Moreover, AI can personalize these prompts based on guest profiles and past behaviour. For example, a guest who frequently chooses eco-friendly options during their stays may receive tailored suggestions to further engage in sustainable practices. This level of personalization not only enhances the guest experience but also fosters a sense of partnership between the guest and the property in achieving sustainability goals.

AI has the capacity to analyse complex data sets to identify broader opportunities for energy savings and operational adjustments that contribute to a reduced carbon footprint. For instance, AI can suggest optimizing cleaning schedules to minimize water and chemical usage based on room occupancy patterns. It can also recommend shifts in operational practices, such as altering HVAC schedules during peak and off-peak hours, to further improve energy efficiency.

These AI-driven insights help properties set benchmarks for energy and resource usage, facilitating continuous improvement in sustainability practices. Additionally, AI can monitor and report on sustainability metrics in real time, giving operators actionable insights into their environmental performance and identifying areas where further improvements can be made. This transparency supports the creation of targeted sustainability initiatives that resonate with both internal stakeholders and guests who value eco-friendly accommodation.

Balancing automation and human interaction

While AI has the capability to automate many tasks in the hospitality industry, maintaining a human touch is essential for providing a memorable and satisfying guest experience. Hospitality, at its core, is about creating personal connections and offering a tailored service that makes guests feel valued and understood. While AI can support these efforts through efficient service and personalization, it cannot *yet* replicate the empathy and nuanced understanding that human interactions provide.

'AI can convincingly emulate "sentiment and empathy" by continual trial-and-error learning analysis of large data sets. This is, in effect, machine learning that allows conversational AI to develop and become increasingly attuned to human interaction, especially in areas of efficiency and responsiveness, for which hospitality has a lot.'

Richard Vaughton, Founding Partner, YES Consulting and The Avio Group

The challenge lies in maintaining the balance between using AI where it serves us best, and incorporating human abilities that are most valuable while also scaling operations. Operators find that they are continuously evaluating the areas where AI adds the most value and where human interaction is non-negotiable. The goal should be to create a symbiotic relationship where AI augments human efforts, allowing staff to focus on high-impact tasks that enrich the guest experience.

KEY TAKEAWAYS

The practical impact of AI: While AI is often surrounded by hype, its practical use in hospitality centres around incrementally enhancing efficiency and guest experiences. Change is happening, but it will be slower than many have predicted.

Enhanced guest personalization: By analysing guest data and behaviour patterns, AI helps create highly personalized guest experiences that are difficult to achieve manually. We are still very much at the beginning here, but the hospitality industry is embracing change.

The democratization of technology: AI makes sophisticated tools more accessible to smaller operators, enabling them to compete more effectively with larger hospitality chains.

Insights that are data-driven: AI processes vast amounts of data to support revenue management, optimize pricing strategies and facilitate smarter decision making in operations.

Balancing AI with the human touch: The key to successful AI integration is finding the right balance between automation and maintaining genuine, personalized human service. AI enhances our ability to provide a more focused human experience.

Ethical challenges need to be addressed: Like every industry, hospitality operators must tackle ethical issues like data privacy, job displacement and algorithmic bias to ensure the responsible use of AI.

AI and sustainability: AI supports sustainability by optimizing energy use, reducing waste and encouraging eco-friendly choices among guests, contributing to a lower environmental impact.

Proactive maintenance and resource management: AI-driven predictive maintenance helps prevent issues before they arise, saving costs and improving guest satisfaction.

Future trends: The future of AI in hospitality points towards deeper integration with IoT, more sophisticated predictive capabilities and a shift from being a support tool to a strategic partner.

Real-World Example – Blueground: This hospitality operator was an early adopter of AI and uses tools across the customer journey and to enhance its Partner Network.

13

Navigating the technology marketplace

Anyone working in hospitality today knows that identifying the right technology solutions can feel like navigating a maze. The sheer number of options has exploded – we've moved far beyond basic Property Management Systems (PMSs) into a world of specialized tools for every aspect of operations and guest experience. Revenue optimization, guest messaging, digital guest journeys, occupancy monitoring, upselling, housekeeping systems, smart room controls – the list grows longer each year.

Over the course of researching this book, I've spent many hours speaking with hoteliers and vacation rental operators about their technology challenges. The stories are often similar: operators know technology can transform their business and so they use it in advanced ways to improve their operational efficiencies and guest satisfaction. However, their 'tech stack' journeys have not been without huge challenges, costly errors and countless frustrations.

Without a clear strategy, operators can face integration issues, underutilized systems and investments that fail to deliver value. The bottom line is that navigating the hospitality marketplace requires a thoughtful approach: understanding what your business truly needs, correctly identifying your pain points and ensuring any new tools align with your long-term goals. Sometimes, however, mistakes and wasted time and resources need to take place in order to get a clear view of this.

As we have explored in Chapter 4, foundational systems like the PMS continue to serve as the operational backbone for hoteliers and property managers. Yet today's tech stack extends far beyond PMS, and, more recently, the lines between core tech categories have started to blur. For instance, Revenue Management Systems (RMSs) now incorporate guest feedback to adjust pricing strategies, and PMS platforms often double as basic Customer Relationship Management (CRM) systems. Operational tech negates some of the need for the PMS and can also double as a guest communication tool. This convergence also reflects the growing demand for integrated, seamless solutions that address multiple needs – just simplified.

Another key point is that in today's hospitality, convergence between different asset classes is growing, which adds to the complexity of what operators need. Increasingly, brands may be operating aparthotels, traditional hotel rooms, single-family homes as vacation rentals, multifamily apartments as short stays and also mixed-stay lengths and selling 'Spaces as a Service'. The tech required to manage all of this is complex, and so far, no *one* provider has fully launched a solution that works across all asset types, all business models and all geographies.

> 'We're constantly on that journey of looking at who's emerging in the space, who's launching new things. How do you stay abreast.'
>
> **Kent Hatcher, Director of Product, Mint House**

Navigating the hospitality technology marketplace

As we've seen, the hospitality technology marketplace is characterized by constant innovation, with several trends shaping its evolution.

AI and machine learning

AI and machine learning have become transformative forces in hospitality. AI tools are upgrading guest engagement and operational efficiency in unprecedented ways. For instance, AI-driven chatbots can now handle a majority of routine guest queries, such as room service requests or check-out times, with accuracy and immediacy.

Beyond chatbots, predictive analytics powered by AI optimize revenue management by analysing historical booking trends, current demand and market conditions to recommend dynamic pricing strategies. Guest personalization is another key area where AI shines, enabling operators to tailor recommendations based on past behaviours, preferences and real-time data. AI tools are advancing even further, incorporating real-time room conditions to refine guest communication and experiences.

Simplified adoption through no-code and low-code platforms

The rise of no-code and low-code platforms has democratized access to advanced technology. These platforms allow hospitality operators, even those with limited technical expertise, to customize and deploy their own solutions without relying heavily on developers. No-code tools empower small businesses to build bespoke solutions. This trend reduces barriers to entry for independent operators who want to modernize their tech.

Integrated ecosystems

Open Application Programming Interface (API) platforms are increasingly sought after in the hospitality sector as they allow for seamless integration of multiple tools. These interconnected systems enable operators to unify their PMS, CRM, RMS and other technologies, leading to a more centralized ecosystem.

Fast-growing companies with modern tech stacks are leveraging open APIs to scale their operations without the need for costly overhauls. For example, integrating a PMS with a guest messaging platform can streamline communications, while connecting a CRM with a dynamic pricing tool means that guest preferences inform revenue strategies.

This interconnected approach helps operators stay agile, adapting quickly to new market demands and guest behaviours. It also ensures a cohesive guest journey, from booking to check-out.

Blurring of categories

The traditional boundaries between hospitality technology categories are becoming less distinct. Tools like the RMS, CRM and guest engagement platforms are increasingly overlapping in functionality.

For example, dynamic pricing tools that were once solely focused on optimizing rates now incorporate guest reviews and operational data to refine pricing strategies. Similarly, CRMs are evolving to include guest messaging and feedback tools, creating a more holistic approach to engagement.

This convergence reflects the interconnected nature of hospitality operations, where decisions in one area, such as pricing, directly impact others, like guest satisfaction. Software companies are leading this shift, repositioning themselves as growth platforms rather than being limited to revenue management, for example.

Consolidation

There has been an increase in mergers and acquisitions of software companies within hospitality technology, with larger, funded businesses buying up smaller competitors or point solutions. This has a significant potential impact for operators.

'It's so easy to be sold to. These tech products that apparently are really easy to use and don't require lots of human resources to run, actually do. You need headspace, you need time and energy to put into these products to really optimize and get the most out of them.'

James Cornwell, CEO and Founder, Curated Property

REAL-WORLD EXAMPLE

Placemakr puts data infrastructure first in blended buildings

Placemakr is a flexible-use property management company and commercial real estate investor that helps transform multifamily properties into a mix of apartment living and hotel stays. It leverages technology to provide optimal experiences for both guests and residents, and combines the advantages of apartment living with the services and reliability of a hotel, all within a single building.

Challenges and opportunities

Placemakr's website tagline is 'Hotel, meet apartment. Apartment, meet hotel.' While apartments continue to be a fast-growing area of hospitality, particularly for business travellers who seek more conveniences and bigger spaces while on the road, large real estate investors need sophisticated platforms that allow them to make returns from this flexible model. Placemakr wants to help real estate investors blend multifamily and hospitality into one property, but needs to convince many in the industry to change their mindset.

The solution

Placemakr is one of a growing number of tech-enabled hospitality brands that work in tandem with investors and development partners, focusing on cities and tapping into trends such as increased demand for apartment-style stays and flexible living. And technology is the key, according to Jason Fudin, CEO and co-founder of Placemakr.

'The notion of combining a hotel or apartment building and blending them is hard for traditional real estate people to wrap their arms around,' he says. Although Covid accelerated the concept, with more digital nomads and cities ready to adjust to new travel and living patterns created by remote work, there continues to be a 'real estate mindset'.

He thinks that, to date, hospitality-focused tech solutions do not support blended multifamily and hospitality buildings.

'I would say that in the hospitality world, there are low expectations of technology today because it's not ubiquitous,' he continues.

Tipping point: waiting for the big brand evolution

Jason Fudin predicts a more digitized hospitality industry will arrive soon, but the catalyst for change will be driven by the major hotel groups.

'There's a tipping point where you need the large brands that do hundreds of millions of stays moving into modernized tech stacks. Until that happens it's going to be a novelty,' he says. 'For that innovation to happen, we've got to wait for the big brands to say: we need it, and we're going to be basically funding it.'

He compares it to the taxi industry in the United States. 'No city was going to change until Uber just gutted it with its much more consumer-friendly, more efficient process.'

In the future, he predicts a new generation of dynamic buildings will emerge, able to produce higher cash flow and meet evolving customer experience needs.

'Whether it's one of those big hotel companies changing their profile and everyone else having to follow, or whether it's an upstart like ourselves, or Kasa Living, or somebody else... something painful is likely going to force change,' he adds. 'And then when that happens, it happens rapidly.'

Fudin aims to bring the concept to life, although it can be complex. Placemakr offers 'home-style' units that can be rented short and long term, furnished or unfurnished.

'Furnished lettings are more complex because of the transaction volume; with hundreds of people showing up daily, charges are different, tax treatments are different and the guest mix will vary, including corporate travellers as well as individual tourists,' Fudin says. 'It's different from getting a rent cheque every month.'

To tackle the complexity, Placemakr uses a number of tools including the PMS Apaleo. 'It is API first, which most of the other PMSs at the time were not,' Fudin says.

'We probably use 18 to 20 different pieces of software and another half-dozen pieces of hardware. What we've built is a kind of data infrastructure, and then we've back-built out certain snippets of code that are required to have the existing tech stacks do what we need them to do, as opposed to what they were designed to do.'

This underscores a common theme among 'tech-enabled' hospitality brands: selecting platforms and systems that can connect seamlessly with other systems.

As ever for an entrepreneur, there's room to improve and Fudin identifies two areas.

'Access control, there's always problems. It's not seamless, it's not beautiful, it's unnecessarily expensive,' he says. 'Managed WiFi. It's not seamless and it can be inconsistent.'

Revenue, pricing and reporting can also be a challenge, due to the mix of a building's guests and residents; each will have different profiles depending on the length of stay and type of customer.

But on an optimistic note he says the industry today is 'really at the cusp of change' and cites one of Placemakr's investors, Steve Case, who was the former CEO of America Online (AOL).

'He brought the US onto the internet. He's fond of saying AOL was a 10-year overnight success, meaning for a decade they worked on the infrastructure for the internet to be able to be a "thing",' Fudin says. 'And then when it happened, it was like wildfire.'

Rapid digitization may then lead to more price transparency, and easier ways to book, arrive and communicate, he adds. Once that sea change takes place, the technology will move into other physical assets in different places, outside touristic hubs of cities.

'Airbnb gets full credit for changing the types of places which you can visit for hospitality, and having a diversity of price points and product types in a way that's much more diverse than the hotels,' Fudin adds.

Conclusion

The clue is in the name, Placemakr. It's notable that the company rebranded from WhyHotel in 2022, coming out of the pandemic. It wants to offer apartment-style spaces in multifamily buildings, adding a hospitality use alongside other purposes such as residential, offices or even hotels, as cities continue to evolve after Covid-19.

Evaluating and choosing technology solutions

With an overwhelming number of technology options available, selecting the right solution is a critical decision. It requires a structured approach, balancing immediate needs with long-term goals and ensuring that the chosen tools align seamlessly with the business's operational and strategic priorities. Below are key criteria that can guide this process:

Cost and ROI: While cost is often a primary consideration, operators should evaluate the long-term return on investment rather than focus solely on upfront expenses. For example, a high-quality RMS may have a significant initial cost but can lead to substantial revenue gains through optimized pricing and better demand forecasting. Operators should also assess the scalability of subscription models. Some systems charge per property or user, while others offer tiered pricing based on functionality. Balancing affordability with the system's potential to boost profitability is crucial.

Integration and open APIs: In today's interconnected ecosystem, compatibility with existing systems is a non-negotiable requirement. Tools that support open APIs facilitate seamless data sharing across platforms, ensuring that vital systems like the PMS, RMS and CRM communicate effectively. For instance, integrating a channel manager with a PMS allows real-time updates to room availability and pricing across all platforms, preventing overbookings and ensuring accurate reporting. Open APIs also future-proof investments, enabling operators to add or replace systems without extensive reconfiguration. Hotels with complex setups, such as those offering co-working or meeting spaces alongside accommodation, benefit particularly from strong integration capabilities. Interconnected systems reduce operational friction too.

Scalability and flexibility: As businesses grow, their technology needs to evolve. Solutions that can handle increased complexity – such as managing multiple properties or incorporating advanced analytics – are essential for long-term success. Scalable tools adapt to changing demands without requiring costly overhauls. For example, a small boutique hotel planning to expand into vacation rentals may benefit from a PMS that integrates seamlessly with short-term rental platforms like Airbnb or Vrbo. Flexible systems ensure that operators can add new features or modules as needed, such as dynamic pricing for seasonal fluctuations or AI-driven insights for guest personalization.

Usability: A tool's usability can significantly impact its adoption and effectiveness. Systems with intuitive interfaces and straightforward workflows enable faster onboarding for new staff and reduce the risk of errors. For example, a CRM system with a clear, user-friendly dashboard allows front-line employees to quickly access guest preferences without extensive training. The language and design of the tool are equally important. Overly technical interfaces or jargon-heavy language can alienate some users, particularly those in smaller, independent properties. Solutions tailored to the end user's capabilities ensure higher adoption rates and a smoother implementation process.

Vendor support: Reliable vendor support can make or break the success of a technology solution. Operators should evaluate the quality of customer service, availability of training resources and frequency of software updates. Vendors who offer proactive support – such as monitoring system performance and addressing issues before they escalate – add significant value. Documentation, webinars and training sessions can help teams get the most out of the tools. Vendors that emphasize no-code platforms allow operators to make changes independently, reduce reliance on external support and speed up workflows.

'Operators do need to invest in technology. I fully understand that the technology up to now hasn't been and maybe still isn't ideal for everyone. There are a lot of silos, there's a lot of old technology. And so it's not as simple as saying: you just need to invest more in technology. I understand there are barriers to it, and obviously, a lot of hospitality professionals aren't tech-first or necessarily tech-savvy. So coming from a tech company, I understand we have a role to play in this as well, in terms of education and making the technology better and more accessible.'

Wouter Geerts, Director of Research and Intelligence, Mews

Operators must also navigate common pitfalls, such as vendor lock-in or tools that are too complex for their teams to manage effectively. Engaging with reviews, case studies and industry peers can provide valuable insights into a tool's real-world performance and how happy current customers are. Attending expos, demos and webinars also help operators see the tools 'in action'.

Every accommodation operator I spoke with during the book's writing told me that they prefer software providers that are prepared to be 'partners' with them. This means that buyers are looking for vendors who are willing to grow and develop alongside them, are open to dialogue and feedback, and see the relationship as a 'win-win' with mutual goals.

When evaluating a technology system, a hospitality business also needs to ensure it meets the regulatory requirements of every country it operates in, and plans to expand to. Compliance with data protection laws, payment standards and operational regulations varies by region, making it crucial to choose systems that are adaptable and consistently updated to reflect legal changes.

Equally important is assessing the long-term sustainability of your technology vendor. Many startups in the hospitality tech space fail within their first year, which poses a risk to operations. Reviewing the vendor's financial health, checking references from existing clients and evaluating their growth strategy can provide insights into their stability and reliability over time.

> 'There's no point in wasting time on tech that doesn't drive a major improvement. In fact, many hotels underestimate how long it takes to sign, implement and train the team on new systems. It can take weeks or even months. That's why we focus on areas where tech can have an outsized impact.'
>
> **Hans Meyer, Co-founder, Zoku**

Overcoming challenges in technology implementation

Adopting new technology can be transformative, but successful implementation is often fraught with challenges. From integration complexities to resistance from staff, operators must anticipate and address hurdles before they can fully realize the benefits of their investments. With careful planning and a structured approach, these challenges can be mitigated, ensuring a smoother transition and maximizing the technology's impact.

Integration issues

One of the most significant barriers to implementing new technology is ensuring compatibility with existing systems. Hospitality operations rely on an interconnected ecosystem, where the PMS, RMS, CRM and other tools must communicate seamlessly. If new technology fails to integrate effectively, it can lead to operational bottlenecks, duplicated data entry and missed opportunities for efficiency.

For example, a new guest messaging platform that doesn't sync with the PMS might result in delayed responses or incomplete guest profiles. To avoid this, operators may choose to prioritize platforms with open API capabilities and a proven track record of successful integrations.

Team buy-in

Even the most advanced technology can fail if staff are not fully engaged. Resistance to change is a common issue, especially when employees are accustomed to long-standing workflows. Without team buy-in, new systems may be met with scepticism or outright rejection.

To improve the chances of buy-in, operators should involve employees in the selection process from the outset. Gathering input from front-line staff who will use the technology daily can help identify practical needs and ensure the chosen tool addresses real pain points. For example, housekeeping teams might highlight the need for a task management system with mobile accessibility and multi-language functionality, ensuring the technology adds value to their workflow.

Training is another critical component. Vendors often provide training resources, such as webinars, documentation and on-site sessions, to help teams get comfortable with new systems. Offering ongoing support and addressing concerns promptly can build confidence and ensure smoother adoption.

Underutilization

Underutilization is a common problem when adopting new technology, often stemming from overly complex systems or insufficient training. If a tool's interface is unintuitive or requires extensive technical knowledge, employees may default to familiar manual processes.

User-friendly platforms are now more common and better cater to the diverse skill levels of hospitality teams. Solutions with simplified interfaces for smaller, independent properties ensure ease of use without sacrificing essential features. Regularly monitoring usage patterns can also help identify areas where staff may need additional training or where the system itself requires adjustments.

Vendors play a key role in mitigating underutilization. Those that offer ongoing customer support, user guides and proactive outreach can help operators maximize their technology's potential. Additionally, creating internal 'tech champions' within the team – employees who are particularly adept at using the system – can provide on-the-ground support for their peers.

The lengthy implementation process

The installation timeline can be significantly longer than anticipated, particularly for larger properties or chains. Signing contracts, configuring systems, testing integrations and training staff are all time-intensive processes that require meticulous planning. Operators should set realistic timelines and communicate them clearly to all stakeholders.

Phased rollouts are an effective strategy for minimizing disruptions. For example, a large hotel chain implementing a new PMS might begin with one property, gather feedback and refine the process before rolling it out to other locations.

Clear milestones and regular progress reviews are also essential. Operators should work closely with vendors to establish benchmarks for each stage of the implementation, from initial setup to full-scale deployment. These checkpoints provide opportunities to address challenges early and keep the project on track.

Beyond these primary challenges, operators must also navigate other complexities, such as ensuring data security and compliance with regulations like the European Union's General Data Protection Regulation. New technology often involves handling sensitive guest information, making robust cybersecurity measures a top priority.

Additionally, operators should evaluate the scalability of the chosen solution to ensure it can cope with future growth. Investing in technology that meets current needs but lacks flexibility for expansion can lead to additional costs and disruptions down the line.

TECH LEADER INSIGHT
Mapping the transformation journey for guests and employees –
Antonia Bernhardt, Head of Sales and Business Development,
Like Magic

When a hotel takes on the arduous task of selecting which software to use, or what to upgrade to, it needs to take employees into consideration just as much as guests. The reason? 'Without happy staff, a hotel won't have happy customers.'

That's the simple message from Antonia Bernhardt, Head of Sales and Business Development at Like Magic, which is a hospitality management and guest experience startup.

There's an ever-growing roster of new hospitality systems and platforms to choose from. Many promise the earth as they look to disrupt the status quo with mostly cloud-based solutions and a Software as a Service approach.

'The reason why hospitality providers need to change is because guests are changing, and employees at the same time,' she says. 'We're all growing more used to modern technology. We're more informed as travellers today than we ever were because of access to information from anywhere.'

Bernhardt joined Like Magic from Mews, one of the fastest-growing hospitality technology companies today, where she spent seven years working with a range of groups and chains. She's also able to lean on experience in previous operational roles, having worked for brands like Radisson and Marriott, as well as hostels and honeymoon resorts, before switching to the software side.

That switch from operations to Mews was predominantly driven by the frustrations she had as a revenue assistant and as a sales manager with the tools that were on the market at that point.

'I felt it first-hand,' she says. 'I never wanted to sell software. But I saw that we could make a real difference with the things we're doing. We're making people's lives easier. People are used to easy and intuitive tools that focus heavily on the UX/UI like Facebook or Spotify in their personal lives, and at work, they're all of a sudden needing to work with old-fashioned and fragmented tech stacks. That is what I wanted to change.'

Blueprint for success

Bernhardt advises that an accommodation provider must first assess how any new piece of software enhances their guest journey. Plan it meticulously because there are different types of guests, she warns. But in the best projects she has been part of, this mapping process simultaneously involved mapping out the end-to-end guest journey with the end-to-end employee journey.

'Take your guest journey. Take your employee journey. Map them together and see in each stage what is actually happening. Because that's your blueprint for your business; you're putting the employee and the guest on the same level of importance,' she says.

The journey will also differ depending on whether it's a business hotel, an economy hotel, a four-star hotel or a five-star hotel. Once it's clear what those stages look like, it's possible to analyse where technology can fill any gaps and gauge what is expected of each employee.

It's a key phase to help bring a team up to speed. 'You have to have a team that's ready to make a certain shift with you, and you have to take your team on that journey with you as to why you are making that shift, and how you are making that shift,' she says. 'Who's going to implement that shift and why is it important to all of us? Half of the work is already done if you have your team onboard.'

And she adds: 'You also want your staff to be happy because it reflects in your guest experience 100 per cent. If it falls down there, no matter how much technology you have, if your staff are not happily deploying it or you've got a big churn, the end service isn't going to work out because there's no amount of technology that can just do it completely on its own.'

A star is born

Bernhardt also suggests that, based on her experience, the opportunity to transform a hotel can elevate staff to new highs. 'The most amazing projects I've seen where companies introduce new technology stacks are where usually a star was born throughout that process. I'm saying "star" in terms of employees shining and being ambassadors for the company within the tech world as well,' she says.

And it can be unexpected too. In some projects, she recalls, it would be the 'calmest person, who was somewhere in the back connecting cables together', who eventually went on to become the transformation project manager – their dedication and approach not only drove the project forward but also earned them the admiration and respect of the entire team.

'That's the ultimate level of employee satisfaction,' Bernhardt notes.

Looking ahead, the technology expert predicts, like many of her peers, that voice-powered chatbots and other types of agents will dominate the technology landscape.

'Your biggest pain point is always the reservation centre, because people still like to call. Because reservation centres will never go away, hotels can leverage technology that mimics a person, and would ask the same questions as a human, so the person on the other end of the call will still have a "natural conversation",' she says.

Sentiment analysis is also in its infancy, she argues, but in a few years, she thinks a chatbot will know so much more. 'It's been tested in the past quite a bit, but now as we're feeding AI and it is evolving, this will become more important over time,' she adds.

Money matters

Payment technology is also going to grow in importance for hoteliers in the coming years. Larger hospitality companies are already embracing a 'unified payment platform' where sophisticated PMSs, such as Mews, Apaleo or Stayntouch, can handle transactions.

'They have understood that building a unified payment platform will help you in the long run. First, in terms of payment processes, which are so closely aligned to everything a staff member does, but also everything a guest does as well,' says Bernhardt. 'They have their own payments platform built in alongside the employee journey, and ultimately the guest journey as well.'

In this respect, the hospitality industry is taking its cue from the likes of Amazon and the wider e-commerce sector. 'That shift had to occur in hospitality, just a little bit later unfortunately, because hospitality is a lot more traditional,' she says. 'It's all about automating payments. We don't want a human being to interact with payments anymore. It's error-prone. And also, it's an unnecessary admin process.'

She expects more hotels to move away from terminal payments too, although in some situations, they may never really be phased out.

'There will always be on-site payments, via terminals, especially when it comes to food and beverage. You have guests who come into the restaurant and they just want to pay on the spot. But I think the solution here is really the whole "tap-to-pay" and making it more instant, even if you have to pull a credit card or your phone.'

She points to the fact that even mobile phones can function as terminals today. 'It's no longer hardware heavy in that sense. You don't have to run around with cables and have a cash register somewhere.'

Having an overview of payment data is also key when it comes to personalizing a guest's stay, as data can reveal insights about their spending behaviour. Additionally, alternative payment methods, such as Apple Pay, Google Pay and other digital wallets, are rapidly gaining traction. These options offer guests a seamless and secure way to pay, often eliminating the need for physical cards entirely. 'It's not just about making payments faster but also catering to guest preferences. Many travellers today expect to use their phones not just for bookings but for every transaction throughout their stay,' says Bernhardt.

As for Like Magic, she believes the company, founded in 2023, is redefining the guest experience through innovative technology and automation. By strategically reducing the dependency on on-site staff, Like Magic ensures operational efficiency while maintaining a personalized touch for guests. Its platform empowers guests to handle various tasks independently, such as seamless check-ins, ordering food or amenities and requesting additional items like linens or pillows. It also facilitates the creation of keyless room passes via mobile devices, streamlining access.

The platform goes beyond operational convenience by integrating advanced guest journey management features, enabling hotels to proactively address guest needs through tailored communication channels. Guests can easily upgrade their stays, request services or make payments with stored details for a frictionless experience. Additionally, Like Magic provides tools for employees to efficiently manage daily tasks, with data and insights centralized in a single application, reducing errors and improving service delivery.

'Operational inefficiencies can arise from high overhead costs and the potential for human error, which is inherent in many processes. Adding more personnel to address these challenges often isn't the most effective or sustainable solution,' Bernhardt concludes.

Building and testing in a sandbox

Implementing new systems can feel like a high-stakes gamble. Building a sandbox – a controlled environment for testing new technology – offers operators a low-risk, high-reward way to evaluate tools before full-scale implementation.

A sandbox allows operators to simulate real-world scenarios and assess how new systems interact with existing platforms, workflows and team dynamics. For instance, a hotel could test a new guest messaging platform within the sandbox to evaluate its integration with the PMS, measure response times and identify any potential disruptions to staff workflows. This controlled setup ensures that operators gain practical insights into the technology's strengths and limitations without affecting day-to-day operations or guest experiences.

The key to an effective sandbox is involving cross-functional teams, including IT, front-line staff and management, to ensure comprehensive feedback. Vendors can also play a role by providing technical support and helping to replicate realistic conditions.

By identifying issues early and refining processes within the sandbox, operators can make informed decisions, reduce the risk of costly mistakes and build staff confidence in the chosen solution.

'Most software companies run an incredible sales process. So it's pretty easy to find yourself signing the contract before even actually really testing out the software. So we've set up an entire "sandbox" and demo environment that replicates our hotel and anything we have come across or that we're interested in, we're happy to try once, but we'll actually put it into the flow of a day-to-day operation. We typically test it overnight.'

Ryan Killen, Co-founder and CEO, The Annex

KEY TAKEAWAYS

Define business needs before adopting tech: Successful technology implementation starts with clearly identifying business goals, pain points and long-term strategies. Without this clarity, investments risk being ineffective or underutilized.

Low-code or no-code platforms for simplified solutions: No-code and low-code platforms lower barriers to entry, allowing operators to customize and deploy tailored solutions without the need for extensive technical resources.

Integrate systems for a unified ecosystem: Open API platforms and integrated ecosystems ensure seamless communication between tools like the PMS, RMS and CRM, streamlining operations and enhancing the guest journey.

Test in a sandbox: Controlled testing environments allow operators to evaluate how new tools integrate with existing workflows, reducing risk and ensuring smoother implementation.

Engage staff for successful adoption: Employee buy-in is critical to technology success. Involving staff in the selection process, providing training and creating 'tech champions' lead to smoother transitions and effective usage.

Prepare for longer timelines: Implementing technology often takes time. Phased rollouts, realistic timelines and close collaboration with vendors can minimize disruptions and improve the likelihood of success.

Real-World Example – Placemakr: Placemakr, with its tech-first approach using open API systems, highlights the importance of adaptability and seamless integration to manage complex operations.

14

Preparing for the future

Hospitality, with its focus on 'real-life' experiences and interactions within physical spaces, is traditional in many ways. It's still about being greeted, seen and provided for. However, while the sector continues to understand the intrinsic value of personal connections and exceptional service, technological advancements are reshaping how hospitality businesses operate and interact with guests. Adapting to these changes is critical for operators if they want to thrive in an increasingly competitive and changing world. The imperative to 'future-proof' hospitality businesses has never been more pressing.

The need to change stems from various interconnected challenges facing lodging providers of all types. Rising costs have placed pressure on profit margins, while labour shortages and constraints have made it challenging to maintain service quality. At the same time, today's guests demand more personalized and seamless experiences fuelled by their exposure to digital-first services in other areas of their lives and a general societal move towards higher expectations for quality and speed. These shifts have created an environment where survival and success will increasingly become more challenging to those who don't adopt change.

For hospitality, technology adoption is becoming the cornerstone of this adaptation. Tools that harness cloud-based software, interconnected platforms, AI, the Internet of Things (IoT) and data analytics enable businesses to streamline operations, enhance the guest stay and remain agile in the face of rapid market and consumer changes. Yet, this transformation requires a cultural shift, on top of more technological investment.

In addition, the move towards a greater focus on sustainability within hotels and short-term rentals (STRs) will grow. As environmental concerns become increasingly prioritized by guests and governments, adopting eco-friendly practices through software will become more of a necessity. From energy-efficient operations to waste reduction initiatives, sustainable practices appeal to eco-conscious travellers and help reduce operational costs. Tomorrow's Gen Z and Gen Alpha teams will also place more value on working for purpose-driven companies that take care of the world around them.

REAL-WORLD EXAMPLE

Kasa's hospitality operating system saves hotels from the tyranny of rising costs

Kasa is a leading technology-driven hotel and apartment-hotel brand and manager for the modern traveller. Its hospitality operating system merges proprietary technology with streamlined operations to deliver exceptional guest experiences while maximizing profitability for property owners. Kasa offers a fully managed and branded version of its product as well as a white-label version of its technology and centralized services called 'Powered By Kasa'.

With over 85 properties across the United States and partnerships with leading institutions like Starwood Capital, Berkshire and Brookfield, Kasa has become a very interesting operator for guests, property owners and communities alike.

Challenges and opportunities

In a previous life, Roman Pedan, founder and CEO of Kasa, invested in hotels and real estate during his tenure at Walton Street Capital and KKR. During this time, he observed the unsettling trend that hotel properties were experiencing existential headwinds driven by the tyranny of rising costs. 'Hotel owners over the past 15 years have experienced the same worrying trends: taxes, insurance and labour costs have all risen dramatically while revenue has not kept pace,' he says. Simultaneously, guest experiences seemed stuck in the past, not reflecting the innovation present in other consumer-facing industries, he adds.

'As an investor, it was frustrating to see our properties not reaching their full potential. As a traveller, it was even more frustrating to experience outdated services and mediocre stays. I knew there was a community of travellers and investors who felt the same way,' he recalls. 'There was a gap between the experience and profitability that hotels offered and the expectations of the investor and the modern traveller.'

In 2016, Pedan founded Kasa to bridge that gap. The aim was to move hotels away from outdated, on-site and inefficient operations towards a centralized, digital-first model. 'We set out to fundamentally lower the cost structure of hotel operations while vastly improving the guest experience,' he says.

Kasa has since built a broad portfolio of boutique hotels and apartment-hotels across the United States. Its success as a third-party manager has hinged on delivering profitability for property owners and improved experiences for guests. Expansion has often come through word of mouth among real estate owners and expanding relationships with existing partners.

An example of Kasa's transformative approach is the STILE Downtown Los Angeles by Kasa, launched in February 2024. Previously known as the Ace Hotel Los Angeles, this property includes a wrap-around rooftop pool/bar, a lobby restaurant, meeting space and a 1,600-person theatre.

'Downtown LA has faced significant challenges post-pandemic. Traditional approaches to operating hospitality weren't working for many owners,' Pedan says. 'In a market where revenues have dropped and operational costs have increased, Kasa offers a solution that turns struggling properties around.'

A sense of wonder

Amid all the talk of technology, it's important not to lose sight of the basics. While hotels do represent a type of real estate investment, they are also places that should evoke emotion.

'In some cases, getting someone into their room represents shelter, feeling like all their basic needs are met and instilling a sense of hospitality, and a feeling of their home being on the road; it really strikes at the lowest level of Maslow's Hierarchy of Needs,' Pedan says.

But at the same time, he thinks there's much more: 'There's a sense of imagination, a sense of possibility, a sense of wonder and excitement about imagining you're living differently, even if just for a night.'

The solution

Kasa developed its own hospitality operating system, anchored by an extensible proprietary Property Management System (PMS) that integrates first-party and third-party components seamlessly.

'We were very selective about what to build in-house. For every component, we asked if it was central to our competitive advantage and if there was a suitable solution available in the market,' Pedan explains. 'Building and maintaining technology is costly, so we had a very high bar.'

Over time, Kasa built a comprehensive suite of systems, including its own PMS. 'We didn't set out to build a full PMS, but we eventually found that to deliver the best results to properties and guests alike, we needed to,' Pedan notes.

Today, Kasa's operating system includes a PMS, channel management, revenue management, a booking engine and modules for accounting, housekeeping and trust and safety, among others. It also features a self-guided check-in system, making self-check-in the default experience. Some of these solutions are deeply integrated third-party solutions and some are first-party.

Did it succeed with the former Ace?

'It usually takes about a year and a half for a property of that size to really ramp up, because it takes time to build the property's reputation and to book future group and corporate business,' Pedan says. Nevertheless, Kasa doubled the profitability of the property in the first year and improved the margin percentage fivefold.

Beyond boosting the P&L, guest experience metrics improved significantly. 'We improved review scores across just about every online reputation channel like TripAdvisor, Expedia, Booking.com and Google,' Pedan shares. 'Higher reviews represent an improved guest experience and ultimately lead to more revenue.'

Connecting the dots

STILE Downtown Los Angeles by Kasa is much more than just hotel rooms. On top of the nearly 200 guest rooms, the property boasts a 1,600-person theatre, lobby restaurant, a rooftop pool with a bar area and 5,000 square feet of meeting and event space.

'It's crucial that the operations team for the hotel is well integrated with the teams handling food and beverage and theatre management,' Pedan emphasizes. 'Cultural and incentive alignment across these teams makes all the difference.'

Conclusion

Kasa takes a holistic view of hotel operations, blending investment insights, operational efficiency and guest experience. Technology is important, but it is not the whole story. 'We offer a physical experience enhanced by technology. The technology is designed to fade into the background for guests, while allowing operators to lower the cost of delivering that experience,' Pedan explains.

By maximizing profitability and reducing operational costs, Kasa has the potential to grow and expand into property types that are often underserved by traditional hotel brands, such as condo-hotels, outdoor hospitality and office-to-residential adaptive reuses. Partners like Greystar, AMLI Residential and Starwood Capital work with Kasa to operate their properties, demonstrating that a well-designed combination of technology, operations and hospitality can drive innovation in an industry often hesitant to change.

Two key trends impacting the future of hospitality

The guests are changing

As the generations of younger travellers rise to become the dominant market segment, expectations for digital-first and personalized experiences will only grow. Social media, user-generated content, influencer marketing and peer reviews will continue to shape booking decisions. This shift emphasizes hospitality businesses' importance in maintaining a strong online presence and engaging with guests across digital platforms. Additionally, the rise of experiential travel underscores the need for hospitality operators to offer unique and meaningful experiences that resonate with this demographic. The key here is to provide exceptional and differentiated experiences but at scale.

Blended hospitality models

Mixed-use properties that combine residential, commercial and hospitality spaces are on the rise. This growth is driven by changing consumer preferences for flexible, multi-purpose environments and the need for asset owners to make the most out of spaces. These hybrid and flexible models cater to guests seeking long-term stays, co-working spaces and lifestyle-driven accommodation in response to changing needs and lifestyle desires. Managing such diverse offerings requires innovative technology solutions that address greater complexity, from shared services to tailored guest experiences.

'We need to use technology to make sure time is freed up from an HQ perspective, to drive strategy, make tactical and reactive decisions, to look at the data and adapt as needed.'

Alessandra Leoni, Head of Commercial, Resident Hotels

Understanding emerging technologies in hospitality

Artificial intelligence (AI)

AI has already begun to transform hospitality in myriad ways, from automating repetitive tasks, to enhancing the guest experience and acting as sales agents. Machine learning algorithms power dynamic pricing models, predicting demand. Natural language processing enables chatbots to provide 24/7 guest support, handling routine queries such as room service requests or booking confirmations. AI also drives personalization, analysing guest preferences to offer tailored recommendations – whether it's suggesting a spa package or adjusting in-room settings based on past stays.

AI's impact extends beyond guest-facing applications. In operations, AI tools streamline workflows by automating administrative tasks such as scheduling and inventory management. Predictive analytics, powered by AI, help anticipate market trends, allowing operators to optimize pricing and adjust marketing strategies in real time. AI is also well placed to improve recruitment strategies and talent management by identifying ideal candidates through advanced data analysis.

Future developments in generative AI could see systems acting as virtual concierges, negotiating rates, crafting itineraries and even providing emotional support to guests. For businesses, the key to leveraging AI lies in understanding where it can provide tangible value without undermining the human touch that defines hospitality.

Internet of Things (IoT)

The IoT is the interconnection via the internet of physical devices, enabling them to share data and automate processes. In hospitality,

IoT applications range from smart thermostats that optimize energy consumption to keyless entry systems that enhance convenience. Properties equipped with IoT devices can monitor occupancy levels in real time, ensuring efficient housekeeping schedules and energy usage.

IoT is also enhancing guest personalization. Imagine a room that automatically adjusts lighting, temperature and entertainment preferences based on a guest's profile. Beyond in-room experiences, IoT devices help hotels monitor energy usage and water consumption, contributing to sustainability efforts. For example, smart meters can detect leaks or inefficiencies, prompting timely interventions that save resources and costs.

By integrating IoT with other platforms, such as PMSs, operators can achieve a seamless flow of data. Predictive maintenance powered by IoT sensors can alert staff to equipment issues before they escalate, minimizing disruptions and ensuring a consistent guest experience.

Blockchain and cryptocurrencies

Blockchain technology offers the potential of secure, transparent transaction methods, reducing fraud and streamlining payments. By decentralizing data storage, blockchain ensures secure access to sensitive information, from payment records to guest profiles. This level of transparency builds trust with guests and partners alike.

Cryptocurrencies, though still in the very early stages of adoption in hospitality, provide an alternative payment option that may appeal to tech-savvy and international travellers. These digital currencies eliminate the need for intermediaries, reducing transaction fees and offering faster payment processing. Blockchain's potential extends to loyalty programmes, where it could enable the seamless exchange of rewards across platforms and partners, creating a unified ecosystem for guest incentives.

Sustainability technologies

As sustainability becomes a core guest expectation, at least in some parts of the world, technology will play a more crucial role in meeting eco-friendly goals. IoT-driven energy management systems and AI-powered predictive maintenance and waste reduction tools can help hospitality businesses operate more sustainably.

For instance, IoT-enabled sensors can track energy usage across a property and automatically adjust settings to reduce waste. AI tools can analyse consumption patterns, providing actionable insights to further optimize energy efficiency. Technologies such as water-saving fixtures and waste-monitoring systems also ensure resources are used responsibly. By integrating sustainability into their operations, businesses not only align with guest values but also future-proof themselves against regulatory changes.

Automation and robotics

Automation is the golden ticket for operations. From robotic concierges handling check-ins to autonomous cleaning systems maintaining public spaces, the future of automation will help businesses reduce labour costs and improve efficiency, allowing business owners and managers to allocate resources to high-impact areas.

Guest-facing robotics, such as luggage-carrying bots or automated food delivery systems, may add novelty, but they could also address labour shortages. In the back office, robotic process automation streamlines repetitive tasks like payroll processing or financial reporting, freeing staff to focus on strategic initiatives.

Agentic AI

Agentic AI is the next frontier – systems that don't just follow commands but can think and act for themselves. These tools are capable of making decisions, learning from what's happening around them and taking action to achieve a set goal – all without needing constant human input. Instead of relying on one-off instructions, agentic AI uses multiple intelligent components that can interpret context, solve complex challenges and carry out tasks in a way that feels almost human in its initiative.

'Some of the best projects that I've been part of, they've mapped out the end-to-end guest journey along with the end-to-end employee journey.'

Antonia Bernhardt, Head of Sales and Business Development, Like Magic

While these innovations enhance efficiency, they also present an opportunity to redefine the guest experience. Robots will handle repetitive tasks, allowing human staff to focus on creating personalized, memorable interactions. However, it should go without saying that the integration of robotics and automation must be approached thoughtfully to ensure they complement rather than replace the human touch that remains central to hospitality. It's important to understand also that robots *will* start to replace some traditional human roles. If a robot can deliver food to a room, there is no need for a room service waiter anymore.

TECH LEADER INSIGHT
Why the future is selling emotions and experiences, not rooms –
Markus Mueller, Co-founder and Managing Director, GauVendi

Attribute-based selling, where hoteliers replace the traditional method of offering rooms by category or type, and instead sell their features, has been gaining ground in the hospitality industry for several years.

It's not such a radical idea and is common in other industries, such as e-commerce (see 'Tech Leader Insight: Attribute-based selling and changing mindsets' in Chapter 2).

But looking further ahead, in a more radical way, is Markus Mueller. His ambition is to help hotels not only adopt attribute-based selling but take that a step further and package (and price) rooms in new ways by tapping into 'emotional trigger points'. In short, he wants hoteliers and apartment operators to rethink revenue management.

Mueller is co-founder and Managing Director of GauVendi, which is a combination of two Latin words: *gaudium*, meaning joy, and *venditio*, meaning selling. The platform is described as a 'next-generation booking, distribution, revenue management and automation tool for differentiated and hyper-personalized guest engagement, built on a feature-based native and dynamic inventory system for real estate-based businesses'.

Commoditization at the expense of differentiation

Author James Burke once said: 'Why should we look to the past in order to prepare for the future? Because there is nowhere else to look.' In this vein, Mueller argues hotels must now regain control over how they sell rooms, because they lost control of their inventory with the onset of digitalization.

With the arrival of the internet, hotels had no choice but to simplify their product, to cater to a sudden huge number of new customers arriving via online travel agencies (OTAs). They had to be able to allow people to compare rooms easily, in order to compete effectively.

'Before, hotels had a lot of different room categories, and there were only a few distribution channels, mainly the Global Distribution System (GDS),' he says. 'There was some standardization, but there was a lot more variety out there. Now with digitalization, this can't be handled anymore. So what did hotels do? They simplified their inventory into manageable categories, otherwise it was impossible to make sure they had parity with the products out there.'

This extent of standardization led to commoditization, which was essential to help hotel brands grow and scale. But in that process hotels lost differentiation and individualization, Mueller says.

'We are sacrificing personalization for automation because we manage categories,' he adds. 'This is where the personalization stops, because we're not managing in a more granular way. What we said is: how do we gain back power and distribution control for the operators?'

Moving away from 'static' inventory

GauVendi has developed a new data infrastructure to allow hotels to adopt attribute-based selling, as well as a sales engine to facilitate the resulting 'dynamic' inventory to be sold. This is in keeping with the dynamic pricing principle, made popular by the likes of Uber. 'It's acceptable in our society to pay different prices for different times based on demand,' argues Mueller.

First, in terms of attribute-based selling, GauVendi's system lets a hotel specify if a room is located on the second floor, for example, or is south-facing. He argues this data context is absent in most PMSs.

'Maybe I want rooms next to each other, maybe I want a quiet location, and I'll be willing to pay for it. Or I don't mind a room facing the street if I save $10,' he says. 'What we have done is change the way we look at the management of accommodation inventory.'

GauVendi is also able to help hotels sell rooms according to the customer profile. As Mueller explains: 'Here's my room of the month. These are the best combinations for families. We could have "The Markus room". And people are willing to pay different prices when we present the same unit that's more relevant to them.'

As another example, a room with a small balcony would not be promoted in winter, or for a family with younger children, as nobody will pay extra for it. So, in this case, a room without a balcony would be more expensive than with a balcony.

Promoted rooms could also include a spa package and dinner reservation, if the system detects that the customer previously booked this combination. Mueller believes the technology is replicating the perfect salesperson, who would show a customer the benefits that are relevant to them. If they sell the same product to somebody else, they will highlight different benefits for that profile.

These so-called 'smart room assignments' could ultimately aid hotels in ensuring the right reservation comes from the right guest, which, as well as maximizing occupancy, maximizes revenue.

'Your cheapest room might not be your cheapest room anymore because you're not pricing categories, you're pricing attributes,' he continues. 'That's the new power of It. A room is not just a room, but a feature combination.'

Avoiding the paradox of choice

With this new perspective on revenue management, there's a risk of overwhelming a potential guest with so many different features and combinations, so GauVendi is adding labels.

'If you offer me 40 different options, I have no clue what I'm going to take and I'm completely confused,' Mueller says. 'So the paradox of choice suggests that we need to put fewer things on the shelf, but more relevant things.'

As a result, its booking engine will not display more than six products, and it includes graded labelling, which involves the use of an easily distinguishable tag, sticker, label, letter, mark or symbol, which identifies the quality or grade of a product being offered.

In GauVendi's case, a label may specify that the room is the lowest price available, or is the most popular, or is the hotel's top recommendation. The lowest price might be a standard room with a view on the street, but the hotel's top recommendation could be a more quietly located standard room – for $5 more.

Transparency is also a bonus, Mueller adds, because the guest knows they are buying the lowest price facing the street: 'Your expectation is managed in the right way, so it moves your guest satisfaction ratio up.'

Looking even further ahead, new data structures, combined with generative AI, could accelerate how hotels frame rooms with more experience descriptions.

Strategies for future-proofing your business

Building agility and scalability

To stay competitive, hospitality businesses must prioritize agility and scalability in their technology solutions. Cloud-based PMSs provide the foundation for this adaptability, allowing businesses to integrate new tools and features as needed. These platforms, increasingly built on Application Programming Interface (API) frameworks, enable seamless connections with third-party software, ensuring a flexible tech stack that can grow alongside business needs. This is particularly beneficial for businesses navigating seasonal demand fluctuations or expanding into new markets.

Scalability also means preparing for unforeseen challenges. Whether it's adapting to sudden shifts in guest expectations or accommodating technological changes, scalable systems ensure that businesses can pivot quickly without overhauling their entire infrastructure. Operators choosing between marketplace models and all-in-one systems must weigh the benefits of customization against simplicity. While marketplace models offer flexibility to incorporate specialized tools, all-in-one systems streamline management for businesses with straightforward needs.

Data-driven decision making

Data is the currency of the future, and businesses that harness it effectively can gain a significant competitive edge. Advanced analytics platforms allow operators to transform raw data into actionable insights. By examining booking trends, guest preferences and operational bottlenecks, businesses can optimize everything from pricing strategies to staff allocation.

Security and compliance

Effective data utilization demands robust governance practices. Businesses must ensure transparency in how data is collected, stored and used to maintain guest trust. Compliance with global privacy regulations, such as the General Data Protection Regulation, is non-negotiable, and operators should prioritize investments in secure systems to protect sensitive information. Choosing software that prioritizes security is vital when selecting a system.

> 'Generative AI is big. It's what's brought AI back into the spotlight again, because it's cool and you can do things with it that were previously thought kind of impossible.'
>
> **David Kelso, Chief Technology Officer and Co-founder, Beyond**

Investing in talent and training

While technology can enhance operations, the human element remains at the heart of hospitality. A well-trained team equipped to leverage new tools can transform guest interactions and operational efficiency. Training programmes should focus not only on the technical aspects of new systems but also on how these systems can complement and enhance staff roles.

Upskilling initiatives can also help mitigate the effects of labour shortages, enabling employees to take on more complex responsibilities. For example, automating routine tasks like check-ins frees staff to focus on high-touch, personalized guest interactions. A culture of continuous learning ensures that teams remain adaptable as new technologies and operational models emerge.

Businesses must also invest in leadership training to ensure that management teams are prepared to guide their organizations through periods of change. Leaders who understand the strategic value of technology can inspire confidence and drive innovation across the organization.

Overcoming barriers to change

Addressing resistance: Resistance to change is a common hurdle in implementing new technologies. Involving staff early in the decision-making process, providing comprehensive training and demonstrating the benefits of new systems can help overcome scepticism. Pilot programmes and 'sandbox' experiments allow teams to experience the advantages first-hand, building confidence in the transition.

Avoiding common pitfalls: Implementing the wrong technology or failing to integrate new tools properly can lead to inefficiencies and frustration. Conducting thorough needs assessments and ensuring compatibility with existing systems are critical steps in the selection process. Choosing reputable vendors with strong customer support can also mitigate risks, as can choosing vendors with robust development roadmaps and backing.

Ensuring stakeholder buy-in: Communicating the long-term benefits of technological investments – from cost savings to enhanced guest experiences – is essential for securing buy-in from stakeholders. Clear metrics for success, such as increased revenue or improved guest satisfaction scores, provide tangible evidence of ROI.

'Investing in technology without the necessary support can result in wasted resources and a lack of return on investment, emphasizing the need for strategic implementation.'

James Cornwell, CEO and Founder, Curated Property

Becoming a tech-forward leader

Preparing for the future of hospitality requires a delicate balance between embracing innovation and preserving its essence. After all, hospitality will always be a 'people business' driven by service, relationships and interaction. Of course, there will always be those customers who simply want a bed for the night and are happy to have no relationship with a provider; however, even those will still want a digital relationship of some kind, even through an app and a chatbot. They will want 'something' to deal with issues and questions.

That said, hospitality business leaders can position themselves for long-term success by adopting emerging technologies, being adaptable and staying attuned to evolving guest expectations. But to truly succeed, innovation must be paired with a clear vision and strategy. Operators would do well not just to follow trends for the latest smart tool or software but to evaluate which technologies align with their brand values and operational goals. This deliberate approach will ensure investments are purposeful and deliver maximum impact.

Cultivating a culture of adaptability within the workforce is equally critical. Hospitality teams must be empowered to experiment with new tools and practices, learning from successes and setbacks. Open communication and feedback loops ensure that staff at all levels contribute to the evolution of the business.

The journey towards future-proofing is not without its challenges, but the rewards – greater efficiency, profitability and guest satisfaction – are well worth the effort. In an industry defined by its ability to create memorable experiences, leveraging technology to enhance operations and human connection is the key to thriving in the years ahead.

After all, as Ryan Killeen, co-founder and CEO of The Annex, told me, 'The future of hospitality is hospitality.'

KEY TAKEAWAYS

The imperative to adapt: The hospitality industry must evolve to address rising operational costs, labour shortages and increasing guest demands.

Technology as a cornerstone: Tools like AI, IoT and integrated PMSs streamline operations and enhance the guest experience. However, success requires both technological investment and a cultural shift towards innovation.

Sustainability as a necessity: Eco-friendly practices supported by technology appeal to environmentally conscious guests and reduce operational costs. Future generations of travellers and workers will prioritize companies with strong sustainability commitments.

Emerging guest expectations: Younger travellers demand digital-first, personalized and experiential travel. Social media, peer reviews and influencer marketing play significant roles in shaping booking decisions.

Blended hospitality models: Mixed-use properties combining residential, commercial and hospitality spaces are growing in popularity. These models require advanced technology to address complex operational needs.

Overcoming resistance to change: Implementing new technologies successfully involves engaging staff early, providing comprehensive training and even using pilot programmes to build confidence.

Future-focused leadership: Leaders must strategically evaluate which technologies align with their brand values and goals. Cultivating a culture of experimentation and adaptability empowers teams to innovate and remain competitive.

Technology enhances human connection: While technology drives efficiency, the essence of hospitality, for some, does lie in human connection. Operators must understand their guests and their needs, and leverage technology to enhance – not replace – personal interactions, ensuring memorable guest experiences and long-term success.

Technology can replace human roles: On the other hand, not every guest wants personal interaction, and for those operators that cater to these guests, full automation is now very possible.

Real-World Example – Kasa: By adopting a centralized, digital-first model, Kasa has successfully transformed struggling properties into profitable, highly rated destinations.

GLOSSARY OF KEY TERMS

ADR (Average Daily Rate): The average revenue generated per occupied room over a specific time period, used to assess pricing strategy effectiveness and financial performance.

Agentic AI: Artificial intelligence systems developed to autonomously handle tasks such as managing bookings, optimizing pricing and streamlining guest communications, reducing human workload.

Analytics and Reporting Tools: Business intelligence platforms that collect, process and display data insights to aid decision making, operational efficiency and performance tracking.

API (Application Programming Interface): Software interfaces that enable seamless communication between different hospitality systems, such as PMS, CRM and booking platforms.

Attribute-Based Selling (ABS): A sales approach allowing guests to select specific room attributes (e.g. view, floor level, amenities), offering customized experiences and maximizing revenue.

BNPL (Buy Now, Pay Later): A flexible payment option that lets guests book and pay in instalments over time, enhancing affordability and encouraging bookings.

Bulk Rate Adjustments: The capability to apply pricing changes simultaneously across multiple properties or room types, ensuring consistency and efficiency.

Channel Manager: A software tool that connects hotel inventory to various OTAs, managing rates, availability and bookings across platforms in real time.

Competitor Pricing: The practice of analysing competitors' rates to adjust pricing strategies and maintain market competitiveness.

Consolidation: The merging of technology companies within the hospitality sector, leading to integrated platforms and expanded service offerings.

Consumer Intent Analysis: Evaluating guest search behaviour, booking patterns and preferences to refine pricing and marketing strategies.

CRM (Customer Relationship Management): Systems that store and manage guest data, enabling personalized marketing, improved guest experiences and loyalty management.

CRS (Central Reservation System): A platform used by hotels and property managers to manage bookings across multiple distribution channels from a centralized interface.

Data Flow Management: Systems ensuring smooth data sharing across departments, enhancing operational efficiency and informed decision making.

Dynamic Pricing: Automated pricing that adjusts room rates based on factors like demand, competition and seasonality to maximize revenue.

Fintech: Financial technology solutions for secure, fast and seamless transactions, including digital payments, fraud prevention and financial reporting.

Forward-Looking Data: Predictive insights derived from market analysis and booking trends, used for future planning and pricing decisions.

Generative AI: AI that generates original content, such as marketing materials, guest communications and pricing recommendations, enhancing operational creativity.

GOPPAR (Gross Operating Profit per Available Room): A key performance indicator measuring gross operating profit per available room, reflecting overall financial efficiency.

Guest Experience Platforms: Integrated software that manages guest communications, feedback and service requests, improving the overall stay experience.

Historical Data: Past booking and pricing information used to identify trends and inform future pricing strategies.

Hyper-Personalization: Advanced personalization techniques that tailor every aspect of the guest experience, from marketing to in-stay services, based on detailed guest data.

IoT (Internet of Things): Connected smart devices that automate and optimize hotel operations, such as lighting, temperature control and security.

Machine Learning: AI systems that learn from data over time to improve pricing algorithms, operational processes and guest interactions.

Marketplace Model: A flexible PMS setup that integrates various third-party solutions, allowing operators to choose specialized tools for different functions.

Market Segmentation: Dividing guests into categories (e.g. business, leisure, groups) for targeted pricing, marketing and service strategies.

No-Code/Low-Code Platforms: Tools that allow hospitality operators to create and customize software solutions without extensive programming knowledge.

Occupancy Levels: A metric representing the percentage of available rooms that are occupied, used to gauge demand and adjust pricing.

Open API Ecosystems: Systems designed with open APIs to facilitate easy integration with other tools, enhancing operational flexibility.

Operational Models: Software managing hotel operations like housekeeping, maintenance and scheduling, ensuring smooth service delivery.

OTA (online travel agency): A third-party platform that lists accommodations and facilitates online bookings for travellers. Examples are Airbnb, Booking.com, Agoda and Vrbo.

PMS (Property Management System): The central system that handles reservations, billing, guest management and operational coordination.

Point-of-Sale (POS) System: Technology managing all on-site transactions, including payments for rooms, dining and services.

Portfolio Analytics Tools: Platforms providing performance metrics and insights across multiple properties, aiding portfolio management.

Predictive Analytics: Advanced data analysis used to forecast demand, optimize pricing and anticipate guest needs.

Prescriptive Analytics: AI-driven tools that suggest specific actions and strategies based on data analysis, enhancing operational decisions.

Pricing Algorithms: Automated systems that calculate optimal room rates based on market conditions, demand and competitor analysis.

Real-Time Market Intelligence: Systems providing up-to-date market data for agile decision making in pricing and operations.

Regulatory Impact: The influence of local laws and regulations on pricing, availability and operational strategies.

RevPAN (Revenue per Available Night): A revenue metric specific to short-term rentals, measuring income per available night including owner stays and maintenance periods.

RevPAR (Revenue per Available Room): A key metric combining occupancy and ADR to assess overall financial performance.

Risk Tolerance Metrics: Tools that evaluate and balance pricing risks with business objectives and market conditions.

RMS (Revenue Management System): Software used to optimize pricing and inventory decisions by analysing demand, competitor rates, booking patterns and other data points.

SaaS (Software as a Service): Subscription-based cloud software that offers flexible, scalable solutions for hotel operations.

Seasonality: Variations in demand based on seasons, holidays and events, impacting pricing and occupancy.

Smart Energy Management: IoT-based systems optimizing energy use, reducing costs and supporting sustainability initiatives.

STR (short-term rental) Lodging accommodations such as apartments or full homes offered for rent for short durations and with 'home-like' facilities.

Supply and Demand Dynamics: Balancing room supply with market demand to determine competitive pricing.

The Taylor Swift Effect: Increased demand and pricing spikes caused by large-scale events such as major concerts.

Unified Commercial Teams: Cross-departmental teams working collaboratively on revenue, marketing and operations.

Unified Payment Platform: Integrated systems that manage all payment processes, enhancing guest convenience and financial tracking.

Virtual Concierge: AI-powered assistants providing guests with personalized service, from booking to in-stay support.

INDEX

Looking for another book?

Explore our award-winning
books from global business
experts in Tourism, Leisure and
Hospitality

Scan the code to browse

www.koganpage.com/tlh

More from Kogan Page

www.koganpage.com

From 4 December 2025 the EU Responsible Person (GPSR) is:
eucomply oÜ, Pärnu mnt. 139b – 14, 11317 Tallinn, Estonia
www.eucompliancepartner.com

www.ingramcontent.com/pod-product-compliance
Lightning Source LLC
Chambersburg PA
CBHW070938050326
40689CB00014B/3260